Wine Girl

ALSO BY VICTORIA JAMES

Drink Pink: A Celebration of Rosé

Wine Girl

THE OBSTACLES, HUMILIATIONS,
AND TRIUMPHS OF
AMERICA'S YOUNGEST SOMMELIER

VICTORIA JAMES

ecco
An Imprint of HarperCollins*Publishers*

Photographs courtesy of the author, except:

pages 9 and 53: photo by author's mother; page 191: photo by Liz Clayman; page 312: photo by Gary He

HarperCollins books may be purchased for educational, business, or sales promotional use. For information, please email the Special Markets Department at SPsales@harpercollins.com.

FIRST EDITION

Designed by Suet Yee Chong

Library of Congress Cataloging-in-Publication Data has been applied for.

ISBN 978-0-06-296167-9 (hardcover)
ISBN 978-0-06-302273-7 (international edition)

20 21 22 23 24   LSC   10 9 8 7 6 5 4 3 2 1

Dedicated to:

Laura James,
for giving me the healing power of your love
(I could dedicate every book I will ever write to you,
and it would never be enough).

Timothy James,
for showing me a strength I still cannot fathom.

Lyle Railsback,
for giving me the courage to be myself.

Simon Kim,
for believing in the unseen.

And to all the women in the world of restaurants . . .

It's our time now.

The best way to find yourself is to lose yourself in the service of others.

—*Mahatma Gandhi*

CONTENTS

Author's Note

This is an account of my experiences as a child, restaurant professional, and sommelier. The stories recounted in this book are based on my memories, stacks of diaries (both mine and my mum's), emails, messages, court transcripts, letters, and public records. All stories have been read and deemed accurate by family members and colleagues. Some names have been changed but this otherwise remains a true narrative. The following persons/places are presented with pseudonyms: Antonio, Chip, Cisco, DeShawn, Ed, Enzo, Finn Ferguson, the Greasy Spoon, the instructor, Henrietta Katz, Joey, Martha Bass, Paul, Reese, Reynard, Shanti, Regina, Tony, the Wine School, and Zef.

WINE GIRL

*T*WENTY-ONE YEARS OLD, *the youngest sommelier in the country and the most foolish. Today my career will end,* I thought.

It was early 2012 during a Monday lunch, one of the shifts given to the newbie (in this case, me), as it is the slowest service of the week and typically safe from any real challenges. Only occasionally would I sell a bottle and get to make the magnificent journey through Aureole's extensive wine cellar. This collection climbed upward and ran the length of the restaurant, holding over fifteen thousand bottles.

Usually, the bottles I sold during this shift weren't particularly fascinating, as it's not a typical American custom to drink well during a Monday lunch. However, this Monday was different. A guest had ordered the 2009 Chevalier-Montrachet from Domaine Ramonet.

Some sommeliers might nitpick that Domaine Ramonet is not their favorite producer in Burgundy (a bit *overrated,* they'll sneer), or perhaps a wine collector will argue that this wine was too young to drink (*infanticide!* at only three years old), but snobbery aside, it was a $650 bottle of chardonnay! Who does that . . . at a *Monday lunch* no less?

I thought of how proud my wine director would be when he saw the sales from lunch and imagined all the wonders the guests would experience when they drank the grand cru white Burgundy. I had never tasted the wine, only read about its notoriety and rarity.

The guest who ordered the Ramonet was at table 100 (in restaurants tables are numbered for practical purposes). It was one of the best tables in our dining room, surrounded by a plush banquette and pillows. Sometimes, this comfort led to loose wallets. The captain scurried to find me after receiving the order. With the wine list still carefully propped open to the correct page, he pointed to "the six-hundred-fifty-dollar one!" His eyes screamed *Ka-ching!*

I held my breath as his fingers scrolled from the price over to the left . . . *2009 Domaine Ramonet Chevalier-Montrachet* . . . ! At first, I was sure this was a practical joke. As the new girl, I had grown accustomed to all sorts of ruses.

"Let me just double-check," I added, hesitant. The captain's face dropped as I took the wine list from his hands and walked over to the table, where four men lounged. They all had slicked-back gray hair and wore dark suits with thin stripes. I presented the list to the gentleman who had ordered. "Pardon me, sir, I wanted to confirm your order of 2009 Domaine Ramonet Chevalier-Montrachet . . ." My finger ran along the name and to the price. He just stared at me with his beady eyes.

Tiny droplets of sweat began to form under my cheap polyester suit. He closed the wine list abruptly with a clap. "Yes," he said with an overt tinge of annoyance, "and hurry, we are thirsty." I managed a nervous nod, rushing out of the dining room and upstairs.

In the wine cellar, there was a corner I had yet to explore. This nook was where all of the high-end wine was hidden, away from light and dangerous swings in temperature. After a few moments of scanning, I found the Ramonets and thumbed my way through until I landed upon the right vintage and vineyard. I gently picked up the bottle and noticed that there were, in total, only two of them. I cradled the wine in my arms as if it were a small child, terrified of what a single misstep might bring.

Back near the table of men in suits, their conversation quieted to whispers as I returned. "Sir, 2009." I pointed to the vintage on the bottle. "Domaine Ramonet." I pointed to the producer. "Chevalier-Montrachet." I pointed to the vineyard. He gave a sharp nod. The eerie silence from the group crept onto my skin and sent a small shiver throughout my body.

Outside the dining room, I placed the bottle steadily down on the gueridon, the sommelier station where wine is opened, prepped, and tasted. To open the bottle, I whipped out my corkscrew and rendered two precise cuts to the foil capsule, removing the top portion that covered the cork. Just in case there was any unwanted residue, I wiped the top of the cork off with a serviette. Once it was cleaned, I dug the tip of my corkscrew in and, with a few twists plus one steady pull, extracted the cork quietly. To be sure, I followed the last step of the sommelier protocol here and wiped the lip again with a serviette. Then, the best part—I poured myself a one-ounce taste.

Believe it or not, a sommelier must taste every single bottle before serving. One bottle in every two or three cases of wine is corked, and even more can be affected by a variety of other flaws. Just as a chef would never send out a rotten piece of fish, a sommelier should never serve a lousy bottle of wine. The chemical compound known as TCA (trichloroanisole) is what is responsible for this "cork taint." It won't harm you, unlike a piece of rotten fish, but it's a horrible taste.

The tradition remains that even after the sommelier—arguably the expert in this scenario—approves the wine, she allows the guest to taste it as well. Here, the guest is merely rechecking to see if it is flawed; it is not a tasting to see if they "like it." Preferences should be established with the sommelier well before the selection. So why even go through this rechecking process? I like to do it because I believe hospitality is about love, not logic. Of course, it would make more sense to skip this step. However, at this moment, the sommelier puts expertise on the back burner and humbly gives the guest the power. The sommelier respectfully bows down first, followed by the guest's reciprocating in appreciation (ideally).

Despite my lack of experience in the industry, I had already tasted thousands of wines and trained myself to commit all "flawed" flavors to memory. Still, I especially honored the tradition of letting the guest approve the wine. Many of my guests were two to three times my age; it would have been disrespectful for me not to bow to them first.

When I tasted the Ramonet Chevalier-Montrachet, there was nothing off about it. The wine was like slipping into a bed made up with silk sheets. In the glass, aromas and memories kept popping out: sour cream spread on toast with honey, butterscotch candies, clotted cream, movie-theater popcorn, sour frozen yogurt, a zing of lemon zest, freshly cracked crème brûlée, warm butter with salt, and mouth-puckering acidity. I could see why people would spend so much money on this wine.

"The glasses are down," the captain remarked, pulling me out of my amorous reverie and back to Monday lunch service. He had placed white Burgundy glasses, specifically made for this type of wine, on the table.

The uneasiness I had felt before crept back. Although my restaurant training had taught me how to suppress nervousness, sometimes my body had a hard time listening. I approached the leader from the right again, pouring a taste quickly but with a calculated precision—*label facing him, two ounces, a quick dip of the neck, twist, wipe with a serviette, cradle in both hands within view.* He brought his lips to the glass, stuck out his tongue a tiny bit, letting the Burgundy inch in. Moments passed; he looked up at me, scoffed, and turned back to his guests. "I think she has too much perfume in her nose, this girl . . ." His glare turned upward and at me. "The bottle is corked, take it back. Bring us another."

With this swift blow, the color drained from my face. *Corked? It couldn't be! The wine was delicious, perfect. Corked? Is he testing me? What kind of sommelier would be caught dead wearing perfume? Corked!?*

I managed to stutter, "Sir, respectfully, the wine has been tested, and it is sound. Perhaps you'd like to try it again?"

His face turned the dark red color of Bordeaux. "Listen, *wine girl*, I have bottles in my cellar older than you. I know when a wine is corked." Flecks of spit sprinkled from his lips. "Our food is about to arrive, and we still have nothing to drink. GET. US. ANOTHER. BOTTLE!"

My torso began to shake, and my knees weakened. I hurried out of the dining room with the bottle. *What just happened?* I kept replaying the series of events in my head.

The captain who took the order was standing at the gueridon with our GM (general manager). He dipped his nose into my tasting glass. I knew the two of them were absolute white Burgundy junkies, and the GM held a particular fondness for Ramonet.

"Oof." The GM puckered his lips and then began to smile. "It smells great," he sang in his soft French accent, adding, "Which table ordered this?" I told them that table 100 *had* ordered the bottle, but they'd sent it back. We all looked down at the dejected bottle. "Did you taste it?" The GM jetted his head forward and furrowed his brow.

"Of course!" I began. "I think it's spectacular, but they don't seem to agree. So . . ." All I could think of was my poor wine director and the pressure the restaurant bosses put on him to meet horrifyingly low costs, already unachievable unless every martini was vigorously shaken until wholly watered down. This would certainly not help. The bottle was unreturnable, as the vendor wouldn't detect any TCA responsible for cork taint. We couldn't salvage the cost and sell off glasses of it—who would splurge for $130 a glass on a Monday? Instead, it would surely go to waste. Half of me was heartbroken, and the other half was afraid for my job. Would they have returned the bottle if the older male captain had presented it? Or were they testing a kid they thought didn't belong? Maybe I *didn't* belong there.

"Let me taste it," the GM insisted. He poured himself a drop. "*Pfft* . . . This is delicious! Serve it to him." No one at Aureole would ever argue with the GM. Before I could ask for help, he walked away with my wineglass. The captain trailed behind him, hoping for maybe just a whiff.

Now abandoned, I racked my brain for a solution . . . how could I make everyone happy? I couldn't just go back to the table and insist that the guest *had* to drink the bottle. But I also couldn't open another Ramonet, as it would taste the same.

The right and the wrong here seemed to be all muddled. Just before table 100's first course was about to land, I came up with a plan. I bolted upstairs and grabbed the last bottle of the 2009 Ramonet Chevalier-Montrachet from the cellar. I presented it, only to be brushed off with a "Yes, yes." At that moment, the servers placed the first course of food on the table in one synchronized swoop. The leader looked up at me in a fury—I was far behind schedule.

In a silent panic, I tried to brush off fearful thoughts. Was what I was about to do ethical? Would this be the end of my just-begun career as a sommelier? I knew that if this didn't work it was my head alone on the chopping block.

The routine of wine service helped calm my nerves for a few moments—*label facing the guest, two ounces, quick dip of the neck, twist, wipe with a serviette, cradle in both hands within view.* The leader brought the glass to his nose and swirled slowly, around and around and around. I felt like a duck swimming on water, calm and collected above while pedaling furiously underneath.

He swished around the wine loudly in his mouth, sucking in air and making a loud *whooooo* noise. With a quick swallow, he burst into laughter and clasped his hands. "Ha! Yes, much better. Finally! Gentlemen, wait until you taste this wine, it is *magnificent*!"

I breathed a visible sigh of relief. Now much lighter, I floated around the table and filled everyone's glass with the wine.

"A woman, a *young* woman . . . probably too much perfume in her nose . . . could there be anything worse in a sommelier?" With the leader's words, my body tightened again, this time in shock and anger. The whole table laughed as the leader went on about how lovely the wine was and how inexperienced I seemed to be. My jaws clenched together to keep my angry words inside. While I was filling the fourth and final glass with wine, the leader added one last comment. "I guess it could be worse, actually." He leaned in and dropped his voice to a loud whisper. "At least she isn't a *nigger*."

My hand jolted, almost spilling the wine outside of the glass. The whole table erupted in guffaws, grabbing their glasses and bringing them together for a cheers. I recoiled in disgust. Before I could escape, the leader narrowed his eyes and said, "Thank you, *wine girl*."

I ran out of the dining room and back to the gueridon. My head lowered as I took deep breaths in an attempt to collect myself. I often faced men who didn't like a girl telling them what wine they should buy. Or worse, their wandering hands. Speaking out against this behavior wasn't an option. The customer is always right, the restaurant would remind us, and the word *no* should never be spoken. I didn't want people to see me as a problem. Being a sommelier was everything to me—I had dropped out of school to pursue wine and I had no family or safety net to support me. Despite the challenges I faced, I loved what I did.

My breathing eventually began to slow. The captain stopped by my side and tried to comfort me. "Well, at least you didn't have to open that other bottle," he said with a wink, pointing at an unopened 2009 Domaine Ramonet Chevalier-Montrachet sitting upright in front of me. It was the first and last time I ever did a bottle bait-and-switch. I nodded and let out a small smile before quickly returning it to the dark and quiet corner of the cellar.

PART I

AGE 7-14

SHUT THE DOOR

WHEN I WAS SEVEN, my father was offered a job in New York City, some five hundred miles from Blacksburg, Virginia, where we then lived. Mum had just given birth to our younger sister, Laura, and was very much still in recovery. She came from a line of aristocrats who'd set down roots, and couldn't comprehend the constant moving around my father demanded.

Since her mother was a countess, Contessa Anna Chiara Francesca Maria de Rege ("of the king") Thesaura di Donato de San Raffaele of Castello di Bagnolo in Piemonte, Italy, Mum said that this made her a lady, and she carried herself as such. She spoke French, Italian, Arabic, and Swahili, having lived in more countries than my father had visited.

My father's mother was an orphaned cotton picker born Willie "Sissy" Lou Ellen Barran in the rural town of Crump, Tennessee. This juxtaposition of blue blood and blue collar is what I believe groomed me for the eventual role of a sommelier, essentially a highbrow servant.

Just as my parents' backgrounds couldn't have been more different, their passions were worlds apart. Once she became an American citizen, Mum went to Corcoran College in Washington, DC, to study art. Painting and reading books absorbed her. In contrast, my father was dyslexic as a child and to this day finds reading an unpleasant task. Instead, he excelled in math and science and self-funded his education at Johns Hopkins University.

In a later court-mandated forensic psychological evaluation, my father described his main reason for marrying my mum as "the fact that she was the first one who loved [him]." They went on to have four children together; I am the second oldest.

Bored after a few years of staying in one place, my father always found another "excellent opportunity" elsewhere. We had already moved three times since I was born. My mum always joked that our life pattern was modeled after one of our favorite children's books, *Make Way for Ducklings*, where the father goes ahead, and the mother has to bring the babies to meet him. Despite her gripes, Mum had resigned herself to being an obedient Christian wife, so she packed our things and drove us up to New York City to meet our father, who was already there. Mum squeezed us four children and two dogs into our blue Ford minivan. Ironically, this was the same car that would later take us away from her.

It was December 1997, a week before Christmas, and the roads were slick with ice. The drive was normally seven hours but ended up closer to nine with the miserable weather. I can only imagine what Mum must have felt, being cooped up and outnumbered by her children on that long drive. Reese, my older sister, was eight and a fierce navigator in the front seat next to Mum, who was frail and hid behind her curtains of long brown hair. Reese had an array of maps strewn across her legs, her feet not quite touching the floor, as she instructed Mum: "*Wrong turn! No! The other way!*" Forever overwhelmed, Mum started to slump down further in her seat until she bent exhaustedly over the steering wheel.

I wish my mum had stood up for herself during these times. Part of me wishes I had also interjected. But just as Reese had inherited bossy traits from our father, I seemed to have inherited my mother's submissive nature. Any controversy made me quiver. If ever I found myself the target of a disagreement, I would completely break down in tears and apologize. My father called me the peacekeeper of the family, as I always tried to smooth out the group members' jagged edges.

On the drive, I sat next to baby Laura, who was fast asleep. Her tiny cheeks puffed with exhalations of air. I remembered holding her in the hospital months earlier, right after she was born. At first, I was annoyed, since I had to put on a bow and an itchy Sunday-school dress to visit our new sister. At the hospital, an overly excited nurse put Laura in my arms. *Weird*, I remember thinking, *she looks like an alien*. My arms began to get tired, and since the nurse had left, I tried to pass Laura to Mum. Then the oddest thing happened—even as a little girl I knew it was strange: Mum didn't want to hold her.

My mum had been bedridden during the last few months of the pregnancy, and the birth was especially difficult. Years later I found in my mum's diary an entry from right after the delivery: "I have great love for this baby. Laura and I have gone through so much together." The entry was particularly startling because I don't remember ever seeing her express those emotions.

Slightly irritated, I continued to hold Laura. I found a chair that supported my arms and cradled her until the nurse came back to put her in a bassinet. Only then did I feel something. As soon as she took her from me, my body seemed to physically revolt. It was as if there were an invisible cord that ran between the two of us. I started crying until I was allowed to hold her again.

ONLY WHEN WE REACHED South Orange, New Jersey, did I realize that we weren't going to be living in New York City. I felt cheated, the visions of vast skyscrapers and bright lights ripped from my head. In the dark, we found the house that was supposed to be our new home. Our father ran outside without any shoes. He waded through the snow, too excited to think of cold feet. I remember wishing that I could feign that same level of enthusiasm but instead only managed to whisper, "*This* is the place?"

Even as I became an adult, this shame remained with me. It wasn't inherently the state of New Jersey that was embarrassing, but rather the next few years that followed. Often, I will bypass these years altogether and tell people I am from New York. Close enough, right? For me, this move signified the start of a downward spiral.

At first, Mum continued to homeschool us, as she had in rural Virginia. She wrote in her diary:

> *One day I was pointing to a four syllable word while I was teaching her to read and instructed "Read this page EXCEPT for THIS word because you'll learn how to read THAT word, later next week." Victoria replied in casual tones while pointing straight to the word, "Oh, you mean 'transportation'?"*

Eventually, though, Mum's reclusive behavior intensified, and we became more self-taught. It started with Mum's hiding in her room after our father left for work. When he went away on business trips, she would sometimes not come out for several days. Frightened of failing our father's "pop quizzes," or worse

yet, of his muttering the words "I am disappointed in your performance," we anxiously studied our workbooks together. Although
my brother, Timmy; Reese; and I were each a grade or two apart,
we all studied the curriculum from Reese's books to be safe. The
neurotic pace of our learning was partly fueled by fear but mostly
by pride. Compared with the other children in our church, we
were odd. And while we accepted that kids could make fun of
us for our behaviors, we swore that they would never be able to
call us stupid. We would never be the coolest kids, but we could
learn more and try harder than everyone else. Knowledge made
us feel powerful.

Meanwhile, my mother became more of a ghost. I would claw
at her bedroom door and cry, but she remained silently locked
inside.

In my diary I later wrote:

> *My sister called you Sleeping Beauty,*
> *But weren't you ugly?*
> *Stacked bones, tired face,*
> *A tiny waist I couldn't hold,*
> *Because I had tried*
> *And you would never*
> *Hold me*
> *Back.*

Restless, we ran wild. The only good part about the house
was that our backyard bordered the South Mountain Reservation, a 2,110-acre nature reserve complete with waterfalls, creeks,
and abandoned cabins. Timmy occupied himself by chasing wild
turkeys, catching toads in the streams, and finding ever-taller trees
to climb. Reese and I would team up as fort builders and trail-
blazers. We once created a rather impressive teepee (really, more
of a lean-to) and lived in it for a full weekend, until it rained.

Together, we created whole worlds for ourselves, ones we would have much rather occupied than the real one.

During these times, we would fortify ourselves by the most creative means possible. We invented our meals—Timmy created brews of milk and ginger ale, Reese preferred handfuls of cream cheese or Miracle Whip, and Laura would lick a spoonful of peanut butter for hours or eat lipstick like it was a banana. I came to prefer pickle juice and clumps of cocoa powder.

My mum said of these times, "The depression had marched across my brain to the point that 'weep-and-sleep and weep-and-sleep' was the way I spent my days, alone in the bedroom behind closed doors."

Without Mum, we resorted to any form of sustenance we could find in the cupboards. As our father's trips away lengthened, we became more desperate. Timmy, who was naturally brilliant at math, once broke down an allotment of saltine crackers for us children based on our weight and age. We had to make the sleeve of crackers last for days.

I CAN REMEMBER ONLY one time Mum cooked of her own accord, although my siblings said it happened a handful of times. Our uncle Carlo and aunt Sue were planning a visit from Italy, and Mum announced that she would make some rendition of savory chicken pockets. The recipe was an "award winner" in a contest that Pillsbury had sponsored. The dough company probably just wanted to sell their product, but my mum fell for the marketing, which claimed that the dish was the newest, most sophisticated, yet hardest-to-mess-up dinner out there. I knew it could only lead to humiliation.

Timmy was sincerely worried there might not be supper at all, and my father began yelling. Little Laura found a hiding place in the pantry and stayed there all day.

Mum tried to explain her reasoning. Aunt Sue was a Cordon Bleu–trained chef (which I didn't completely understand, but it sounded impressive), and Uncle Carlo was a count of Castello della Manta, a twelfth-century fortress tucked into the snow-capped foothills of the Alps. Our grandmother the Countess Anna had grown up with Uncle Carlo. I urged my mother to consider a more "beginner" recipe. Instead, she made those horrible chicken pockets.

When Uncle Carlo and Aunt Sue arrived later that evening, I had never seen a better-looking couple. It wasn't so much their features but rather their presence. Uncle Carlo seemed taller than the oak trees Timmy loved to climb, and Aunt Sue had a laugh like a movie star's. He wore an abundant array of textures and fabrics I had never experienced—cashmere, wool, and corduroy. She wrapped a silk scarf around her shoulders, which seemed the most elegant thing I could possibly imagine. Next to them, I felt unimportant in my raggedy church clothes.

Uncle Carlo quickly put me at ease: "You have the face of a de Rege!" he told me as I touched my cheeks, trying to find the Italian "of the king" part. He also told me the history behind a print Mum had hung on our wall that we called "the Pink Lady." "This is from Castello della Manta, where your grandmother Anna was so happy, where your family is from." He pointed at me, and I leaned in with awe. My family was from a castle?

Of the countless rooms in the *castello*, there was one, in particular, the Salone Baronale, that my grandmother Anna loved. In it were ancient frescoes depicting heroes and heroines throughout history. Completed in 1420, the murals included renderings of King Charlemagne; Julius Caesar; Tamiris, queen of the Shiites; and my grandmother's favorite, Teuta, queen of the Illyrians, or "the Pink Lady." Teuta wore a long rose gown and looked toward her left with an outstretched hand, as if saying, *Come with me*.

After graduating from high school, Anna went to Oxford

University. She soon dropped out of college to marry a "commoner" from Canada, the first in the family to marry outside of the nobility or aristocracy. "It was quite a scandal," our mum said. Now our family history was so watered down I hadn't even heard of Castello della Manta, let alone visited.

DURING DINNER, Mum was resolutely apologetic. Before anyone had even taken a bite, she was sorry it wasn't more "highbrow," sorry it might be a bit "dry," and sorry she didn't have time to try something a bit more "challenging." Biting into the chicken pocket was like grabbing a bit of sorrow and being forced to swallow it. Here it was, pure humiliation. I felt it flooding our faces in front of Uncle Carlo and Aunt Sue.

What I didn't expect was the reaction from our Italian relatives. For me, adults fell into two camps: the criers and the yellers. I was sure Aunt Sue would start crying over how horrible the chicken pockets were, and Uncle Carlo would yell at my mum and storm out.

Instead, they were both enchanting and warm. It radiated from them like microwaves of hospitality. Aunt Sue always seemed to have the right knee-jerk response to all of Mum's laments ("Something a bit more *challenging*? Well, I'd rather have something that goes down *easy*!"). Uncle Carlo changed the subject and asked us children questions about ourselves. He remarked on how big we had gotten, how everything we were doing was just great, just *great*. No one had ever spoken to us like this before. We were floating on a cloud. When Timmy asked if Uncle Carlo was a count, he replied with a chortle, "A count of no account!" The response made Timmy giggle and draw closer to him.

That night, I realized that food was only a part of dining.

Previously, I'd fixated on when I would eat next, not *how* I would do it or with *whom*. Unlike my mum's apologies, which created a tense and awkward air, Uncle Carlo and Aunt Sue's reassurance had made us feel light and carefree. With good company, dinner even seemed easier to digest.

AS MY CURIOSITY ABOUT food and drink began to evolve, I started running a lemonade stand on the weekend. My father insisted that the profits from my "small business" would have to cover costs—lemonade mix, paper towels, ice, cups, and the table rental. Our father believed everything in the house belonged to him. If we wanted to use something, we would have to pay for it.

There were few things thus far that I had been able to control in my life. Admittedly not my father's temper nor my mother's absence, and certainly not the way kids looked at me in Sunday school. But the money I clenched in my sweaty palms after a long day working the lemonade stand was something I had earned and received. Pride trickled in as I counted the cash. I knew this was something I could control and do well.

I sorted out a payment plan for the table, and within a month, it was paid off. The paper towels, the lemonade mix, the cups— soon I started purchasing everything in bulk to get a better deal. I combed the supermarket to find the lowest prices. The different brands and flavors of lemonade were all taste-tested and ranked. I found the ubiquitous pink lemonade was a crowd-pleaser, but I could charge more for the real deal—lemon juice and sugar—if it was called "homemade." Although I didn't know it at the time, this was an early lesson in marketing. What I did know back then was that working and crunching costs made me feel useful.

By the time the wind started to hold a chill and the leaves began falling from the oak trees Timmy loved to climb, the lemonade stand was a well-operated and successful business. My first job, as an unknowing "beverage director," left me as all lemonade does—thirsty for more.

⚜

Shortly after the dinner party with Carlo and Sue, my parents began to seriously unravel. We would go to bed, pretending to be asleep, but instead listen to screaming and slamming, thuds and bangs, then cries and apologies between my parents.

An excerpt from my diary reads:

> *They didn't know I was listening, but I'm sure they had some idea. His voice was raised, hers probably fighting tears. The crack underneath my door was the only light in the room. He yelled, things were hit. . . . She choked back tears with apologies. She was always sorry, he never knew how to fix it.*

"You can't feed your own children?" we heard my father bellow about how the money he brought in fulfilled his husbandly duties and she needed to be a wife.

"I need to see a doctor," Mum begged.

Our father bellowed back, "Prayer"—he hit something loudly—"is what you need, not medication or someone in your head!"

Religion was a weapon swung at us. I hated the churches we were forced into every Sunday and the fact that our father wouldn't let us leave the sermons halfway through with all of the other children. He complained that they took the kids away to fatten them up with cookies and sing songs. *Uh, yeah!* I thought. *That sounds amazing.* Instead, we had to listen to the sermon with the adults and pay *very* close attention. Afterward, he would give us all a quiz on the car ride home. If we didn't know the proper answers, we would surely burn in hell. From this, I taught myself to listen to the pastor's buzzwords and repeat them later to my father.

We never questioned our father's words. We believed Mum was sick because she didn't pray enough. Soon, our father became aloof and distant, traveling on increasingly frequent business trips. Mum would sometimes come out of her room and feed us, but mostly it was to go on errands to the bank or the post office. In my mum's diary she wrote about a time she came out of her room:

> Victoria noticed that our neighbors had a really beautiful garden because they were retired and "because they had no children." One day Mummy and Victoria were cuddling and snuggling and Mummy said lovingly, "Oh Victoria, where would I be without you?" Victoria answered helpfully, "You would have a beautiful garden."

In what later was described to me as a "political move," our father came home one afternoon in late May while Mum was out on an errand and told us, "Kids, you have three minutes to pack up all of your belongings."

It took a few moments for his announcement to sink in. We froze while holding our Beanie Babies in our hands. He had interrupted a pretend wedding where the spud was marrying the brown dog. Questions leaped out of our mouths faster than we could think. Our father ignored them all and added, "Now you only have two minutes left, you had better hurry."

I scrambled to pack up Cookie, my guinea pig, who would die only days later of explosive diarrhea, while Timmy made sure to secure all of his toy soldiers. Reese packed a box of seedy romance novels she had collected from Grandma Willie, and all Laura wanted to bring was a blanket. I helped her carry out some clothes anyway. Although we weren't quite sure what was happening, we knew it wasn't rational. Even as an eight-year-old, I felt our father saw those in his life as pieces on a chessboard. He was always moving us around, on the offensive.

We stuffed all of the belongings we deemed worthy into our blue minivan, the same van that had initially brought us to the house in South Orange. Our father shouted, "Get in! Get in!" In all of the excitement, I threw myself into the passenger seat, the most coveted placement in the car. Reese protested but was quickly shut up by our father; there was no time to argue. Laura and Reese sat in the middle seat and Timmy hid in the way back. Cookie was on my lap.

Our father revved the engine, and we flew down South Mountain. "Where are we going?" Reese said, demanding an answer from our father. When there was no response, she kept asking. He met her eyes in the rearview mirror with a dead-set stare. She knew what that meant and quickly became quiet.

Cookie *wheeep wheeep wheeep*ed as guinea pigs do in times of distress and pooped little pellets on my legs when the back tires of the blue van came crashing into the road. Timmy laughed. "You are in deep shit, Victoria. *Literally!*"

The car jerked left, now bounding into the parking lot of the bank, where we saw Mum exiting from large brass doors. She was wearing her peppermint shirt, a nickname I had given it, since it was striped white and red. Now I understood why our father hadn't let me go to the bank with Mum that morning. Usually, if anyone was allowed to go on errands with her, it was me. I liked to tell myself that I was her favorite, but really I knew she chose me because I was the quiet one. My secret to being preferred, which I had picked up from a church sermon: "It is better to remain silent and be thought a fool, than to speak out and remove all doubt."

"We are leaving," our father bellowed at Mum from the car. The way he said *leaving* was what made it all click. He didn't mean the sort of leaving one does for a vacation or for an errand but rather a leaving that meant *gone*. Suddenly I realized that the late-night fights, the slamming and crying, the months of Mum alone in her room while our father was elsewhere—they all added up to this exodus. When someone no longer obeyed our father, they were taken off the chessboard altogether. Mum had been a "broken" piece for years now. The speedometer zoomed forward as a look of recognition dawned on our mother's face. She ran alongside the car and screamed, "Do not take my children!"

I had never seen my mother run; I had never seen her do anything with much speed. Her moves were always slow and fragile; even holding her hand felt like grabbing on to a limp rope. But here she was, sprinting, her legs flicking past one another like a gazelle's. It really looked like she was going to catch up with the van. I was shocked; I hadn't realized until now that Mum cared for us. Most of the time we seemed a nuisance to her, and I had been sure that if we left, she might not even notice. But here she was, running. I mean, *really* running fast.

Our father looked ahead, so as not to hit anything, and turned around in the parking lot. The turn was an opportunity Mum seized and she yanked open my door. She met my eyes, and I met hers—brown like mine, with flecks of green and a red rim that gave way to small lashes. The look they held said, *No, not this.*

"Shut the door!" our father yelled at me. My head snapped around and I looked at his eyes, fiery and piercing. I pulled Cookie tightly toward me with my left arm and extended my right. Mum was running alongside the car, her body a blur of red and white, now pink. Her arms were flailing like ribbons, trying to grab the door of the moving van.

"Shut the door!" On repeat. I extended my hand closer to the handle, my fingers dangling over the plastic loop. Mum was not crying, but she was looking at me as if she would or could.

I didn't know if I would rather be with her outside the car, *running and running,* or inside and running away. The whole thing was confusing to me. Why did our father feel the need for these dramatics? Why parade our departure in front of her? He could have just left a note. Instead, I was stuck in between a woman I had only just seen display maternal instincts for the first time, and a man directing an unwarranted emotional scene. And of course, I had to choose.

"Shut the door!" My father's screams shook my hand outward. I grabbed the plastic handle, wrapped my little fingers around the loop, and with all my might swung it toward me. After a powerful *slam,* everything was silent. A pit of regret began to swell in my belly. Maybe I shouldn't have closed the door. I looked in my side mirror and watched Mum slow and then stop altogether, becoming a little pink speck, a paint drop in the suburban landscape.

THE POOR KIDS

WE MOVED BACK TO MARYLAND, near where I was born. At first, we lived in the basement of our aunt Betty's house with my father's mother, Grandma Willie, the long-since-retired cotton picker. Her sweet Tennessee drawl and habit of handing out chewing gum from her purse made her a favorite among the grandkids.

Willie's comforts remained simple: her five children and grandchildren, peanut brittle, Pall Mall cigarettes, dollar-store romance novels, and white zinfandel on ice. She would sit on the porch, the air around her thick with cigarette smoke and Chanel No. 5 perfume, and slowly sip wine. When her cup would get a bit low, I would bring it back into the kitchen and sneak a watery sip. I was amazed that the pink juice could taste so sweet yet sour. Then I would quickly go about making her another drink—fresh ice, a new glass, and a splash of some more rosé.

"Well, isn't this full service?" Willie would laugh as I handed her cup back. "You got it," she would remark, "makin' yourself useful and thoughtful." She took a small sip of her wine and smiled. "Well, that's the best you can do in life."

THROUGH THE NASTY DIVORCE battle that ensued, Willie raised us, along with our aunt Betty and aunt Kathy. These three wildly different women somehow morphed into one temporary mother for us.

We spent a long summer making mud pies by the Potomac River, wondering if we would ever see Mum again and feeling guilty for not especially missing her. She saved a letter I sent to her, in which I wrote: "Laura says every day 'Where Mummy where?'" I also asked her, "Because you don't have children now, do you have a beautiful garden?"

After a few months of basement living, our father rented a house and instantly announced that it was something we couldn't afford. A sense of unworthiness hit the bottom of my stomach and stayed there. Since there was no money for furniture, we had only a few beds from Goodwill and secondhand dishware no one else in the family wanted.

Now without a job, our father spent his days tutoring us four kids (which we interpreted primarily as punishment). He decided we had been focusing on "fluff" in our homeschooling studies and bought thick math and science textbooks for us. All I wanted to do that summer was disappear into a stack of Nancy Drew novels.

Instead, he forced us to fill out countless worksheets. If we failed to solve a problem correctly, whined with exhaustion, or tried to ask one another for help, a series of punishments would be handed out. His first resort was the rod. It began as a wooden spoon, but when that broke from all of the spankings, he used the metal handle of a flyswatter. The latter left a stinging pain on my backside that throbbed for days. Quickly growing tired of the physical exertion of whipping, he soon had us sprint around the house thirty times (I laughed like a crazy person whenever the neighbors saw, hoping they would think the running was a game). Or, the worst because of my bony knees, he would make us kneel on a bag of rice.

When my mum asked about these punishments, she recorded six-year-old Timmy talking about "time-outs":

> For how many years old you are, that's how many minutes you're in time-out. Then you have your arms up the whole time, then Daddy send someone to check on you. It's painful to hold your arms up. Very painful. And you can't like, be swinging around in like a spiral 'cause it makes it easier. For double time-out you have to sit on the edge of the bathtub with your arms straight out and your legs out. Most of the time we're punished.

Mum also recorded me saying, "Daddy's a little overstrict."

But the worst punishments were psychological. These were "disappointments" our father heaped upon our shoulders. He pitted us against one another, comparing our behaviors. He would call me "stupid" if I didn't finish math problems as fast as Timmy and a "cheater" if I did. The tasks he assigned us were beyond impossible, but we so desperately sought his approval that we did them anyway. I remember thinking that if I just did all of the math problems correctly, my father would finally love me.

About these times, my father says that he wishes he had made better decisions. That the burden of raising us alone led him to favor strict regimens and that he wasn't able to talk about his emotions. In retrospect, there is a lot he wishes he'd done differently.

Within a short period of time, we went from forgotten to micromanaged. I quickly wished I was back with Mum, neglected but free, running wild in the South Mountain Reservation and drinking pickle juice for dinner. That summer, for the first time, I missed something I didn't even know I'd once had— independence.

By the time September came around, instead of transitioning from the inflicted summer school to local classes, we were yanked back to New Jersey by court order. The judge ruled that my father couldn't kidnap and move us across state borders. After a long legal battle, the divorce went through, and sole custody was given to our father. After this, Mum was effectively out of the picture.

Our father and us kids moved back into the old South Orange house. We had only been gone a few months, but things had turned on their head with no explanation. I had to learn to adjust to change quickly—and to loss. All of the furniture Mum loved, including the Pink Lady print from Castello della Manta, was gone. A white square remained on the wall where she used to hang.

IN INTERVALS, Grandma Willie, Aunt Kathy, and Aunt Betty would come to stay with us. The first to leave was Aunt Kathy, who felt no need to hide her opinions about our living situation. My father was the youngest of five siblings. Aunt Kathy was the oldest, and as such had a solution for everything. I always admired her doesn't-take-shit-from-nobody attitude and how she preached, "Do not let a bully win, stand up for yourself!" Aunt Kathy stood up to our father, even though this led to his banning her from visiting for the remainder of our childhood.

Next was Aunt Betty. She was closest in age to my father and the opposite of Kathy in many ways. Whereas his older sister was fierce and strong willed, Betty was soft and open-minded. She didn't speak much, like me, and I felt safe around her. Betty made herself most helpful in making our meals (our first time having fresh peas!) and taking us shopping for clothes (my first pair of new sneakers!). Eventually, she had to return to her own family and seven children, but she would visit and check in on us, take us out for a nice meal or buy us clothes for school. Although she would ask how I was and how things were at home, I never told her the whole truth, thinking that to complain would be selfish. Fear of being a bother was a feeling I carried with me well into my career as a sommelier. Keeping things bottled up inside seemed easier than causing conflict. Looking back now, I wish that for my sake and my siblings' sake, I had just spoken up.

UNTIL HER DEATH six years later, Grandma Willie kept hope in our hearts. We would wake to her singing with the sizzling of fresh sausages on the griddle. Sleepy-eyed, Reese and I would crawl to the breakfast table in our matching pink nightgowns, Timmy in his dinosaur pajamas, and Laura in her diapers. *"I love you, a bushel and a peck, a bushel and a peck and a hug around the neck,"* she would sing, and ask us each how we wanted our eggs cooked.

Never before had anyone asked us *how* we wanted our food prepared. "What are the choices?" Timmy asked first, carefully taking mental notes as Grandma Willie went through the variations.

At first, I didn't want to make a decision. I worried that if we all chose different options, it would make breakfast a nuisance for Grandma. I didn't want her to go to extra trouble for me, so I let everyone else choose first. They all chose differently! Reese picked over-easy eggs, poking the yolk and watching with glee as it ran about her plate. Timmy loved scrambled eggs, mainly if he was in charge of whisking the eggs briskly with a fork. He wiggled and writhed like an electrical current was moving through his dinosaur pajamas. Laura also went for scrambled eggs, always keen to follow in Timmy's footsteps, hers with cheese.

When it was my turn, I apologized for my siblings, all the extra work they'd given her, and said she should make whatever was easiest. "Nonsense, you silly girl!" Grandma Willie began. "Fixing your breakfast the way you want it, now, that there is what will bring me happiness. No trouble at all." I will never forget how good she made me feel.

With Willie, food became a joy. Every morning before school we had a proper breakfast of eggs with toast and often hotcakes, sausages, bacon, biscuits, and fruit. We learned that pears needed to spend a day or two in a brown bag on the counter before eating. Clementines were like oranges but smaller, sweeter, and only available once a year. There were also different types of apples— Golden Delicious, Honeycrisp, Granny Smith—with different flavors.

On our birthdays, she would prepare a special meal of our choosing. I always asked for her "Tennessee green beans," which were practically fried in bacon fat, alongside roasted chicken and potatoes. The bird was doused in so much lemon juice that the spuds at the bottom would suck up the acid and all the chicken fat, becoming the best part of the dish—little zippy, oily bites. Whenever she was cooking, it was as if the whole house filled with the smell of a home. Aromas of crispy chicken skin and crackling bacon fat told us that someone loved us so much, they were going through all of this trouble.

I can remember only one instance of seeing my granny Anna and my grandmother Willie together. This was before they both lost all their hair and started undergoing chemotherapy, before my parents divorced and became caricatures of themselves, their

eccentricities turning into full-blown mental disorders, and before I could realize how phenomenal these women indeed were.
I was six.

They were both at Granny's house in Lake Monticello, smoking cigarettes at the kitchen counter, propped up on stools and
leaning into the radio. Don McLean's "American Pie" started to
spring out of the speaker, and Anna quickly turned the knob to
the right. The song grew louder until it seemed to reverberate in
my bones.

Willie tapped her cigarette into an ashtray and slowly let
out lyrics with her warm southern drawl. She sang along about
maybe being happy for a while, her Tennessee tone dripping like
melted butter. Anna's voice, perched high and soft like a mourn-
ing dove's, chimed in. They both crushed their cigarettes and
hummed along until the chorus, when they both stood up and bellowed, "Bye, bye, Miss American Pie . . ."

They started patting their hips and swaying to the left and
right. Necklaces shimmied across sweaters and slippers twisted
back and forth. These two women, both in their seventies, suddenly became teenagers over cigarettes and rock music.

They both carried out the last note and then collapsed in their
chairs, laughing until tears started to swell in their eyes. Anna
lit another cigarette and handed the matches to Willie, who took
them gratefully.

"You have such lovely hands," Anna remarked. She always
handed out compliments, little genuine morsels, that delighted
everyone around her. Making others happy will make you happy,
she always told me.

Willie struck the stick against the side of the box, a tiny flame
appearing at the tip. "These are cotton-picker hands"—Willie
laughed—"all torn and pricked . . . Now, your hands are the
good ones, pretty things with blue blood runnin' through 'em."

Anna took Willie's hands in hers. "You are kind, but no, mine are chubby from too much biscotti." Anna looked over at me, where I sat wide-eyed and quiet in the corner. "Victoria, what do you think?"

Upon hearing my name, I obediently walked closer and looked up at their hands, intertwined in one another's. Small brown spots dotted their skin, and bright indigo veins popped up like mountain ranges. Over time, their hands, which belonged to such different people, had started to look the same.

"Which old lady do you think has the better hands?" Anna smiled at me as Willie winked and slid in, "The contessa or the cotton picker?"

I studied both of their hands closely. Was there a difference? My love and admiration for them both had sunk so deeply into my bones that I knew I could never see one as better than the other. I looked up at their anticipatory grins and shrugged. "They look the same to me."

With roots in both of their worlds, I grew up with the knowledge that one's social class did not define one's character.

Most important, on that afternoon, when the two of them jumped up together to dance to "American Pie," I realized that some joys are universal. Like music, the wonders of art, food, and beverage can transcend all boundaries. I remember thinking of this day when I became a sommelier. I wanted to capture that feeling, the exhilaration of familiarity, and bring people together through wine.

⚜

Since we were a "low-income household," us kids received free meals when we began public school. I was eight. Normal school lunches were already a travesty of the culinary arts: processed and canned food served without concern. But even worse were the school lunches set aside for the "poor kids," which we soon learned meant fewer comforting, recognizable food options, such as apples and chips, and more mysterious blobs of brown paste.

Worse yet, children who received low-income-household lunches were served last and forced to stand in line after all of the *regular* kids went past the lunch counter. I was one of three poor kids during my lunch hour, so we stood out.

The mush was sour, the meat was tough as jerky, and the diced vegetables were soggy and free of any flavor. Having been told that only selfish and ungrateful children would refuse food, I guiltily pushed everything around on my plate so I would appear agreeable.

Grandma Willie occasionally gave me money to use for lunch when our father wasn't looking. In my diary I wrote:

> *I took the dollar bill and slipped it into my sock and ran to the cafeteria. I entered the lunch line proudly clutching my treasure. Suddenly I felt an elbow in my side and an empty apology. "Get out of the lunch line. We all know you don't have any money." I tried to ignore him, but he kept saying it, calling me poor, making fun of my hand-me-down jeans held up by a thick knotted rope and my dirty sneakers with holes in the bottom. When I came towards the lunch lady, I grabbed a carton of milk and just shoved the money into her hand. She gave me a cold face and remarked that chocolate milk was an extra 25 cents. Tears welled up in my eyes when she said they didn't have any other milk left, and that I owed her 25 cents. I dropped the carton and ran from the cafeteria, into the girl's bathroom. I sat there for hours, ignoring the deep rumble in my stomach. I was used to it. The next day I told my grandmother that milk was now free, and I didn't need money.*

This was our first foray into a real school, and we were socially inept. Our only interaction with kids our age had occurred for brief moments during church. We couldn't afford lunch, our clothes weren't from the right shops, and we didn't own a television or have AOL instant messenger. I wished I could follow my father's suggestion not to let the other kids make me feel embarrassed, but it doesn't quite work like that when you're a kid.

Each of us was the youngest in our grade, which didn't help our attempts at social acceptance. We'd all tested high and skipped a grade when entering the public school. Timmy was called a pipsqueak in the second grade, and I was a ragamuffin in the fourth grade. Our father's demanding lessons had at least taught us intellectual discipline. Classwork seemed a joke in comparison to the hours of intensive exercises he had heaped onto our plates. For the rest of my schooling (and later in my sommelier studies) I found that because my father had drilled into me a relentless focus, I always forced myself to learn at an unusually accelerated pace.

WHEN GRANDMA WILLIE MOVED into a retirement home, the kids took over the kitchen. My father set up a rotation and each day of the month was a different kid's turn to clean. These "cleanup days" were split between Reese, Timmy, and myself.

One evening on Timmy's cleanup day, bowls, cutlery, and plates were piled high, and we all had to watch—myself in sadness—while Timmy pulled over a tiny step stool and got to work. None of us were allowed to help the others. Halfway through, his legs started to shake in his dinosaur pajamas. He had to go to the restroom. I begged my father to let him take a break, but he had a strict rule that no one was allowed to leave the kitchen until their duties were complete.

Timmy's legs began to violently twist, and tears began to stream down his seven-year-old face. "Please!" I implored my father to see reason. But my father was not one for concessions.

Little rivers of yellow began to trickle down the step stool. Timmy was sobbing now, the humiliation all-encompassing. I leaned against the door frame and cried with him. Our father walked away.

OUR FATHER TOOK OVER the food shopping when Grandma Willie left. Every other Saturday we would head to the grocery store with a box full of coupons and a carefully curated shopping list. Before the trip it was my job to clip deals from the paper and compile a list of necessities. The first part of this job was particularly tricky, as our father believed the newspaper to be another waste of money. As a result, I was instructed to go through the neighbors' paper-recycling bins and fish out their gently used glossies for coupons. I wore a baseball cap low, to hide the top half of my face. I must have looked absurd, a tiny girl upside down with her legs in the air, diving deep into large blue tubs on the side of the street.

Necessities in shopping meant just that. There were no frills here. Our father believed it was his sole duty to put a roof over our heads and to clothe and feed us (both done as frugally as possible). When the free-lunch program was cut from school, our lunches became throwaways from the deli counter after he discovered that for a few dollars, he could score a bag of meat and cheese "ends"—the small butt of the ham or cheese that didn't make it through the slicer. These meat pieces were tough, and the cheese slabs were often just rinds. Biting into a sandwich made with these ends was a nasty endeavor, as it took forever to chew through the rough chunks. "Are you even supposed to eat these?" Reese would say, grimacing at our father. I spent lunches alone at a cafeteria table, pretending to be so engrossed in a book that I "forgot" to eat. I was too ashamed to gnaw at a bark-like lump of a sandwich in front of my classmates.

Impressively, our father was able to feed the whole family on a monthly budget of $400 throughout the late 1990s and early 2000s. Never more and never less. If we went over the limit at the register we were questioned and had to return an item (*Did you not calculate the tax correctly!?*). I always opted for the meat and cheese ends to get cut but it was usually the paper towels (just *throwing* away money, our father would say). Timmy was always the best at math, but I started to take joy in budgeting and crunching costs as I had with the lemonade stand. If we were able to balance everything just perfectly, I could find a way to allow us a few luxuries.

During these childhood shopping trips, if I had been especially good at pinching pennies and coupon clipping, our luxury treat was a small New York strip steak, slathered in Worcestershire sauce and lots of pepper. There was only enough for each of us to have a few bites, but it was a flavor so fulfilling that the taste lasted for hours. This small reward made everything else disappear. Our mother's absence, our father's tyranny, the friends I didn't have—all of it melted away. Was this what a good bite of food could do? Maybe, but it wasn't just the steak that gave me this sentiment. The Dumpster diving, coupon clipping, and graph-paper planning were what made the steak taste not only delicious but also deserved.

THE GREASY SPOON

IN THE SPRING OF 2003, I graduated from lemonade stands and started a pet-sitting business with Reese. I was twelve and she was thirteen. We printed out one hundred flyers and soon found ourselves with an impressive list of clients. Our rotation included cats, dogs, guinea pigs, mice, an ant farm, and a plant collection. But the business was short-lived.

On occasion we would speak to Mum over the phone, and she would press us for details on our lives. During one of these calls she recorded the details of the pet-sitting business's downfall:

> Over the following weeks Reese made two runaway attempts, the last one was 6/29 and she was returned to her father by the police. She left a note to her father "I've left. I'll call you when I get settled."
>
> She took several trips on her bike in the middle of the night to bring her belongings over to a neighbor's house. This house

was unoccupied. Reese had been cat-sitting while the owners
were away and so she had their keys.

When the news spread that we were more squatters than sit-
ters, and that the cat owners had unknowingly harbored a run-
away child, our neighborhood credibility was ruined. Our father
was furious that Reese had caused such a scene, so he shipped her
off to Virginia, where she spent the next few years being tossed
around like a hot potato between Aunt Betty, Aunt Kathy, and
finally, Mum. I don't know how this made her feel, and I never
asked. Our relationship fizzled in and out over the years. Still,
my heart broke for her.

Now that I was the oldest sibling in the house, I spent the next
few years teaching Laura to read and trying to keep hyperactive
Timmy entertained. Childhood slipped away, and soon I was a
teenager. More than ever before, I yearned to fit in with my peers.
High school meant cliques that formed around clothing, music,
and movies. But all of these things involved money. More and
more, I began to count on the prospect of work to provide me
with an escape from home and school.

THE GREASY SPOON WAS located near the railroad tracks that led
to New York City. It seemed one step closer to the city that I was
sure held my future. Hearing the rumble of the arriving trains on
the platform filled me with hope.

The air was a soup of hamburger grease and filled with the
never-ending ringing of a little bell from the kitchen, followed
by a gruff *"Order up!"*

The diner maintained a questionable level of cleanliness, the
walls yellowed from years of frying oil, and it was well known
that the bathroom should only be used in case of emergency. Regardless, it was the neighborhood spot: where teachers went for

coffee before school, where kids cut classes and smoked cigarettes, where families would celebrate birthdays, and where I
desperately wanted to work. The whole place seemed like a party
you could disappear into, a way of hiding in plain sight.

Months after Reese ran away, I turned thirteen and walked
into the Greasy Spoon clutching a freshly printed résumé. With
no official prior work experience, I instead highlighted my pet-
sitting business, babysitting gigs, church volunteer work, and
straight-A report card.

Upon entering, I was struck by the smell of wet, mildewed
rags. At the counter that separated the eatery from the kitchen,
I asked for Ed. Everyone in town knew Ed was the owner, and
I hoped that dropping his name would make me seem confident.
My hands began to shake as an Indian woman behind the counter
looked me up and down.

Meeting Ed sent a chill running down my spine. I was almost
a woman and had learned what certain *looks* meant. Ed was full
of those looks and more. He was entirely bald (save for a few hair
plugs that looked as horrific as those in the scene from the film
The Fly when the character begins to grow setae, little clawlike
hairs). His small facial features combined with his thin figure
made him look a bit like a weasel. The only times I saw Ed outside the restaurant were when he was driving around in his shiny
convertible, always with a different girl by his side. I quickly
blurted out that I was looking for a job, and I tried my best to
imitate my childhood pastor, using a confident sermonlike tone
and buzzwords that I thought sounded impressive.

Like the woman at the counter, he gave me an up-and-down
look, but his eyes seemed to rest uncomfortably on my developing chest before moving upward. I was well aware that by thirteen, I'd grown into my looks. Still, being attractive hadn't been
a positive thus far in my life. My appearance made Reese resent
me growing up, and as a result, I tried to hide in dark clothes and

under curtains of hair. Recently, men had started taking notice of me, but this attention only made me even more uncomfortable.

"Yeah, some bitch just called out, so we need another girl. You can start tomorrow, four P.M." Ed smacked gum and cracked a foreboding smile. The Indian woman behind the counter rolled her eyes. I was elated. I thanked him numerous times and quickly left before he could change his mind. An entry from my diary says: "*I went to the Greasy Spoon & I was HIRED!*"

I SPRINTED HOME TO tell Timmy the excellent news. My mind raced along with my body as I trekked for miles up South Mountain. I thought of all the horrors I might commit—dropping a tray, forgetting someone's order, slipping and falling, burning myself with a pot of coffee. I shook the possibility of failure out of my head and swallowed my fear.

At the time, I chalked up my good luck to the fact that I was a go-getter. Only later did I realize that it was probably my vulnerability that led Ed to hire me at age thirteen.

I found Timmy at home, crouched over an impossible pile of homework, my father carefully watching from across the table. Timmy was a boy of impressive intellect, with the ability to ace exams without studying. Still, our father found this to be without merit. "You have to force yourself, train yourself, to do what you aren't good at or don't like," he would say. Upon investigation, he would find months of homework piled up in Timmy's backpack and force him to do it all in one sitting. For a boy who could never sit still, concentrating for hours on menial assignments was torture.

Timmy straightened from his hunch and looked up at me, his face streaked with tears. My first instinct was to scoop him up, but I hesitated as I saw my father watching us from across the table, his face as firm as a rock.

My father is a man who likes to be happy but more often than not found himself otherwise. The firmness of his stone face began to loosen, and his eyes shifted from my brother as I told them my news—*I got my first job!* Timmy jumped up and hugged my lower waist, burying his head in my side. Even amid stress, Timmy always found a way to be genuinely happy for others. I admired his ability to remain warm during cold times.

I could tell my father was proud. Hard work and good grades were the way to his heart. When he was happy, he would shed his hardened skin. He wasn't without skepticism, though. "Be careful," he started in a grave tone, "your good looks will get you in many doors, but only your brains will keep you there." He added, "And *never* let Ed drive you home."

EVEN BEFORE MY FIRST shift, I was in debt. The uniform of a shirt, apron, and matching visor (yes, a visor, even though I would work indoors) put me out $50. I would work it off, Ed informed me with a wink that made me uneasy. I wondered if his actual business was hiring naive girls, making them buy silly diner gear, and then firing them.

Since no one wanted to train me—"Not my problem, I already got my two girls to care for at home" or "Princess isn't about to slow *me* down"—Ed said I would just observe for the day and then "wing it" tomorrow, for my first live shift. To observe meant to try not to get shoved, punched, hit, burned, cut, or scraped, or topple a tray of hot food. I pressed myself into corners and against walls to avoid these mishaps. During the busy after-school rush, I wished the walls could have absorbed my body, which always felt in the way.

Everyone was fully "in the weeds," which, as I later learned, meant fucking busy. Each server had five or six tables asking for a million things at once—more ketchup, no salt in their soup, another coffee refill, their check, an ice-cream sundae—and I was not to meddle. However, I didn't know this at the time. Instead, I did what I always tried to do and made myself useful.

A nearby table asked me for ketchup, and without thinking twice, I brought a bottle to them. Apparently, doing so was stepping on someone else's turf. I felt a shoulder clip my arm as a server pushed me to the side and slammed a bottle of ketchup on the table in front of me. The guests looked at the two bottles of ketchup in front of them, confused. Loudly, the server exclaimed, "Oh! You were already brought ketchup. *I didn't know*, my apologies." The server shot me a furious look. "So sorry to waste everyone's time here." I pressed my body back against the wall and mumbled a series of apologies.

My second mistake was smiling at a seated family that acknowledged my awkward presence, squeezed in between a pillar and the cash register. The family smiled back at me while their server was looking. This did not sit well with the server, who proceeded to walk up to me, shove menus in my hand, and say, "Well if you want them so bad, you can have them," adding under his breath, "*Burn, baby, burn.*" The server walked away and joined a group of two other aproned employees. They stared at me with crossed arms. I could tell they wanted me to fail miserably and, humiliated, never come back again.

I took the server's challenge and walked over to the smiling table. All of a sudden I was drenched in a shower of requests— *Two iced teas (do you have Sweet'N Low?), a Diet Coke, no, scratch that, a Sprite, and an egg cream.*

A *what?* I wrote it all down, smiled, and walked away in a silent panic.

I stalled on preparing the egg cream as I put together the iced teas (with Sweet'N Low) and Sprite. The night before, I had studied the take-out menu, but I couldn't recall a drink with egg and cream. I thought that perhaps this was something ordinary people ordered, something so intuitive that it needn't be listed on a menu, like soda. Therefore, I grabbed an egg from the cook, who seemed puzzled and annoyed by my request, and cream from the coffee fridge. I mixed the two in a plastic cup until it appeared a drinkable texture. *Voilà!* An egg cream. The guest was not pleased.

From this enormous embarrassment, a beautiful thing happened—the servers grew to *like* me. Shanti, the woman who'd looked me up and down when I first walked in and had paw prints tattooed above her breasts, scooped up my gummy glass and replaced it with an *actual* egg cream. (Apparently, the *real* drink is made with seltzer, chocolate syrup, and milk.) She placed my concoction on the counter and erupted in laughter, calling over the rest of the servers to "see what this crazy little girl just made." Their tables now abandoned, they bent over in hysterics. My face flushed red. It seemed everyone in the world knew what an egg cream was, except me. I tried to bury this shame and let myself join in on the laughter. The drink *did* look ridiculous.

"The girl's got balls," a wiry server named DeShawn chimed in.

He patted my back, and Shanti added warmly, "Next time, ask for help." I looked back at the ragtag diner staff, their faces now sincere with pity. As the night sped forward, my gluey drink remained on the counter for comic relief. Whenever a server walked by, they let out a small chuckle. The egg cream had succeeded in breaking up the tension of my first shift. With all of the pressure the diner created throughout the day, I could tell it felt good to laugh.

THE COOK,
THE DISHWASHER, AND ME

THERE ARE TWO PEOPLE YOU have to befriend before anyone else," Shanti told me. "The cook and the dishwasher." My first actual day of work opened with a swarm of advice from everyone, but this is the one message that stuck with me. The cook and dishwasher had the most brutal hours; they were the first people there and the last to leave. At around six A.M. every day they would drag their bodies in, make coffee, and flick on the grills. The cook would then place a cigarette in between his lips and bring his face to the flames for a light. The dishwasher would turn on the tiny radio in the kitchen and salsa music would cough from a rusty speaker.

With music echoing around the diner, the cook would fly through prepping hundreds of poached eggs for Benedicts— dropping them in boiling water, waiting three minutes, then transferring them rapidly to an ice bath. The eggs swam in a bucket of ice and water, perfectly preserved, until ordered. Cans of hollandaise were opened, sprigs of parsley were plucked, peppers were sliced, and pancake batter was mixed. The cook could cut an entire bag of yellow onions in under five minutes, without a single tear welling in his eyes. Later, I learned his trick was to freeze the onions before chopping them. As a result, not a single painful vapor would escape from the bulb.

Meanwhile, the dishwasher went about cleaning the restaurant after the atrocities committed the night before. Billows of chemical clouds formed as he generously applied bleach, Lysol, Windex, and other chemicals one probably shouldn't mix. With the chairs propped up, he mopped the floors and scraped gum out from below the tables. *Sixteen!* the dishwasher would scream to the cook, his daily inventory of scraped gum.

When other staff started arriving, the dishwasher retreated to his station in the back reaches of the restaurant. There, in the dark dish pit, he would put his head down and scrub plates for hours. The cook, separated from the dish pit by a walk-in fridge, would keep up with the tickets thrown in the window with heated fury. Whenever an illegible order was received, the cook would let out a wild scream and send the request back through the window as a giant spitball. As the day grew into night, he would become more ferocious, gnawing at a T-bone while flipping hamburger patties and slamming pots. The dishwasher was the opposite. By nighttime he was already a ghost of himself, drifting to sleep over the churning of the dishwashing machines.

During my first week at the diner, I ventured into the kitchen in search of coleslaw. The cook's eyes jerked toward me, and he spun around and looked at the empty bowl I held in my hands. Without words, he pointed toward the walk-in fridge with his greasy spatula, flinging flecks of oil onto my apron. I smiled nervously while the splatters soaked into the fabric of my clothes. I could feel his eyes burning holes into my back as I walked past him and into the fridge.

When the fridge door swung open, I was overwhelmed by the pungent aromas. Inside lay the most massive bucket I had ever seen, filled with a creamy lake of shredded cabbage. A couple of flies were currently in the process of drowning, a few others buried underneath. I felt silly for not bringing a utensil, but since I was fearful of walking past the cook twice, I just dunked the bowl in the bucket, attempting to dodge the flies.

For my next few shifts, fetching coleslaw was the only time I entered the kitchen. Each time, I tried to connect a bit more with the cook through either a smile or a greeting. His response was always an annoyed grunt. I thought maybe I could help them mop the floors or wipe down part of the kitchen but it seemed like I was always getting in the way. Only later did I learn that long after the servers left, they would get down to their respective final duties, each duty the last for the same reason—it was the worst.

I would never have discovered these final duties had I not forgotten my house keys one night. In the beginning, Ed would send me home around nine every evening due to child labor laws. But when I started to ask for more shifts, all *off the clock*, of course, I would leave work later and later. Going home meant trekking for miles in the dark up South Mountain. I was careful to stay on the busy street. Certainly, no one would try to kidnap me with so many potential witnesses?

Just in case, I kept my keys in between each finger, pointed outward, my fist becoming a makeshift weapon. I thought about actually punching someone with my tiny wrists and long fingers— the idea itself was laughable. Still, I kept the keys pressed along the webbing of my fingers. One night, after walking past a particularly ominous set of hedges, I became frightened and reached into my bag to find my keys. They weren't there. Panic spread through my body; without them, I didn't think I could mentally handle the rest of the walk home. I realized I must have left them at the diner.

The Greasy Spoon wasn't a traditional twenty-four-hour diner. I wondered if anyone would even be there if I headed back. I sprinted back as quickly as my wobbly legs could carry me. When I arrived at the Greasy Spoon, the lights were off in the front, and Ed's convertible was no longer parked outside. *Shit.* I knocked on the front door and kept yelling, *Hello, hello, hello.* No one answered. As I neared the rear of the building, I heard a faint sound. I listened closely. What was it? *Salsa music.*

I crept around the back and started banging on the door. I was still terrified of the cook but much more so of the unknown outside. The cook's frightening demeanor was at least familiar. The door swung open, and my thoughts of comfort disappeared. The cook was drenched in sweat. Beads of water fell from his brow, under the gold chain hanging around his neck, and into the forest of chest hair poking out from his white tank top. I rapidly mumbled about my missing keys—they might be on the counter, maybe in the office, I wasn't so sure anymore. Did he even speak English? He stepped to the side with a grunt.

Just past the dish pit I found the dishwasher on all fours. He was leaning over a drain underneath the dishwashing machine with a flashlight and a long, thin wire. His hands wiggled the wire around a bit, then froze, as if he had caught a large fish. He carefully pulled the wire back out toward him. It brought up bits of washed and chewed food, swaths of tangled hair, and bent straws, vomiting from the drain. I covered my mouth with a clap as small roaches scurried about the dishwasher's hands. I was going to either throw up or scream. Maybe both.

The dishwasher looked at me, flicking the roaches from his hands, and started to chuckle. He nodded his head toward the cook. "White girl never seen no one snake a drain before," he said, and they both let out enormous laughs. The roaches were dancing around the bits of chewed food, merrily going about their lives. One started to scurry up his arm.

"There's one on you!" I screeched, pointing. The cook lunged toward him, his palm coming down with a loud slap.

The cook brushed off the dead roach. He motioned for me to follow him, saying, "This way, white girl." It was the first time I'd spoken with them directly. He explained to me that almost every night the dishwasher had to snake the drain, to get rid of all the large bits of things that could cause a much more serious clog. "A big clog"—he looked at me with utmost seriousness— "would really suck."

While the dishwasher did his final duty, the cook had something just as unpleasant on his hands. He passed me a flashlight and told me to get on the ground, by the stoves. Was he serious? I looked at him with disbelief. The floors looked filthy, covered with a full day of business. He didn't waver and motioned for me to get down. Scared of disobeying him, I timidly moved downward. My cheek near the floor, I looked through a thick sea of oil that coated the floor, islands of crumbs, and muck of unknown origin.

He passed me a flashlight and said to look underneath all of the stoves. My long brown hair mopped up the grease on the floor. Lost French fries, tops of English muffins, and lettuce leaves appeared in the spotlight. Then, all of a sudden, a pair of illuminated red eyes looked back at me. I let out a startled shriek. The cook laughed and simply asked, "Dead or alive?"

I shuffled back up to my feet, shaking. "*Very* much alive," I managed to croak out.

The cook suddenly got angry. "*MIERDA!*" he screamed, and started banging on the stove. "Come out, come out, you little shit." He looked back at me and said, "We should check the trap."

I gulped at his use of the word *we*. He got down on all fours, yelling at me to do the same again.

With the flashlight, he pointed to a spot about a foot in underneath the stove, right around an old burger bun. When I looked closer, I could see a small wooden rectangle.

The cook caught my eyes, our heads now inches apart, and smiled. "The trap." He held the flashlight steady and passed me what had once been the end of a broom and was now simply a broken stick. "Get it." He pointed to the trap.

I banged the stick around frantically, trying to smack the wooden rectangle closer to us. Instead, I merely angered a pack of roaches, now wildly running in all directions. I winced and tried to abandon the stick altogether. My stomach started to ache, and I felt nauseous.

"*No, no!*" The cook took the stick from me. I had to be more careful, he instructed. I tried to stop shaking as I watched him bring the stick closer to the trap. With one soft tap, he shot the trap flying toward us until it hit my hand and came to a halt. This time, I screamed, far beyond a yelp, as the trap revealed a bloody mouse smushed in half. I jumped back to my feet and ran to the sink to scrub my hands. *Gross, gross, gross.* The cook scooped up the trap and held it up for the dishwasher to see. "Victory, *paisano!*" The dishwasher grinned wide.

I dried my hands as I watched the cook shove a new trap under the stove, with a dollop of peanut butter on it. He turned to me and said, "Okay, now we look for your keys together." Thankful to be through with the horrors of their tasks, I promised myself I would never complain about server work again. He flicked on the lights in the dining room, and we paced around the restaurant. I eventually found my keys crumpled into a pile by the bar.

I secured the keys between each finger and made a fist, walking home silently and slowly up the mountain. The two men had finally told me their names. The dishwasher was named Antonio, and the cook was Cisco, which I assumed was short for Francisco. How strange that only after I'd watched them battle roaches, mice, and particles of rancid food had they revealed their names. I felt honored with the information, wondering if Shanti and DeShawn or even Ed knew their names. I had only heard Ed scream slurs at them.

But by the time I got home, I had decided that to secure my friendship with Antonio and Cisco, I had to show them that I could be useful. I had to fight the roaches with them.

"PUT A LITTLE BIT of *ketchup,* instead," I told Cisco as he was setting up another mousetrap to sling under the stove. He looked at me like I was crazy. "The peanut butter doesn't seem to be working anymore." I crossed my arms and widened my stance. "Let's just try something else." I held out the ketchup bottle in front of him.

He shrugged his shoulders as if to say, *Why not?* With a solid thrust and a plop, the ketchup fell on the trap. "Like blood." A smile blossomed on Cisco's face. "Foreshadowing."

I nodded, impressed by how clever he was and ashamed that I found it surprising. I remembered my grandmothers and how they had both shown me that character is not determined by one's class. In the whole diner, the two people I found the most inspiring were Antonio and Cisco. Despite their grueling tasks and long days, they never complained. Sometimes the more honest the work, the more honest the people.

On days I could stay late, I kept Antonio and Cisco company during their final duties. At first, I was extremely unhelpful. I would pull the snake out of the drain too hard and splatter Antonio and myself with the dregs of dinner service. The wet mush from the pipe, Antonio flecked off like it was nothing. I, however, keeled over, revolted and incredibly sorry. Cisco insisted that I scared away the mice by banging around the broom handle too furiously.

Eventually, I wasn't as clumsy, and my presence became more than comic relief. I was elated to be a part of a group. Antonio and Cisco might not have been the typical companions for a thirteen-year-old girl, but I loved our bond.

We would sit on milk crates in the back alley, smoke cigarettes, and sip on (properly made) egg creams. They would give me life advice and tell me stories about the last place they'd worked (which played out like a horror story), and I would listen. I didn't have any real friends at school. Most girls my age poked fun at my worn clothes, and boys joked that my gangly arms made me look like Gumby. In restaurants, I finally found people who accepted me.

Antonio and Cisco also enjoyed my company, but they would remind me constantly during my year at the Greasy Spoon, "Save up your tips from here, go to college. You don't want to be in this business your whole life." I nodded while thinking, *Would that really be so bad?*

PART II

AGE 14-19

DRINK GIRL

MY FATHER, WHO'D NEVER BEEN especially healthy, underwent triple-bypass surgery just as I was starting my teenage years. He brought home with him from the hospital his room-mate's sister, a Brazilian woman named Lucy. Lucy wasn't quite fluent in English yet, so when my father told her during their whirlwind romance that he had four children, she thought he'd said four *brothers*. Imagine her surprise when she walked in to find his quartet of clamoring kids.

When we first met Lucy, she was wearing a bright yellow blazer with thick shoulder pads, metallic-purple lipstick, and eyeliner that extended far beyond her lashes. We had never seen anyone like her. Reese looked her up and down once, and that was it. In her fury, the only word she managed to get out was a solid NO.

Reese had just come back to live with us after a string of unsuccessful stays with relatives. Still stinging from rejection, she carried what I felt to be a bitterness aimed at anyone and everything. Her new goal became breaking up the blossoming romance between our father and Lucy; she would fail.

Lucy sent me into bone-shivering, heart-exploding, cold-sweating fear. She was a hot-blooded don't-look-at-me-the-wrong-way kind of lady who once told us, "My brother, one time when we fighting, I bit his arm and took a chunk of his skin . . . with my teeth. My brother, I love him, what you think I do to *you?*" Around her, we sat up straight.

Once, I woke up to find Lucy pulling our babysitter's hair and pinning her down. They rolled around on the floor, Lucy winning the battle. I was frozen in fear until the police arrived. Lucy was carried out in handcuffs and spent the night in jail. Although her fury was white-hot, she loved just as passionately. I quickly made sure I was on her good side.

LUCY WAS THE ONE who brought alcohol into our everyday lives. Before that, only Grandma's white zinfandel had been in the fridge. My mum was a teetotaler, and my father never sipped alcohol until he was thirty-five. My father later said that without my mum, he started drinking to help him sleep. When booze alone no longer did the trick, he began to mix Ambien and vodka. Regrettably, he says that he doesn't remember many of the instances that follow.

His social gateway drink was sangria. Lucy made a version that was laden with fresh fruit and at least six different types of booze. Her extended family would come over, and she would straddle a colossal plastic tub in the kitchen, stirring her concoction for the thirsty masses. I feared this sudden introduction to something we had always been told was evil. With Laura and Timmy, I hid in my room and watched through a door slightly ajar as people started dancing, falling over, laughing loudly, and throwing bottles around the house like gum wrappers. It was the first time I had seen drunken behavior.

Timmy snuck out occasionally to bring back provisions. We discovered a whole new cuisine—Brazilian street food. *Kibe* were deep-fried croquettes of beef, bulgur wheat, garlic, onions, mint, and cinnamon. "It looks like poop!" Timmy would exclaim in delight, slathering it in ketchup and going back for seconds. *Coxinha* were little fried wonders that resembled chunky teardrops filled with shredded poultry and covered in dough. Post-Lucy, food was plentiful. It was as if alcohol loosened our household's purse strings. Now it was all about excess.

For the first time, I realized that food and beverages could carry a sense of place. The ingredients that went into Lucy's sangria, for example, spoke of local resources and tradition in Brazil. Drinking something familiar brought Lucy back home.

Our father, who had never drunk before, had suddenly found this magical elixir that seemed to solve all of his woes. For hours, he would disappear into a numbed state. Hours became days.

Soon, sangria became screwdrivers. Made up of only two ingredients—vodka and a splash of orange juice—screwdrivers were a more convenient drink that he could easily craft. He began buying booze even if we weren't having people over. "Are we having a party again!?" I would groan in fear of having to dodge flying cans, all-too-friendly hands, and the sticky-sour breath of drinkers.

"No, this is just for us." He unpacked a gigantic plastic bottle filled with vodka. *Us,* of course, meant him.

Soon a jug of vodka wouldn't last a week, then a day. Real juice as a mixer suddenly became Crystal Light powder with no added water. Essentially, he was flavoring vodka and then downing it. In a short period, my father had gone from totalitarian teetotaling ruler to an intoxicated ghost of himself. In the morning

he would work from home on his computer. Then he would sleep
for the rest of the day on the couch, waking up only to eat or pun-
ish us for something.

In my teenage diary, a poem about him read:

> *Cozy, you are now*
> *Huddled on our sunken couch with*
> *Your swollen face, and eyes*
> *Red and puffy, like a tomato*
> *Before it's juiced.*

He had been tough before, but at least he had been predict-
able. Now he weaved in and out of personalities, at times giggly
and stumbling and other times exploding in a matter of moments.
I found myself wishing he would sleep all the time as Mum had.

AFTER A YEAR, WHEN I was fourteen, our family moved farther
south to a small town called Metuchen. Lucy had given birth to
a girl named Angela and did not want to raise her in a house that
contained the remnants of a life with another woman. I was furious that I had to leave my friends at the Greasy Spoon and that
we were now even further away from the possibility of New York
City.

Metuchen was a doughnut-hole town, surrounded by the
larger city of Edison, named after the inventor Thomas Edison.
However, it didn't appear that any brilliance had occurred here.
Instead, strip malls and chain restaurants reigned supreme. Edison
might as well have been any other town in suburban America.

My mum visited us there only a couple of times. Timmy re-
calls that it wasn't that Mum didn't want to visit but that she was
frightened of Lucy. He distinctly remembers Lucy's saying on

multiple occasions that if Mum dared come into *her* house, just wait and see what she would do. As a result, if she did visit, we met her at a local McDonald's. One excerpt from my diary read:

> *Mum came up for like, a second. And we had to meet her at a McDonald's again. UGH. It's annoying because she keeps saying she is so poor, and makes us pay for everything. I am 14! I don't have any money either. Anyway, Timmy had to bring his piggy bank to pay for HER hamburger. It made me so mad.*

Once, she came and took only me out to a McDonald's. I remember thinking, *Something horrible is going to happen.* And I was right. On a grease-stained napkin, she drew the female reproductive system and described the birds and bees to me. The oil on the napkins made the ink run, and the ovaries came out looking like distorted mutants.

Aunt Kathy had already told me about sex seven years ago, but I didn't dare say this. I knew it would just make my mum sad, and I couldn't deal with her crying in public.

AFTER THE MOVE TO Metuchen, Laura essentially gave up speaking. The stresses of our home made her burst into tears constantly. She later remembered one time when our father held up a single pin and claimed, "Look, everyone! Laura is so sensitive, I bet she will cry at the drop of a pin!"

"And I did," Laura told me, "because it was just so mean."

Timmy had shot up to over six feet, his height belying his fragile emotional state. If he was around my father for more than a few minutes, it would end in wails or screams. My father always was the toughest on Timmy.

It wasn't just us kids who were lost. My father swung in and out of favor with Lucy, one day her drinking buddy and the next just a lowly drunkard. Once on our father's birthday, Lucy threw a vodka bottle furiously upon the ground. If it weren't plastic, it would have shattered into a hundred pieces. Then she took Angela and said she was leaving forever.

She begrudgingly returned after one weekend away. My father made her apologize to each of us, one by one, for causing a spectacle.

IN ADDITION TO DRINKING, another newfound vice entered the family—gambling. I have no idea how the idea came to my father, but somehow, one weekend, we found ourselves dragged to Atlantic City.

Our father called the trip a *vacation*, but once we arrived, the glitzy image of a holiday quickly vanished. Atlantic City was a frightening place with syringes littering the boardwalk and more abandoned buildings than inhabited ones. We checked into the Trump Plaza, which Lucy had chosen because it looked the most "glamorous." Fake gold paint covered every surface, and a cloud of cheap perfume stung my nostrils.

Looking back, it would have been better if our father had lost that first night. Instead, the next morning we went home victorious. To be defeated by victory is perhaps the most damaging.

It wasn't even a month before our father was itching to go on another "vacation." I didn't want to go, but without me, there was no one else to watch Timmy and Laura. So I went. As I did all of the times that followed.

After a while, Trump Plaza even began sending limousines to pick us up. The first time, we all went bananas. A *limo*! But soon, the fancy factor wore off and a feeling of dread set in. Just how much money was my father spending in Atlantic City that Trump Plaza figured the expense of a limousine was justified?

SOMETIMES HE LOST A lot of money, sometimes just a little. Every so often—and this was important—he won. It was never chump change either, but rather splurge-worthy, payday money. During those times he wore a wide, deranged smile and let us order any room service we liked, purchase any toy we could dream of on the boardwalk, and even buy pay-per-view movies.

There was one particularly bad streak during the summer. Our father kept losing, and so he kept going back. It was during one of these desperate visits that I hatched a plan. When Timmy and Laura were tucked into bed upstairs, I headed down to the casino.

I expected the casino to be a mecca, given how much time and money my father spent there. Instead, the elevators opened on a dusty old parlor that stank of stale cigarettes and shoddy booze. The dealers, hidden safely behind the tables, all wore gaudy, shiny vests.

"Wuuldd ya like a drink?" an older waitress with blue hair rasped. I politely shook my head and started searching for my father. As I walked around I began to hear whistling, then a few comments: "Damn, girl," or "Come over here, pretty lady," and even "Hey, you wanna blow on my lucky chip?"

I adjusted my sweater to make sure my chest was completely hidden and pulled my long brown hair in front of most of my face. All of a sudden, someone grabbed my elbow tightly. I swung around to see a hunched-over man who could have been my grandfather. He asked if I was lost. I started stammering about finding someone.

He dragged me along by my elbow, and I went along, feeling paralyzed. We circled rows of slot machines and tables filled with men who had the same expression that my father did when he won. Creepy casino faces all started to blend together.

"There!" I pointed to my father in the distance. Relief flooded my body.

The man let go of my elbow and shrugged. "Seems your fellow likes the blackjack tables. I seen him there all night." He took my hand and pressed a black chip in its center. "Maybe that and a pretty girl will bring him some good luck."

I closed my fingers around the chip and made a fist. A black chip, $100! I was lucky if I made that much in a week at the Greasy Spoon. But this was so easy; it felt almost like I had done something wrong.

There was no grin on my father's face. His eyes furiously darted between the table and his hand. "Hit me!" he yelled just as I crept up behind him. The dealer gave him a sad look and revealed his losses. I tapped his shoulder. "Victoria?" His eyes were wild with shame.

I knew there was nothing to say, so I just handed him the black chip. He looked down at the token and smiled, happy again; this was his ticket back in. What had I done?

I watched as his stack of chips went rapidly from high to low.

"Maybe," I started gently, "we should stop playing."

My father didn't seem to like that response. He shook his head and got back to the game. He lost everything within minutes.

Near the blackjack table, I watched as he sucked down one screwdriver after another. I was scared, because not only had he lost, again, but this time it was my fault. I was the one who had given him that extra chip.

"Well, you're sad I lost . . . too bad, why don't you ask your friend for another chip?" He slurred the suggestion at me, and I recoiled. His voice became louder and more insistent. His face tightened. "You can spend money on room service, but you don't want to earn it?"

"That's not fair—" I started.

"Just pretend you're at the diner, it's the same as working for a tip."

I WISH I COULD say this was the end of the merry-go-round of gambling for my father, but it was just the beginning. During the next few years, trips to Atlantic City would come and go in waves. Sometimes we wouldn't go for whole months. Other times we would spend every weekend there, often extending into a Monday or Friday for just a bit more time.

"Well, won't our teachers wonder?" Timmy asked our father one weekend that stretched until a Tuesday.

"Forgiveness is easier to obtain than permission," our father would always say. Timmy shook his head and got back to the math problems he'd scribbled on hotel stationery. He was too smart to argue.

Things were getting worse, quickly. The look of excitement that used to creep across our father's face when he was winning was no longer present. Even if he was ahead, by thousands of dollars, it no longer brought that rush of ecstasy.

One weekend I decided to take matters into my own hands. I could no longer sit in the hotel room while my father spent all of our money. I decided to heed the nagging voice in the back of my head saying, *Well, do something!*

I headed back down to the casino. Everyone was fixated on the numbers on their slot machine, the deck of cards, the set of dice, the drink in front of them, or the chips in their hands. A waitress offered me a rum and Coke, which smelled like putrid suntan lotion, but I took it anyway. It was an excellent prop; I felt it made me look older than I was.

At a poker table, the players' eyeballs were so bugged out it seemed they might pop out of their skulls. How did my father do this all day!? Cards came and went, chips tossed about like tumbleweeds. I found the game boring but people's reactions interesting. I watched their eyes tighten and lower, eyebrows dancing like loose threads, lips crinkling, then widening, jutting out and puckering or bitten with a set of top teeth. Backs would bend like question marks, straighten up tall, or move about tensely.

A man in front of me began to sniff the air. "Rum and Coke?" he asked. "Can you get me one, too, when the waitress comes by?"

"Here, take this one, I don't drink." I handed him mine. Throughout the next hand, he sipped on the cocktail until it was gone.

"Fetch me another, will you?" He passed a blue chip— $10!—to me and smiled. "Thanks."

As soon as the chip landed in my hand, everything clicked. This was how I was going to be useful. Finally, something I knew how to do: take orders.

I started to flag down waitresses and place drink orders for not just this one man but others around the casino. *Make yourself useful.* Grandma Willie's words echoed in my head.

It turned out that the casino waitresses, who theoretically should have been aiming to get their patrons as drunk as possible so that the house could win a bit more foolish money, didn't seem to care. More often than not, they were on smoke breaks or gossiping in a corner.

I was able to identify a demand and a solution. People wanted to drink, and I could get them a drink.

By the end of the night, I was the unofficial drink runner. While delivering a drink to one gambler, another would pat my shoulder and say, "Hey, drink girl, can you get me another?" and point to their empty glass. After each run, my tip would be a chip.

Bloody Mary, no salt. Banana daiquiri. Long Island iced tea, top-shelf only. G&T. Martini, extra dry. Merlot. Vodka on the rocks. Kir royale. Cosmo. Beer. Sidecar. Lemon-drop martini. Vodka cranberry. Old-fashioned. Margarita on the rocks. Scotch and soda. Pinot grigio. Manhattan. Bourbon and ginger.

One drink usually yielded one chip. It was often a white or blue chip but, if the gambler was doing well, maybe a green or even black one. I counted my earnings and found myself smiling. It was a *lot* of money. That I could control one good thing in life was all I needed to keep going.

Whenever my father would lose, I would sneak my chips in to soften the blow. I am not sure if they helped all that much, since, if anything, I just gave him more to lose. But I couldn't just sit around in the hotel room all weekend. These years developed a sort of grit in all of us kids—me, Laura, and Timmy—that I now know is invaluable, though I resented it at the time. It is what makes us resourceful and sets us apart from others. Even when a situation felt impossible, I learned not to give up. Instead of escaping into the relief that distraction would bring, I found that there was an absolute beauty in facing what is hard, or sad, and trying to change it.

Also, as time passed, my Rolodex of drinks expanded rapidly. No other fifteen-year-old knew more about classic cocktails than I did.

THE LOVE CYCLE

DON'T COME HOME UNTIL YOU have a job," my father would say, and he meant it. Poor Timmy, always the last person to find one, once had to sleep outside for a few days until he secured a job at a local sub shop.

Enamored of the energy of twenty-four-hour establishments, I started at the Plaza Diner when I was fifteen. It looked like any other diner on a highway in New Jersey, and the crowd ranged from truck drivers to early birds, late-night drunkards, and college kids.

Every surface was shiny, due to either plastic mirrors or polished metals. There was a long bar made out of Formica with stools that spun. The first thing everyone noticed upon entering was a massive, curved glass display case. Crammed inside were elaborately decorated desserts that all somehow managed to taste the same.

The walk to the diner was just over a mile and a half from my house and another mile on top of that from school. If I hurried, I could get there right after classes.

WHEN I ARRIVED, FRANKY, the most senior waiter, would be on a tear. He worked six A.M. to six P.M. and had every day for as long as he could remember. Barely over five feet, Franky was well into his sixties, with a full head of white hair and a thick mustache that looked like a comb over his lips. You couldn't see his mouth unless it was cracked open wide in a smile that exposed the few gray teeth he had left.

Usually, he was going on in his raspy Long Island accent about "mothafuckahs here for the early bird, whirling away in hot soup all afternoon, hoggin' [his] good booth."

He enjoyed his guests but was also a businessman. So, he would cozy up tableside and somehow manage to get the early birds out, miraculously happy. As they left, they would say, "We just love coming and visiting Franky!"

And he would wave to them, saying, "Buh-bye, folks! Come back tomorrow!" Then he'd turn around and whisper, "They're goddamn cheap bastards, but I love 'em," all the while sitting another table down in his "good booth."

Franky would spend all of his energy trying to think of ways to make his regulars feel special, ways he could show them he cared. When six o'clock would approach, Franky would recall the day's events to me and impart bits of wisdom, almost sad to leave. "The sugar packets, never let the sugar out of your sight," Franky would say. "You let that sugar sit on the table and next thing you know the caddy is back—no sugar! Those bitches will rob you blind every time. And that's a life lesson: watch your sugar." I came to learn that guests would take anything that wasn't nailed down.

Franky took me, a complete novice, and molded me into a real hospitality professional. At first, whenever I was in the weeds, I felt nauseous. I couldn't both move and think fast. Franky taught me to embrace this carsick feeling and ride past it. The unnatural feeling of being overwhelmed soon felt less so. I was lucky to learn to move and think this way at an early age, at a place where it was okay to embarrass myself.

THE ADVICE I MOST appreciated from Franky was about customers.

"You gotta love 'em, I mean it. You gotta. Tell 'em you love 'em, too. Let 'em know. Look at this one," he said, and pointed to a table of football players from my school. "Okay, what do you love about these guys?" They were chowing down on a platter of burgers, fries, and towering onion rings. I watched as grease dripped down their chins.

"I don't know, Franky. Let's try another table . . ." Sometimes I would become annoyed by how intense Franky was. After all, I was a teenager, and genuinely mustering up a passion for every guest seemed exhausting.

Franky crossed his arms and leaned in so close I could smell stale cigarettes on his breath. "I don't think so, dollface. You gotta find something to love in each of these guys. You just gotta, that's your job."

I looked again.

As the footballers were polishing off their feast, they stacked up their plates, one on top of the other, and carefully poked their crumpled napkins into their milkshake glasses. "They are considerate," I started, and looked at Franky. "The way they stacked those plates for me and tucked away their napkins, so I don't have to touch them."

By looking closely, I saw something I wouldn't have otherwise noticed. It wasn't just about carefully watching people to make a sale but about appreciating them. Franky forced me to be empathetic instead of bitching in the corner with the other diner waitresses about how annoying our guests were. He was building a specific strength in me—it takes a strong person to be kind to those who aren't.

"You don't get to choose your guests . . . ," Franky began, "some are sons o' bitches, pompous assholes, dirtbags, swindlers, pervy bastards, drunken buffoons, jealous bitches . . . you don't have to like them as people, but find *something* to like, something to talk about. Got it, dollface?"

I nodded, soaking in his advice. He looked over my shoulder. "Looks like you were just sat."

I always requested the smoking section. I only occasionally smoked at the time, mostly to look cool, but I found that the most exciting people sat in this area. As I walked toward my new table, one guest lit up. A super-thin cigarette rested in between her long, polished nails painted red. The other woman was noticeably younger; I guessed it was her daughter.

I tried to study their mannerisms. The daughter fidgeted and couldn't seem to decide where to place her hands. The mother sucked on her cigarette like she was trying to pull a milkshake up with a straw. She looked stressed, like pulling her smokes in deeper would help alleviate something.

I welcomed them while distributing menus. The mother didn't respond but instead kept sucking on her little cigarette. Her daughter smiled at me. As I was walking away from the table, Franky followed me. "So? What do you love about them?"

I grew irritated. "I don't know, Franky. I just met them. The mom seems stuck-up, and the daughter is quiet. I don't think I like them much at all, honestly."

Franky's face hardened. "Listen, dollface: this job ain't easy. Ain't many good people out there, but they are still people. Each and every one of them is just wandering around, asking to be loved, to be told they're beautiful, they're great, they're the best . . . and it never happens. But here, it can. At least for one meal."

As Franky went on, I started to think of my father, Lucy, Mum, and Reese. People who sometimes frustrated me to no end, but Franky was right; they were still people. It broke my heart to think of how much they probably wanted to be loved and accepted. "Make 'em happy, c'mon, it's not that hard. It'll be good for you, too, how ya think I got this big grin on after all these years?" Franky looked at me then quite seriously. "If you make them happy, you're happy. Don't forget, only happy people can give good hospitality." His words made me recall my grandmother Anna's advice—that making others happy would in turn make me happy.

Franky was undoubtedly good at his job. The other servers would become furious with jealousy that even in the dog days of summer, his section was packed. I asked him one day how he'd amassed such a huge fan base. He laughed hoarsely and let me in on his secret. I carefully wrote down every word he said in my notebook: "Shit, anybody can sling eggs and pour a pot of cawfee. That's why all these servers are here, right? They think, oh, that's easy money, I can do that. Then they do. Maybe for a while. And then they all burn out. Dummies don't got anything to drive them anymore. Even money only drives you for a while. You know what I got that they don't?" Franky grinned wide and pounded his chest above his heart. "I got purpose. That's what drives me. I created my love cycle, of lovin' people, and maybe one or two will love me back. It makes it all worth it. I ain't got kids but I been told that shit is fulfilling, too, it's kinda similar."

I thought about this when I walked back to the table. When I arrived, only the daughter looked up at me, and proceeded to order a Coke. The mother cut her off quickly. "Oh, you are not having a Coke, not with all that caffeine! Give her a Sprite."

An awkward silence followed.

I considered Franky's number one rule—always be authentic. "People can smell shit. It stinks. Don't bullshit them," he would say.

I scanned for clues. She was definitely the mother, but her daughter didn't look that much younger than her. Maybe she'd had her when she was young? That was probably hard, and maybe it toughened her up a bit. No wedding ring on her finger; perhaps she had to do it all alone. *Aha!* That was how to love the mother, by loving the daughter.

I noticed the daughter's water was empty. Just like that, I found an in. "I never see that much, people who drink a lot of water." I motioned from the mother to the daughter. "It's so good for you, and yet so few people do it. It's nice to see." I put their water glasses back, took their order, and walked away. I looked over my shoulder, and the mother gave the daughter a soft wink. The daughter smiled and gulped down her water obediently.

Something profound happened at that moment. I felt a joy so complete I began to crave it always. I would continue to use Franky's cycle of love, not just at the diner but throughout my life. Although I had initially fallen in love with food and restaurants as a means of escape, the cycle of love kept me in it. Making people happy in turn made me happy. It gave me purpose and people began to love me back. I'd finally found a place where I belonged.

THE GRAVEYARD SHIFT

WHEN FRANKY LEFT THE DINER each day, other veterans took the lead. All the waitresses were nicknamed Flo, except me. I always felt like an observer, taking notes on my diner notepad. Franky and all the Flos loved giving me life advice. I was their ticket out of the Plaza Diner.

"If you get out," a Flo once told me, "then with all the stuff we given you, a little piece of us gets out, too."

I started working the graveyard shift on the weekends and eventually during the week. The shift began at four in the afternoon and went until four in the morning. I looked old enough, so the owners never seemed bothered by the restrictions of child labor laws. When I returned home early in the morning, our father would be passed out on the couch, his cup of vodka either finished or almost empty.

For the night shift, an affable young Albanian named Zef would take the reins. Zef would help me with my leftover homework, and I would help him with his crossword puzzles.

"How are you with calculus?" I thumped my textbook down on his table one night, where he hunched over his newspaper.

"Hey!" He rearranged his paper and coffee so I could sit with him. "Why don't you ever do that stuff after school with your parents or friends, like a normal kid?"

I scooched in next to him and looked at his paper. "*Tarantula*," I said, pointing to the crossword. "Eight across—'A hairy arachnid.'"

Zef looked back at his paper and nodded his head, adding a smile as he scribbled in the word. He then looked back at me and gave in. "Okay, calculus . . . let's see what I can remember."

Together, Zef and I would observe the waves of the evening with avid curiosity. On weekends, drunk patrons leaked in from two to four in the morning (after the bars closed). They ordered strange creations like fried eggs on ice cream. With them, I learned what disco fries are, gobs of gravy and cheese slathered on top of potatoes (still a perfect creation to me), and that onion rings with blue cheese are a crunchy, creamy dream.

If the postbar crowd got rowdy, Zef would take out his fake gun (which, to be honest, looked incredibly real) and scream, "Pay up and get out!" It worked every time. With Zef, I felt safe.

When the drunks got tired, we just let them sleep it off. "The breakfast crowd will wake them," Zef said. We watched once as two boys nestled up in the booth together and slept until Franky hovered over them at six in the morning, cigarette in his mouth as he sang, "Wakey, wakey! Eggs and bac-y!" They decided to stay for breakfast, too.

The hardest part of the graveyard shift was leaving. At four in the morning, my body ached, and my head was in a fog. I would walk if it was warm outside or otherwise call a cab. Then I would sleep for a few hours and go to school.

AFTER A FEW MONTHS, I had a regular fan base of locals and truck drivers who popped in on their routes. Franky and the Flos taught me old-fashioned quips, and soon I was in my element. As a waitress, I tried to channel the energy I felt from my first dinner party with Uncle Carlo and Aunt Sue. They'd made the meal an event through warmth and charm. My work personality was who I ultimately wanted to be, versus who I was at school, where I barely spoke and no one talked to me.

What Franky's love cycle hadn't prepared me for were dangerous guests. He was a tough guy, and I can't imagine that people ever gave him trouble. Or perhaps deceptive visitors were what made him tough, over time.

ONE GUEST IN PARTICULAR kept visiting during my graveyard shifts. He would show up around two or three in the morning, hang out by himself in a booth, and drink coffee while reading. He never ate anything, just smoked cigarettes. My curiosity started to build, and I wondered who this mysterious man was. After a few visits, I asked him his name.

"Tired," he said, and smiled wearily.

I looked at him. "Well, you probably shouldn't stay here all night, then, drinking coffee." He laughed and went back to his book. I could never quite see what he was reading.

Zef and I would look at him from our booth and try to guess who he was or what he did. I imagined he was a traveling poet, staying up all night with ideas that gnawed at his mind. Maybe, like me, he liked to hide in plain sight.

I tried to follow Franky's love cycle. While watching the mysterious guest, I decided I liked the way he would quietly sip his coffee, never looking up from his book or around the room. It was rare to see solo guests. Most people are too self-conscious to dine alone. I was envious of how brave he was.

When he got to the end of a chapter, he would look at his watch and decide whether or not it was time to go. When it was, it always made me a little sad. He held a fascination for me, and I hoped I was the reason he kept coming back.

One particular night in the middle of winter, he kept looking at his watch at the end of every chapter and deciding to stay anyway. The time crept past four in the morning, and although I was looking forward to his always-generous tip, I was also weak and ready to head home. I let him know that I was leaving and that our morning server, Flo, would take over. He nodded and quickly got back to his book.

I waited for my taxi inside the diner. It was a cold January night, and the beginnings of a snowstorm crept in. After a half hour of waiting, I called the car service. "Yeah, yeah, just sent a guy . . . he should be there any minute." I bundled up and headed outside so as not to miss the cab. The cold slipped in through my gloves and chilled my hands. I shook my body to muster up warmth and waited. Moments that seemed like minutes dragged by.

Suddenly, from behind me, a voice called out, "I thought you left." It was the regular from inside. I never really saw much of his face, as it was always in a book, and now he was especially unrecognizable; a black scarf was wrapped around the lower half of his face and a knit cap covered the top of his head.

"Where are you headed? I can give you a ride." He pointed his thumb back toward his car. I looked behind the diner and saw a lone car parked toward the shadows.

"Thank you, but my taxi should be here any minute." He waited alongside me.

After a few minutes of silence, he said, "Listen, you're welcome to freeze to death out here, but I'm going to head out. You sure you don't want a ride?" I looked back at him and then at the empty highway in front of me. There was something about the cold that made me crazy, torturously uncomfortable. I was all knobby knees and jagged elbows, with no meat on my bones for insulation.

I gave in. The drive was only a mile and a half away; what could go wrong? My father's words ran through my head: *Don't ever let Ed drive you home.* But I shook the thought away. Ed was creepy, and in comparison, this man seemed safe. Sensing my hesitation, the guest waved his hand, motioning me forward.

As I walked around the diner, it became progressively darker. My steps crunched through shards of ice and with a sudden mis-step, I wobbled on a patch of black ice and slipped, falling on my left hip with a thud. A flash of pain launched from my leg and ricocheted throughout my body. The man immediately bent over to help. My pain was only matched by my embarrassment.

He put my arm around his shoulder and hoisted me upward. "You okay?" he asked as I caught my breath. Being near him was a strange feeling. It was the closest I had ever been to a man, and I couldn't help but feel nervous. There was a slight stench to him, a bit of the diner—stale cigarettes, coffee, and grease—mixed with oniony perspiration.

He opened the car door and helped me in. Outside, I had felt gratitude toward him. When he had helped me after my fall, I'd felt warmth. Now, inside the cold car, which had been chill-ing in the January night for hours, I winced as I fell onto the seat cushion. With one powerful flick from his strong shoulders, the door slammed shut. Instantly, my mind flashed back to my father screaming *Shut the door!* and the regret that flooded my tiny body afterward. I felt the same remorse rush in. What had I agreed to?

My trembling fingers searched for the door handle. It wouldn't open. I was locked inside. I was shaking uncontrollably, per-haps from the cold, but definitely from a wave of panic. My eyes followed the man as he walked around to the driver's seat and climbed in. When he caught my gaze, I immediately looked away, frightened.

Normally, the drive took under ten minutes, but the man seemed to drive unnaturally slowly, as if purposely trying to scare me. My whole body was frozen, with only my lips moving to give directions—*Right, right, left, then another left. You can stop here.*

When we were a few houses away from home, I asked him to stop the car. I didn't want him to see where I lived; it seemed too intimate.

"Let me help you out," he said, as if he hadn't locked me in. I waited for him to walk around to my side and tensed up further. I was freezing and nervous; my body felt so numb it was as if it weren't my own. Which is why, when he swung open the door and reached down toward me, I imagined that the body he began to pin down wasn't mine at all.

His left hand pulled the lever underneath my seat, catapulting me downward. In one swift motion, he climbed on top of me, his dense shoulders like a paperweight on mine. I stopped shaking. The car door swung shut behind him. That thud, when the door met the car, that deep and cavernous bellow, I will never forget.

His face, pressed against mine, smelled like the diner's coffee I had just served him. There were notes of cigarette smoke, too— the ones he had smoked in my section. His mouth was suffocating mine. I couldn't even think about screaming; I only wanted to breathe. I felt my lungs being pinched tighter and tighter. Then he bit down on my tongue, flooding the taste of blood into my mouth. I gasped from the razor-sharp pain, the metallic liquid washing down my throat. "Quiet!" he yelled. Like my mum, I was always obedient. I hid behind a curtain of long brown hair and did as I was told. Because it was safer that way.

My winter layers were jerked off, unleashing an aroma of

French fry grease. I imagined that maybe Zef had followed us, having heard me fall outside of the diner, and, suspicious, trailed the icebox of a car. Or that perhaps Franky had come early for his morning shift and had decided to kill time by smoking out behind the diner. He had seen me fall, too. Then he'd watched as this man helped me up and loaded me into his car like a wounded calf for slaughter. Franky would, of course, have found us here, and maybe with Zef's help they would pry open the car door, rip it off altogether, and collect me from inside. Zef's fists would fly, and Franky would give me his jacket. We would watch as Zef used his fake gun to scare the man away. Then, safe, we would all go back to the diner for a hot coffee to warm up.

None of these things happened. Instead, I lay there, still and sobbing. Again, a flash of pain lit up my body. A ripping tear from below, and thrusts. Now I knew what my father had meant when he said not to get into Ed's car. What I didn't know was what this whole thing meant in Franky's love cycle. How did I mess that up? I blamed myself, the fact that I was too nice to him, that I'd led him on.

WITH ONE LAST HOWL from the hinges, the car door slammed shut and he drove away. I don't remember how long I was in the vehicle, but soon after I was on the ground, just outside where he had parked. Part of me wanted to get up, but mostly I wanted to lie there. Possibly forever. Although it was still freezing outside, I couldn't shake any more to warm myself up. There was no energy left in my bones.

The wind carried specks of snow. As they landed, I tried to count each flake, but there were too many. When the snowflakes stopped melting on my face and began to pile up, I realized it was time to move. I walked past the couple of houses that separated the attack from my home. I wondered, if I had screamed, would my family have heard me?

Once in the house, I walked through the living room. The space was lit by the television screen, giving the air an ice-blue tint. A cup of vodka that had been dyed red by Crystal Light powder had fallen over, the crimson color leaking onto the couch.

My father wasn't on the couch but instead was on the floor next to it. He must have fallen over in his sleep. I thought about how I had been lying on the ground, moments before, also intoxicated, but by pain. He looked contorted, all twisted in a flannel blanket. His snores ricocheted from floor to ceiling. I debated whether or not I should wake him up, if I should tell him to take me to the hospital, to call the police. I looked back at the pool of Crystal Light–dyed vodka and realized he would probably be too drunk to help.

If only I had never fallen in love with diners, with working long and late hours, with escaping into hospitality, with loving others, then maybe I wouldn't have gotten myself here. Like my father, I was extreme in my decisions. I had to give all of myself to my studies, my work, or nothing at all. So on that night, I unknowingly decided to let the pendulum swing the other way. I stopped caring.

A small trickle of blood began to inch down my legs. I went upstairs to take a shower.

THAT NEXT YEAR WAS my last at home before moving to New York City, at seventeen. Perhaps in anticipation of this, the chaos at home began to crescendo. I didn't talk to anyone about the rape. Instead, I did what I had been taught to do—suppress. I had problems sleeping and took anything that would make the nightmares stop.

My diary read:

Going to bed is the hardest thing for me. I'm pathetic and get tired around 9:00 pm, however, it takes me forever to get to sleep. I usually am scared I'll have a bad dream. Recently my nightmares haven't been so bad, but they used to be. I would wake up in a cold sweat, petrified, and scared to death to go back to sleep. Sometimes I take things to help me sleep. Those work.

I tried to go back to my normal diner routine, but I had lost all interest in the love cycle. It had betrayed me.

Sick of Zef and Franky's trying to cheer me up, I left the diner altogether and went to work at Uno's Chicago Grill & Pizzeria, on a different highway in New Jersey. Squeezed between two other chains, a Famous Dave's and a Bennigan's, in a mall parking lot, it was the perfect place to drown in indifference. The corporate nature of the restaurant meant there was no owner on the premises and few cared about hospitality. The job was a paycheck, nothing more. Mostly college kids worked there, and with them, I began smoking pot and drinking.

On our break, we would head to the Bennigan's next door and order a Swift-Kick (vodka, orange juice, and Red Bull) and then go back to work at Uno's. I hated that I had begun drinking my father's screwdrivers, albeit mixed with an energy drink. Drowning myself in booze was how I coped with emotions I couldn't face.

Besides liquor and sometimes pills, I barely put anything in my body. I struggled with eating. I thought that the less space I could take up in the world, the better. My hope was that eventually I would disappear completely.

I also started writing. I had always kept a diary, but now it was filled with poems. These came together in a poetry anthology, "French Fry Grease," about the diner characters I missed but couldn't face anymore, like Franky.

If he was Saint Nick, then I was an elf.
He taught me everything I somehow knew.
Everyone laughed like Christmas,
Forgetting to tell me the truth:
We're never too young to lose innocence,
But always too old to go back.

My English teacher recognized that writing was a form of therapy and encouraged more. I won local poetry contests and wrote voraciously. When I woke up with a nightmare, I tried to write it down in an attempt to get it out of my head:

Late nights,
Graveyard shift,
I chose.
I was still in high school
But you didn't know
Because you never asked.
Outside the diner,
Cold, black air.
From behind
You found me and told me
Not to scream.
But I did, inside,
And still am.

WHAT THE PSYCH
WARD TAUGHT

SINCE UNO'S WAS FARTHER FROM HOME, I needed a car. With my diner money, I purchased a car from an ad in the newspaper. It was gray, and I liked that it smelled like lemons. I paid in cash and, without even a learner's permit, started driving. Lucy, who claimed she'd started driving when she was nine years old in Brazil, was all too happy to teach me the rules of the road.

Timmy had grown his hair long and at fifteen looked like a young John Lennon. Perhaps because he was the only boy, our father was especially tough on Timmy. Timmy was brilliant, but he had a lackadaisical personality. All he wanted to do was play the piano. If he didn't do his homework or if he lost one of his many after-school jobs ("He was going on philosophical rants to our customers!" one boss said), my father would ban him from the piano.

At first, he just stayed longer after school, using the orchestra's piano. When he was kicked out, he used a friend's. Learning this, my father imposed a curfew. Timmy used music as an emotional release. Without it, he must have felt trapped.

Timmy and I started smoking pot together after school, before I had to work, late at night, or even early in the morning. I would show up at Uno's stoned and munch on cold pizza crust throughout the shift.

When Timmy went through a long jobless phase, he sat on the roof, lit matches, and watched them burn before tossing them out. He would spend hours on the roof like this, alone. Without the healing time spent on the piano, he had no release. In an attempt to gain control over Timmy, our father had lost him. Our father still didn't understand that people weren't chess pieces.

"COME HOME NOW!" LAURA called me at Uno's one summer afternoon. She stuttered about police cars and people in the house.

My first thought was that DYFS (Division of Youth and Family Services, now known as the Division of Child Protection and Permanency) had shown up again. Child protective services had come to our house more times than I could count—a relative or teacher of ours seemed to call in weekly. There were no physical signs of abuse, no broken bones or cages for us to sleep in, so the service always left quickly. I remember a representative once chastised me on the way out saying, "*You*, young lady, should be *grateful* . . . you can't even imagine the horrors that are out there."

Then our father would accuse us of sabotage. When I told my aunt Kathy, she encouraged me to keep records of everything. I kept an inventory of the number of bottles of vodka consumed weekly. The times Lucy trapped squirrels and then killed them. The exact words screamed at us and what our father's unique punishments entailed.

One evening when Laura was too scared to go home, we went to the police station in Metuchen. We spent all night there, begging them not to send us back. I told them about my records; I showed them messages and emails. I had collected so much, but still they found it to be too little. We were returned home.

This time was different, though. Our father had turned the accusations on us. Laura was in hysterics, stuttering, and sobbing, *"The police are taking him away."*

I ripped off my apron and told another server to cover for me. Within ten minutes, I was at the house. By the time I arrived, Timmy was already on the stretcher, tied down with thick gray straps and loaded into the back of an ambulance. He wasn't trying to escape, but rather just lay there, fat tears rolling down his cheeks. I imagined I must have looked the same right after I'd been raped—paralyzed and scared. What else could he have done? I felt the helplessness radiate from his body, the fear.

"What's happening?" I started screaming. "Where are they taking him?" I frantically asked my father, Lucy, the police, firefighters, and ambulance workers who were all there. No one would answer me.

Right before the ambulance doors closed, I caught Timmy's eye. He looked just like the little boy who whisked eggs in his dinosaur pajamas and climbed tall oak trees—just a kid. The doors slammed shut with a mighty *thud* that knocked all of the wind out of me. Shutting the door on my mum, the car door slamming to a close on my rape, now this.

I turned to my father, furious and crazed. "What have you done? Where are they taking him?"

Our father, eerily sober and ferociously calm, stood tall with Lucy by his side. He told me that Timmy was playing with matches again, that he would have burned down the whole house, and that this was for his own good. His claim was that the fire department recommended a psych evaluation of Timmy, and that this was all just protocol. I shook my head in disbelief and sought out Laura, who was crying in the corner of her bedroom.

Laura had seen the whole thing. The smoke billowing from the basement and Timmy frantically rushing upstairs. He had played with one too many matches and tried without much luck to fix his growing mistake. "But he was calm," Laura said, "and composed. He told us what he did and asked for help. Everyone was safe." Laura's little mouth jutted out and opened wide; she broke out in sobs, shaking. "Timmy would never hurt anyone, Dad is saying that Timmy is dangerous, but you need to tell them, Tor . . . that he would never hurt *anyone*."

Having grown increasingly frustrated with Timmy, my father didn't know what to do. There was nothing left to take away from him except for his freedom. A deep bitterness began to form inside me. With Timmy gone, I felt utterly lost. As I held Laura while she also mourned the absence of our brother, I promised myself I would never leave her behind.

Aunt Kathy and Betty both drove up right away. I called them as Laura and I locked the door and hid in her room. Neither of them could make my father budge.

"Is he ever going to come back?" Laura wept for days.

THERE WAS NOTHING ANYONE could do. Our father had sole custody. It was frightening that I had compiled so much evidence for the police, but it had been too little to separate us from our parents. Now, when our father had so little, it was more than enough to send Timmy away.

When I was allowed to visit Timmy, it had to be with our father. He kept claiming it was all in Timmy's best interest, that this was some goddamn security crisis. Maybe something about

Timmy, about not being able to control and command respect from his only son, really got under his skin.

"I don't belong here," Timmy pled. He took a deep breath, trying to explain calmly. "The *screams*, the things these people *say*, it's horrible." With my father's testimony that Timmy was dangerous, they had placed him in an especially frightening wing of the psych ward for troubled children with sadistic tendencies. Timmy couldn't sleep, as the screams from the other patients would keep him awake all night. The walls were yellowed and torn with small scratch marks.

Eventually, the doctors released him. At that point it was already too late—what had been done was unforgivable. Timmy had gone from hysterically crying to begging and pleading, and finally, to nothing at all. When he came home, he was calm. Our father was proud that the dramatic decision had yielded his desired results. After all, Timmy was now obedient. Perhaps he felt extremes would settle things into place, like when he jerked us children around a bank's parking lot, Mum running after us in panic. But just like with his blackjack games, he was defeated by victory.

It wasn't until Timmy left the house for good that some of his old charm started to return. The softness that he had always had, even when times were difficult, came back as well.

"What the psych ward taught me," Timmy later told me, "was that I had to get out. I had to take control of my own life." So he waited it out for another two years, unnervingly quiet around our father, and then got as far away as he could. With his perfect SAT scores and musical talent, he received a full ride to Rutgers. This school was still too close to home for him. He declined admission and instead went to a school so far north that it was practically in Canada.

"What's two years?" Timmy said about his time in the mental

institution and trying to survive at home afterward. I wished I could have been like him and not let myself become lost in sorrow.

"After all," Timmy said, "however unpleasant, sometimes you have to do something you really don't like in order to get to a much better place . . . far, far away."

PART III

AGE 19-20

CAN YOU BARTEND?

A T SEVENTEEN I FINALLY MADE it to New York City. I received a scholarship to Fordham College at Lincoln Center. Within a year, my studies had become nonexistent and, instead, my time was filled with drugs, alcohol, and partying. After an especially rough summer, I was broke. My aunt Kathy swooped in and brought me to California for rehabilitation. Things got much worse before they got better.

I stumbled around in a drug-induced haze. At first, I tried to work in a local restaurant on the beach, but I couldn't hold the job down. My nerves were frayed, and I kept dropping dishes and trays.

Then I took a job dressing up as princess characters for children's birthday parties. With our proximity to Disneyland, demand was high. However, Disney princess names are trademarked, so the company I worked for had to call their eerily similar-looking characters different names. At Karacters 4 Kids, I worked as the "Blue Princess" (definitely Cinderella), the "Snow

Princess" (definitely Snow White), and the "Yellow Princess" (definitely Belle). Things went well for a few months until at a five-year-old's birthday party where I was the Snow Princess, I decided to take a quick cigarette break.

The birthday girl, dressed as a mini Snow White, went exploring to find me. When she saw me leaning against the back of her house, sucking on a freshly lit Parliament, chubby tears began to roll down her heavily made-up cheeks. "Why are you smoking, Snow White?" she asked, curious and distraught.

"I'm not Snow White," I retorted, attempting to save the situation but making it worse, "that name is trademarked."

I returned my bobbed wig and yellow-and-blue dress to the company after that. They never called me back for another gig.

AT THE SAME TIME, I found an older boyfriend who idolized Bukowski and lived at home with his parents. After I was raped, men could smell the vulnerability on my body. The attack left me with so much shame that my confidence was completely destroyed. I thought that I deserved abuse. This feeling of worthlessness opened me up to those who were keen to take advantage.

For money, the boyfriend and I drove over the border to Mexico, and before I knew it, I was selling freshly stamped ecstasy for cash in Orange County. Here, my pricing and budgeting skills came in handy.

Then I started smoking black-tar heroin in the backseats of cars. Once, I couldn't find a straw and some aluminum foil to smoke it, so I used a hollowed-out old apple that I found on the street. If that wasn't already a low point, weeks later a series of cop cars chased me along the Pacific Coast Highway. The caravan had been following me for miles, quickly adding on units and even an ambulance. After bombing the DUI test, I was brought into the police station. Even in my drunken stupor, I remembered that I was entitled to a phone call. Unfortunately, the only number I had memorized was my father's. With shame, I called him.

My license was taken away. Since I could no longer drive, living in California seemed pointless, so, full of self-hatred, I moved back to New Jersey to live with my father again. My bedroom still held all of my old books, journals, and secret cubbies with stale weed. Across the hall was Laura, who was now a teenager. I wanted to give her a role model she could look up to, not a washed-up diner druggie.

We started spending more time together, and slowly, Laura healed me. We took long bike rides together and read books out loud. At night, she ran across the hallway, crying that she'd had a nightmare. Soon this became nightly, and I would take her back to bed. To help her sleep, I would stroke her soft blond hair and tell her she was safe. She needed me, and I needed her. It was a reminder that my future was not just my own. If I didn't pull myself together, I would be letting her down, too.

With her unconditional love, I felt less of a need to do drugs. Also, my father, after seeing me struggle in California, offered to pay for counseling. It was a turning point for our relationship that he gave me a chance to seek help. Therapy allowed me to work through all of the emotions I didn't know how to express and gave me the mental tools to recover.

Eventually, I saw no point in drugs altogether. When I moved out of the New Jersey house a few months later, to return to New York City permanently, Laura and I remained close. We both tried to make each other happy, and this, in turn, made us happy.

At nineteen, I was supposed to enter my junior year of college, but instead, I decided to defer for a semester and save up money. Channeling my resourceful self, I printed out a hundred copies of my résumé and walked around New York, handing them out to any restaurant that would take them.

My experience thus far was rather unimpressive—two diners, a corporate pizzeria chain, and a grill on the beach (I kept "illegal casino-waitress liaison" off my résumé). Within a week, multiple places contacted me. It seemed that New York was desperate, like me.

Lattanzi was a small family-run spot on Restaurant Row (a city block of watering and feeding holes squeezed between Eighth and Ninth Avenues on Forty-Sixth Street). Their primary clientele was the theater crowd, eager to down a plate of pasta before the eight P.M. Broadway show. Then came tourists, old-timers, and finally Broadway actors, who arrived late, after their performances.

Lattanzi was one of the first to settle on Restaurant Row. Only Barbetta (one of the first restaurants in America to serve truffles, Barolo, and other Piemontese specialties) could boast a longer tenure. Newcomers certainly garnered more attention, like our next-door neighbor Becco, which had superstar chef Lidia Bastianich at the helm. But there was something indisputably endearing about the less-famous Lattanzi. The white tablecloths, burgundy carpets, and linen-covered lamps seemed like an old-world dream. In a place like Lattanzi, you felt at home the moment you walked in the door.

A MAN WHO I learned was named Luan greeted me at the entrance: "May I help *you?*" His accent reminded me of Zef, from the Plaza Diner. Like Zef, he seemed earnest yet impatient. Luan was wearing a black suit, but unlike all the other men in the restaurant, who wore bow ties, he had on a dark red tie that matched the carpets. The contrast meant he was the boss, I assumed. When he smiled, I could see a row of teeth that looked

like well-spaced Chiclets. I smiled in return and said I was looking for a job.

"We need a bartender. Can you bartend?"

Without even a moment of hesitation, I said, "Of course."
Then honesty crept in: "Well, I can learn." This seemed good
enough for him.

The twenty-four hours before my first shift were a cramming
session. I scrambled to study classic cocktails, spirits, liquors,
and beers. Some of what I researched was familiar from my casino days. *Long Island iced tea, cosmo, Manhattan.* However, back
then, I had only been memorizing names and the appearance of
cocktails.

Though I knew what some cocktails looked like, I had no idea
what was actually *in* them. So I dove into a stack of books and
websites. At first, I went about my normal studying routine of
reading and memorizing. Then something happened. I became
interested in what I was learning and started understanding. The
history behind the spirits left me spellbound: monks who survived on beer for nutrition, the medicinal recipes that led to many
digestifs, Prohibition, and bathtub gin. And curious tidbits—
red beetles were used to dye bitter drinks; the evaporated portion
of whiskey is the "angel's share"; a Creole apothecary in New
Orleans created the aromatic and legendary Sazerac—all of this
sucked me in. The centuries of tradition, innovation, and stories
behind every drink were fascinating.

My anticipation grew (as did my stack of flash cards), and
when it was time to return to Lattanzi, I had committed all the
classics to memory. Confident in my abilities, I strutted past their
wrought-iron gate and down a set of stone steps.

Since it was between lunch and dinner, the restaurant was almost empty. Luan led me to the bar, which was a long L of black
marble and could hold fifteen people. The wall behind the bar
was exposed brick with three glowing shelves of bottles. My jaw

dropped. There was a hanging metal shelf that held even more bottles and wrapped around the length of the bar. There must have been hundreds of spirits there, and from my studies, I only recognized a few. Suddenly, my confidence began to drain.

"Massimo here"—Luan pointed to a round boy behind the bar with a single spike of hair gelled together—"is the worst bartender we have ever had." He burst into a fit of laughter. "But he is the boss, so we keep him around!" His shoulders bopped up and down with his deep laughs.

"This crazy Albanian," Massimo responded, "we keep around for entertainment."

Massimo was the son of Carla and Vittorio Lattanzi, who had opened up shop there in 1984. I could see what Luan meant about poor Massimo; he was sweet and seemed infinitely trustworthy, but his movements lacked care. He kept knocking bottles over and obliterating measurements.

"The basics are pretty much all you need here," Luan reassured me. "Cosmopolitan, old-fashioned, the Manhattan, and a martini. Know those four, and you are more than halfway there." I did a victory lap in my head and wanted to scream, *Yes! I know those!* Because I did—or at least I did on paper.

I inspected the tools Massimo was using—an hourglass-shaped jigger for measuring, shakers both big and small to build the drinks in, a strainer, and a spoon with a long twisty handle.

"Okay, a cosmopolitan," Massimo started. "Watch me closely. One and a half ounces of vodka, a half ounce of Cointreau, a half ounce of cranberry juice, and a half ounce of sour mix," he instructed as he counted, poured, and shook with his whole body. I recalled the cosmopolitan recipe in my head. It seemed that his measurements were a bit off—didn't the recipe ask for lime juice, not a premade mix?

When I asked Luan about this, he laughed. "What do you

think this is!? The Waldorf-Astoria!? The ingredients, the exact measurements aren't so important, a little bit of this and that. So long as it is pink and sweet and you cannot taste the alcohol, it's good."

We tasted the cosmopolitan together, and I winced a bit on my first sip. A rush of candied sugar flavors washed over my lips as a sourness prickled my tongue. The cocktail tasted like soda and smelled like the ball pit at McDonald's, candied plastic. "You definitely can't taste the alcohol," I said, struggling to find something honest and positive to say.

"*Ha!*" Luan clapped. "Success!"

Now it was my turn. Eager to impress, I methodically went through the recipe. Each measurement was exact. I strained the cocktail into a martini glass and garnished it with a wheel of lime. The men both took sips.

"Not bad, not bad," Massimo finally said.

"Okay, maybe for you kids not in a rush, it's okay," Luan added, "but I am an old man . . . waiting two hours for this drink! I could have died of thirst!" He threw up his hands in exaggerated disbelief.

We practiced like this for a few hours before people started to trickle in. Around three in the afternoon, hurried staff members buzzed around the restaurant, making sure everything was in its place. I made sure to introduce myself to everyone and learned their names. Not long after, a wave of hungry and dolled-up patrons burst into the restaurant. A few people came and sat at the bar, but the majority of my work was done at the bar station, building drinks for the dining room.

Waiters scurried up to the counter and shouted, "Two Manhattans!"

Massimo moved as fast as his pudgy little hands allowed him to.

"Come on! Come on!" waiters shouted. "How am I supposed to get three drinks in them if you can't even make one!" At least at the diner, we'd written down our orders, and at Uno's we'd punched them into a computer. Lattanzi was old-school. Every request was verbal.

Drink orders escalated as we approached the pre-theater rush. "Two cosmopolitans, one Grey Goose martini with olives on the side and slightly dirty, one old-fashioned, and pass me the pinot noir . . ." Massimo furiously tried to keep up, but it became all too clear that this was a job he neither wanted nor was good at.

Luan sent me home that night with one word of advice: "It is better to be fast than good." I mulled over this, hoping I could be both fast *and* good, as I spent another night hunched over flash cards.

THE NEXT DAY AT Lattanzi, I met Ulderico. Like Luan, he wore a thick tie instead of a bow tie, but unlike Luan, he was actually the boss. Ulderico had slicked-back hair and a parrot nose. He wasn't very tall but was extraordinarily confident and handsome in his sureness. Every time he entered a room he would click one foot on the ground, announcing his presence. He did the same when leaving a room.

When Carla and Vittorio Lattanzi were in Italy, Ulderico was in charge. In fact, even when they were there, he was in charge of the restaurant. They trusted him entirely, as he had somehow managed to wrestle the team of around twenty men to respect and trust him. I hoped that one day I, too, could command this type of respect.

Aside from myself and a rotating set of hostesses, no women worked in the restaurant. As in Italy or the Old World in general, waiters were typically *waiters* and not *waitresses*. I was an exception.

"The first rule," Ulderico said, and paused while he carefully held my focus, "is never to go in the kitchen. It is not a place for women. You would distract the cooks, who I insist you never meet." And so, in all the time I worked at Lattanzi, I never saw even an inch of the kitchen, nor a single person who worked in there. I longed to meet the cooks, remembering my days of setting traps and snaking drains with Antonio and Cisco, but I couldn't bring myself to disobey Ulderico.

While the rest of the staff would have a meal together in the kitchen around four in the afternoon, I would set the bar up for service. Since the nameless cooks inhabited the kitchen, I wasn't invited to this meal. I survived instead on the mixed nuts we stored behind the bar.

"You don't want to overeat anyway," Luan would say, picking his teeth after a big feast. "You have a nice figure, keep it so you can get a man. Then you don't have to work like this." He wouldn't have been able to comprehend the fact that I *liked* working, especially like *this*, in a restaurant.

Setting up the bar meant a quick inventory (*How did we go through* fifteen *bottles of amarone yesterday?!*) and restocking from the cellar downstairs. The only person who had keys to the cellar was me. They hung on a small hook behind the bar, and except for Ulderico, everyone had to ask my permission to use them. The power that came with my first set of cellar keys was invigorating. I controlled one of the restaurant's most powerful assets—the alcohol.

During dinner service, I followed Luan's advice that *fast* was better than *good* and churned out drinks at a pace the waiters had never seen before. Exact measurements went by the wayside, and a few drinks indeed came back as "too sweet" or "not enough alcohol" (although this could have just been greed). After a while, though, I became both fast and good. It filled me with adrenaline to find something I excelled in. From my perch, I loved looking out and seeing guests enjoy my creations.

I HAD BEEN AT Lattanzi for a full week before I had a chance to finally meet a Lattanzi legend—Enzo. He had been away on vacation, and Luan took this opportunity to fill my head with stories. "Keep him away from the good stuff!" Luan whispered. "He is Albanian, like me, and likes to drink. But make sure Carla Lattanzi never sees it."

All of the guests loved Enzo. There was a particular crew that trickled in late-night in search of him. One night while Enzo was away, a man in a midnight-blue suit asked me where Enzo was.

"I got some Cuban cigars for him. He was gonna show me how to fix them nice with cognac."

Ulderico snapped, "Vacation! Come back next week!"

The next day someone else came by for Enzo. This guest wanted to propose to his girlfriend at Lattanzi, and apparently, Enzo had promised him a VIP setup. "Vacation!" Annoyed, Ulderico instructed, "Come back next week!"

People wandered in and out like this. An older woman even refused to eat, since she only let Enzo pick out her food. She tossed back two vodka martinis and stumbled out.

Most impressive was when Lorne Michaels, creator of *Saturday Night Live*, stopped by for Enzo. Every Tuesday he would bring the *SNL* cast and other celebrities into Lattanzi. But only if Enzo was there. Like Franky at the diner, Enzo had built up a huge fan base of regulars. He was indispensable to the business.

When Enzo was finally back from vacation, I could not match the figure who entered the restaurant with the image I'd created in my head. Enzo wasn't a theatrical giant but instead was thin, with hollowed-out cheekbones, slate-gray eyes, and silver hair. He smiled with only half of his mouth.

"*Nervoso,* when he is not drinking," Ulderico whispered as Enzo entered.

The next time I saw Enzo was halfway through the pre-theater rush. It was as if he had done a grand costume change while remaining in the same clothes. The nervous gentleman was now lit up like a bright star.

"My darling, you look *wonnnnderrrfulll*!" he exclaimed to a blushing lady with bright white hair and dark jewels glittering on her fingers. "Let me fix you up with a drink, your usual, of course." He pulled out a chair, laid a napkin on her lap, and tucked the woman into the table.

Enzo waltzed over to the bar and ordered, "Grey Goose, three olives, extra dirty, extra cold, straight up, straightaway—please!"

I quickly began to make the drink. After only a few moments of waiting, he seemed bored. Without asking, he grabbed a wineglass from beside the bar and helped himself to a bottle of amarone. "The best," he said, winking at me. "I only drink the best."

He downed a healthy glug of wine and hid the empty glass behind a few bottles. "You can just keep those there," he said, pointing to his glass and bottle of amarone. I nodded, eager to show the midnight boss that I was obedient. Enzo scooped up the vodka drink and carried it to his shimmering guest.

Throughout the night, Enzo would continue glugging wine until I lost track of the glasses (and bottles) consumed. No one at Lattanzi was allowed to drink during their shift except Ulderico, who only occasionally had a glass of Frascati or Sancerre with his clam pasta. Meanwhile, Enzo was downing bottle after bottle while everyone turned a blind eye. When I asked why Enzo was allowed to behave like this, Ulderico laughed. "He's better when he drinks!"

I WATCHED AS ENZO sold an old bottle of Gaja to Bill Murray one night just by saying, "Well, this is what you should drink," and then popping the cork.

"What was that?" I asked Enzo.

"Some Merlot, I think, good stuff," he replied with a wink. I later learned it was an $800 bottle of nebbiolo. To Enzo, the good stuff equaled the expensive. It didn't matter what it was; he would sell the priciest dessert, pasta, wine, or cocktail available.

"It's not ripping people off," he told me one day when he sold a third bottle of costly amarone to a guest who was already belligerent. "That woman will wake up the next day and think, *Man, that was the best time!* She will come back in here again and again because she wants that experience, and you cannot have that unless you pay to play, baby."

I looked back at the guest in question. She had her hand on the back of her partner's neck and she was booming, "I am gonna fuck you so bad, I am *gonna fuck you so bad*!"

After the third bottle, she overpaid her check ("The best part!" Enzo added), grabbed her date's hand, and led him to the bathroom, where they remained for the next hour. After that night, she came in at least once a week. Each time, Enzo made sure to show her a better time than the last. More outlandish displays of frozen strawberries and gobs of whipped cream, more champagne poured into overflowing glasses, more shots of grappa being sucked back with lemon twists, *more, more, more*. She never grew sick of it, and neither did Enzo.

Every night with Enzo was like this. "How is he still alive!?" I asked Chowdhury, one of the servers, in awe. Enzo had just polished off six bottles of amarone with a guest, and now they were sipping on Louis XIII cognac ($230 for a two-ounce pour)!

Chowdhury laughed. "Enzo is a beast. He is the reason we all still have a job."

In a way, Enzo's life seemed glamorous. He was able to show up to work, drink the priciest booze, eat fancy foods, and hang out with illustrious guests. His liquid courage helped him garner the trust of people I was much too timid to even look at.

Enzo was not just a walking bottle of amarone—he had his tricks, too.

"You want people to keep eating, keep drinking . . . ," he told me one day as he popped a bottle of amarone and sliced a large chunk of Parmigiano Reggiano into small pieces. "See, if I just gave them this wine"—he pointed to the bottle of amarone—"it would be too much." The thick red wine clung to the side of the glass like glue. It reminded me of drinking soup, rich and warm. "And if I gave them this cheese, well, they would die of thirst!" Sure enough, the hard cheese was crunchy, salty, and left my mouth dry.

After a bite, he looked at me and smiled. "See? What do you want right now? Some wine?" I nodded, and he poured me a glass. In a wave of relief, the amarone coated my palate, bringing moisture and loads of dried-fruit flavors.

I swallowed and looked back at Enzo. "You want more cheese, don't you?" He was right. All night I could have sat there and just eaten the hard, salty cheese with the full, raisiny wine. Enzo had essentially given me the grown-up version of milk and cookies.

Milk and cookies, warm pie with ice cream, grilled cheese dipped in tomato soup, peanut butter and jelly, French fries and ketchup—I knew these went together, but I'd never stopped to think about why. Wine-and-food pairing is the very foundation of a sommelier's career—serve wine and make it taste even better with food.

Enzo made me question why we like what we like together.

The exploration became addictive, and I began to try different sips of wine and think, *What do I want to eat with this?*

A bracing pinot noir made my mouth feel sour, and I longed for a creamy dish of pasta. A glass of port made me want something equally sweet and powerful, like a stewed fruit pie.

On the flip side, a glass of heavy cabernet sauvignon with grilled fish made me want to vomit. A metallic taste flooded my mouth—it tasted like I was eating my fork! The iron found in the tannins of red wine, when mixed with fish oils, created that metallic taste. I searched for low-tannin red wines like gamay and grenache that didn't cause an off flavor. The rule of white wine with fish and red wine with meat, I realized, could be broken.

One day, I watched as Ulderico enjoyed a chilled glass of Sancerre with a warm goat cheese salad for lunch. He took a small bite, chewed slowly, and then allowed himself a sip of wine. He noticed my interest and offered me a taste. The mesclun was unlike any lettuce I had tried before—herbal, bitter, almost spicy. It was also my first time trying goat cheese, and I found it comparable to licking the side of a smelly barn animal. I instantly began to frown in disgust. Ulderico laughed and offered me his glass of Sancerre, saying, "I know, but try *this*."

Desperate to wash down the stinky cheese, I grabbed his glass and took a huge gulp. The wine did something I hadn't expected: it made the cheese taste *better*. Separately the two things made little sense to me—the wine was tart and light, and the salad was intense and rich. But together, there was a balance. All of a sudden, wine became something more than just a tool to get drunk; it became an ingredient in a good meal.

WHEN I FIRST STARTED BARTENDING, my aunt Kathy asked, "Do you think being around all that alcohol is a good idea?" With our family's history and my previous DUI, she was worried.

In church growing up, I had been told liquor was evil. I'd become frightened as I watched sangria transform Lucy and my father. Fear had evolved into shame. Screwdrivers had propelled my father's gambling habit and the sadness that followed. Shame had become disgust. I was repulsed that I had turned to drink as a coping mechanism.

At Lattanzi, the shame and disgust I'd previously felt about alcohol turned into respect. Alcohol wasn't inherently evil, just like food wasn't inherently bad. Yet there were those who suffered from eating disorders and those who suffered from drinking disorders. Unknowingly, as my self-prescribed therapy, I dedicated my life to respecting the drink.

One evening, I found a dusty copy of *Wine for Dummies* tucked behind the cash register at Lattanzi. Previously I had only studied cocktails, spirits, and beer. There was an intangible element to wine. It was an intimidating subject; I thought I was too young and too poor to understand the concept.

I ended up surprising myself. By the end of the week, I had ripped through *Wine for Dummies*. Next, I purchased *The Wine Bible* and started to grow more curious about all these wines I had never tasted. I asked Ulderico and Enzo about some of the wines from the books.

"Have you ever tried a—Brunello di Montalcino?" I asked.

They snorted and chuckled loudly. "Well, of course!"

They told me that this wine was one of the "best." Excited, I asked what it tasted like, my pencil ready to jot down their reactions. They stumbled a bit, and eventually, Enzo chimed in with, "It's just one of the best. Very good, powerful, dry wine. Very good."

My pencil was unmoved; their tasting notes were a bit underwhelming. Why was it one of the best but they couldn't articulate what it tasted like?

I learned rather quickly that wine tasting is based on a

vocabulary not many are taught. Whereas you learn as a child that lemons are tart and milk is creamy, no one tells you that Brunello di Montalcino has high acidity and tannins, and smells like potpourri and tomatoes.

At Lattanzi we had only twenty wines I could taste. There were just two champagnes—Veuve Clicquot and Moët & Chandon. So sure of my evolving palate, I declared one day to Chowdhury that Veuve Clicquot was my favorite. I learned a couple of years later that the same company owned them both.

I began to realize that the world of Lattanzi wasn't as big as I'd thought. I would never be able to taste everything I wanted to there and needed more.

It was a bittersweet moment when I realized that I'd outgrown Lattanzi, a place that was safe and easy. It was now time to take a risk.

THE WINE SCHOOL

I FOUND THE WINE SCHOOL (WS) from an online search. Countless schools offered wine classes, but this one looked the friendliest. Their website advertised a two-month basics course, a six-month theory class, and a four-month tasting class. They also promised additional resources such as tastings and access to the "sommelier" community. The what!?

I searched the dictionary for a definition. *A sommelier, or wine steward, is a trained and knowledgeable wine professional, typically working in fine restaurants, who specializes in all aspects of wine service as well as wine and food pairing.*

I thought about the Sancerre and goat cheese salad, the amarone and Parmigiano Reggiano. I couldn't believe that this was an actual job, that people could serve guests and taste wine for a living. Something clicked inside—the love cycle, the food pairings, my bookworm tendencies—and it all made sense for me.

Now if only I could figure out how to pronounce the word.

Sommalia? Sommuhhlllleeir? I spent the next ten minutes repeating after a YouTube recording, "Some-all-yay, some-all-yay, some-all-yay."

The WS classes were way out of my price range, close to a thousand dollars. However, something on their site did catch my eye—an upcoming tasting with wines from Chile, *free* to members of the trade. I figured, I was a bartender; that's the trade. Perhaps I could slip in unnoticed, taste quickly, take notes, and leave, one step closer to this sommelier community.

ON THE DAY OF the tasting, it was over a hundred degrees. You could see waves of heat coming off the pavement, and the subway poles were as hot as a pan in the oven. Due to the scorching summer weather, I wore cut-off denim shorts (a.k.a. Daisy Dukes) and a tube top.

In retrospect, not the most professional wine-tasting outfit, but I was new to this world and didn't think twice. Needless to say, when I walked into a room full of men in suits, everyone turned to stare. So much for going unnoticed.

Eyes zoomed in on my tight top and the bottom curve of my shorts. I crossed my arms and brought my long chestnut hair forward to cover my breasts.

"*Ahem,*" a man with a clipboard grunted, "name, please!" He started clicking his pen, *click, click, click.*

"My, uh, name?" I began, quivering. "Um . . . why do you need to know my name?"

His eyebrows raised and his left hand rested on his hip. "Did you RSVP for the tasting?" His pen clicked, clicked, clicked.

I stammered about the website and the ad for the tasting.

"Righty, mate. I got her. She's with me," a chipper New Zealand accent interjected. Suddenly, I was pulled right past the man with the clipboard.

The New Zealander was named Grant and was at least a foot taller than me with fiery spiked hair and freckles covering his arms and cheeks. He was the only one there, besides me, who wasn't wearing a suit. Instead, Grant wore a button-down cowboy shirt that was shiny, utterly ridiculous, and instantly made me like him. He grabbed a glass and started to pour me some wine.

"Tell me then, you a hooker, eh?" Grant chuckled. He caught himself, quickly adding, "Sorry, not a funny bit there. What I meant is, *who* are you?"

"Victoria." I extended my hand cautiously. "I bartend."

"Well, nice getup. You're the only one here not dressed like a dullard." He paused, then launched back with his thick accent, "Except me of course." I couldn't help but laugh. He was right, I did look ridiculous. It felt good to laugh at myself, just like when I had made the world's worst egg cream.

"Some savvy B?" Grant pulled out a bottle of sauvignon blanc and poured me a taste.

The wine seemed to jump out of the glass and punch me in the face. It felt like taking a quick huff of perfume (but nicer). I couldn't put the smells into words, so thankfully he did—fresh-cut grass, white flowers, wet rocks, chives, herbs. I nodded in agreement, then took a big swig.

"Whoa!" he shouted out. "Down the hatch! Well, I guess that's a compliment!"

My cheeks turned scarlet. "Is this your wine?"

He laughed and nodded.

Because of the way he was dressed, I hadn't even considered that he could be the winemaker! I was ashamed that I had done the same thing to him that everyone else in the room had done to me.

"It's quite nice," I added, trying to recover from my chugging faux pas. He thanked me, and we moved on to the next wine, a chardonnay.

"So, these wines are from Chile, but you sound like you're

from New Zealand. How does that work?" I hoped this wasn't a stupid question.

He chuckled again and warmly said, "Thank you for not calling me an Aussie. Yep, I started making wine in Chile a while ago; there is a lot of cool stuff happening there, it's home now."

I nodded and furiously swirled the chardonnay, trying to find any aromatics. Compared with the last wine, this one was so neutral. Unable to say much about the chardonnay, I started to ask him questions and take notes. Interest in the wine lit his fuse, as he quickly launched into a spiel on everything from the grapes to the cellar. I circled words I had to look up later: *malolactic, cold stabilization, pyrazines.*

While we were on the chardonnay, two gentlemen flew in. "Grant, my man!" one of the men exclaimed.

Grant placed his hand on the first gentleman, who was just shorter than me. "This here is master sommelier and troublemaker Finn Ferguson." *Master sommelier?* Was that like a Jedilevel wine server? I made a note to Google the term later.

The other gentleman introduced himself as an instructor at the Wine School. My body went numb. An instructor!? Now I was stuck in a tight circle with a winemaker, some sort of master wine person, and an instructor at the school! My plan of going unnoticed was definitely ruined.

"So are you a sommelier?" the instructor asked me.

Before I could answer, Grant chimed in, "Not *yet.*"

The instructor lit up and moved closer. "You should sign up for our basics class. We have a series that begins in a few weeks."

My palms began to sweat furiously. I stammered, "I—I did see that online. I am still deciding."

The instructor went into full recruiter mode. He lectured me on the value of education in today's world. "While you decide," he added, "why don't you sit in on a class?"

Sit in? Meaning, for free? That I could do. I jotted down the time, place, and date.

"Also," the instructor began, "when you show up, don't wear so much perfume. It's hard to taste wines properly with *that* in the air." He pointed to my neck and hair, which I became increasingly aware of. The chamomile water I was wearing all of a sudden jumped out as offensive. I swore to never again wear anything with fragrance.

The next few hours were a blur. I tasted ten different wines. I tried not to speak at all but rather listen to how the men described the wines, taking mental notes. One was "especially slutty, all oak and ripeness," while another was "a blast of pyrazines" or "fecking good shit."

A couple of people were spitting out the wine after tasting, something I had never seen before. The instructor had an especially impressive spit, launching a perfect stream into a bucket like a water gun. Others dribbled, some blasted, a few squirted. Since I was way too nervous to attempt to spit in front of a room of men in suits, I just swallowed—all of the wine.

By the seventh or eighth pour, I realized this had become a problem. My cheeks grew red, and my thoughts began to mush together. It was time to go. I somewhat remember high-fiving the master sommelier goodbye and thanking Grant, who handed me a bottle of sauvignon blanc to take home (I must have lost this on the subway because I couldn't find it the next day). Right before I left, the instructor shook my hand and looked me sharply in the eye, saying, "See you in class."

⚜

The Wine School met in the dark basement of a sushi restaurant in Chelsea. The environment seemed like more of a speakeasy than a classroom. Still, who was I to judge? As a novice, I realized I had to be open-minded.

When I walked in, the instructor was busy organizing bottles with a group of students. Everyone in attendance had brought their own wineglasses. Had the instructor told me to do the same? Our first meeting was still fuzzy, and I couldn't remember his exact instructions. Was I allowed to even taste when I was sitting in?

I looked around the room filled with about thirty students. Each person had paid about a thousand dollars to be there—$30,000 worth of commitment surrounded me! I felt like a kid in the lunch line at school again, *low-income household* written on my forehead. Here I was, butting in around week six of eight, unpaying, and with no glasses of my own.

The instructor looked at me and hurriedly pointed to an empty chair in the far corner. Without his two male buddies by his side, he was much more serious.

"Are there any glasses I can borrow? See, I don't—"

He cut me off, instructing a woman beside him to fetch me glasses from upstairs. I scurried away to the corner obediently.

The person to my left forced a small grin when I sat down. When glasses from upstairs arrived for me they were nubby, dirty little things. I peered enviously at my neighbor's pristine, tall stemware. A student came around to pour wine. He paused briefly, looking down at the stubby stems, then me. I might as well have had a giant *X* on my head.

Hoping to get a head start, I grabbed the bowl of the first wineglass. I shook it around, trying to imitate the swirling that was happening around the room. A student to my left chuckled to his friend, "Look at how she's holding the wineglass!"

Self-conscious, I copied their hand placements and moved my fingers down to the stem of the glass. Apparently, they'd learned in an earlier class that holding the bowl of the wineglass heats the wine, destroying the delicate aromas and structure.

My swirl also needed work. I sloshed the wine around until it jetted out, splattering me and the table in front of me. The student to my left tried to stifle laughter. I pretended my faux pas had never happened and looked away.

"Okay, class!" The instructor commanded attention from the room. He dove into the topic of aromatics in regard to floral notes and oak usage. I furiously scribbled down each word he said. *I'll make sense of it all later,* I thought.

Some grapes apparently had more floral notes than others, although he didn't explain why, and there were different ways to describe the aromas: white flowers, yellow flowers, purple flowers, desiccated flowers, and "soapy."

We all picked up the first wine, and the instructor asked the group, "What type of flowers do you all get here?" The group closed their eyes and poked their noses deep into the glasses, sniffing with total focus.

"White flowers," someone called out; a few others added, "Yellow flowers." I stuck my nose in my glass, trying to detect a lily or a sunflower. Wait, what does a sunflower even smell like? What do yellow flowers smell like anyway versus white flowers? I definitely could not identify what type of flower was supposedly masquerading in the golden juice.

"Exactly. Jasmine, buttercup, chrysanthemum . . . ," the instructor went on. What? Chrysanthemum? What the hell does a chrysanthemum smell like? All of the students began nodding their head and scribbling down notes. I wrote down, *Go to a flower shop!*

"Is it a Riesling?" one student asked calmly, while another scoffed, "The acidity isn't there, maybe a muscat?" I looked at the two students and then the instructor in perplexity. It couldn't be a Riesling, I thought, the one we had at Lattanzi was sweet.

"Riesling," Luan would always say, "we give to the ladies, they like the sugar."

As if he could read my thoughts the instructor asked the class, "How many people think Riesling is always sweet?" I jutted my hand high in the air. No one else raised their hand.

So apparently Riesling didn't have to be sweet. The wine in the glass was a Riesling. It had aromas of white and yellow flowers and no perceptible "residual" sugar. The instructor went on to explain that veteran tasters can perceive residual sugar (RS) at around four grams per liter, and beginners (as in, me) starting at around ten grams per liter. Since this Riesling had only three grams per liter of RS, it was technically dry, or *trocken,* as the Germans would say. My pen frantically skated across the paper. A dry Riesling. I couldn't wait to tell Luan.

Next, we tried a wine that showed evidence of "oak aging." Essentially, the wine was in a barrel. Okay, that I could wrap my mind around, but then it got complicated. There were ways to tell, just by smelling, what type of oak was used (French, American, Slovenian, Hungarian, etc.) and how big the barrel was. It was almost like a detective game, deciphering small clues that most people would miss. The darker color "could indicate some oxidative aging," a student added, holding the glass up to the light. I circled *oxidative aging* in my notebook to look up later.

"Or perhaps just age," another student countered. "White wine gains color as it ages, red wine loses color." The instructor agreed that age and/or time spent in oak could be responsible for the color. If it were an older wine, though, the instructor explained, it wouldn't be this fruity.

"The first thing to go is the fruit," the instructor said, and talked about youthful fruit aromas and how these become dried or tertiary notes over time.

"I am picking up on notes of vanilla, caramel, baking spices," the instructor began. "This is the trifecta of new oak." If one could find these aromatics in a wine it meant that the juice had spent time in new oak barrels—when an oak barrel is brand-new the juice leaches these aromas from the wood.

After a few uses, the wood starts to lose its flavor and provides merely a porous container for the wine to round out in. If the wine feels round but doesn't have aromas of vanilla, caramel, and baking spices, old oak had probably been used. *Okay, okay*, I thought, *but round? How can you tell if a wine is* round?

I swirled the wine through my mouth, cutting my teeth, tongue, and gums. Did it feel rounder than the first wine? The student next to me remarked on how creamy it felt. *Creamy wine*, I wrote down. The instructor went on to explain that oak tannin you perceive on your gums, whereas grape tannin you perceive on your tongue. Everyone else in the room nodded in understanding. Meanwhile, my forehead was scrunched in confusion as I scribbled down the word *tannin* and a picture of a tongue and gums. What was tannin and how did it feel?

Later, I would learn that much of the WS curriculum was out of date (like the tongue-and-gum tasting note). The more I learned about wine, the more I realized that things are continually changing. For example, for the longest time, zinfandel was thought to originate in California. Many considered it the one true all-American grape variety. However, genetic tests soon revealed that it was the same grape as primitivo, commonly found in Puglia, Italy. Sommeliers began to tell their guests, "Zinfandel is actually Italian!" Then, years later, it was discovered that zinfandel was not Italian in origin. Instead, primitivo and zinfandel are both clones of a rare indigenous variety from Croatia called crljenak kaštelanski. First it was Californian, then it was Italian, now it's Croatian! In the wine world, you have to keep learning to stay relevant.

Our second wine was a chardonnay, which everyone in the room guessed, except for me. I had no clue at all. Overwhelmed,

I picked up the third glass and hoped for some obvious hints. Usually, in classroom environments, I excelled. I was always the one who had the answer. Here, I was definitely the stupidest in the room. It was a horrible feeling I never wanted to experience again.

I dug my nose deep in the glass and commanded it to speak the answers to me. The wine was both floral and oaky. Everyone in the room seemed confused. At least it wasn't just me! Pleased that he had stumped his group of followers, the instructor grinned from ear to ear. "Which white wines are classically both floral and aged in new oak?" The whole room began to stir with whispers.

Eventually, a cluster of students timidly put forth a guess. "Rhône whites? Like marsanne and roussanne?" Here were three words I had never heard before. Apparently, they were correct! Whatever was happening here, I wanted in.

AFTER CLASS, I hung around until the instructor was finally free. Students flocked to him like disciples, and in a way, the group seemed more like a cult than a classroom. Especially prevalent in the group were young women, like me.

"Thank you," I said, and found myself vomiting words of praise and excitement uncontrollably.

The instructor eventually interrupted, "So, sign up for the class, then." I promised that I would.

The next day at Lattanzi, I begged Ulderico to help me pay for the expensive class. "Think of how much more knowledgeable I'll be with our guests," I added. "It will definitely help sales!"

I could see that I had lost him. Overall, he was happy to hear that I liked wine, but he insisted that my job was to make drinks and look pretty. He explained that for a woman being too curious is a bad thing, that men would take advantage of me. Further, he insisted that no one, especially the men, wanted me to outsmart them. "Best to not know," he added, "for a girl, anyway."

My body began to shake. I was going to either cry or punch him. I felt like my mum, with my father putting me in my place. It seemed I was the wrong gender for the wine world. But I didn't care. My whole life I hadn't fit in, so why worry about fitting in now?

I was going to take that class, I told myself, with or without the help of Lattanzi. That month, I was ferocious with my hospitality; I made sure that every customer felt loved. I worked seven nights a week. Soon, I had enough money to negotiate a payment plan with the WS.

ALMOST AS IF THEY were encouraging me to leave, things started to become unpleasant at Lattanzi. A new manager was hired by Carla to "keep the boys in line." When Ulderico wasn't there, the new manager ruled like a dictator, and a creepy one at that.

"How long are your legs?" the new manager asked me one day as he inched closer behind the bar. The weight of his presence made me feel like I was being locked in a car again and pinned down. He came closer and closer, telling me a story about the first time he watched the movie *Pretty Woman*.

"That scene," he began, "where she says her legs are forty-four inches, hip to toe, eighty-eight inches wrapped around him for a bargain price of three thousand dollars . . ." He then looked at me from hip to toe. "So, how long are your legs? And how much do they cost?"

When no one else was around he breathed down my neck. Every so often he would touch my arm, hip, or hands for no reason at all. To guests, he referred to me as "*my girl* behind the bar." I knew that it would only be a matter of time before there was a cold night when he would offer me a ride home. I had to get out, fast.

Diving into my wine books helped me escape. I slowly started to absorb information, fascinated by glamorous-sounding wines and vineyards. The WS course helped fuel this fury. Once a week, I headed to the sushi restaurant's basement with my very own pristine wineglasses.

Every week there was a different teacher, only occasionally would the instructor (who recruited me) lead a class. Still, I felt myself getting sucked into the cork-dork cult, worshipping every word that smoothly escaped the instructor's mouth. Through the course, I gained not only knowledge but a bit of confidence.

Toward the end of the eight-week class, I told the instructor that I wanted to taste more wine, to be in a place where I was continually learning and growing. Lattanzi didn't exactly have a fascinating rotation of wines. I could tell the instructor liked being asked for help. He told me to send him my CV. I nodded, not daring to ask what the hell a CV was.

CELLAR RAT

THAT WEEK, SOMEONE NAMED REYNARD reached out to me from Harry's at Hanover Square. He had received my CV from one of the instructors at the Wine School, and by the end of the week, I was hired as a bartender.

When I told the instructor the good news, he replied, "Oh, Reynard will love *you.*" The way he said *you* made me nervous.

Still, I took the job because Harry's held one of the largest wine collections in Manhattan. Harry Poulakakos, a native of Greece, had come to America with a dream. After working at an ice-cream parlor and then at the nearby Delmonico's, he finally had enough cash saved up to open Harry's in 1972. The restaurant soon became a Wall Street institution. According to their website, "Harry's was immortalized in novels such as Tom Wolfe's *Bonfire of the Vanities* as well as Bret Easton Ellis's *American Psycho.*"

Harry had started purchasing wine in the seventies when first-growth Bordeaux and grand cru Burgundy were no more than a couple of bucks a bottle. His cellar now spanned multiple floors in the historic India House in the Financial District. Rumors circulated on the collection's value (*eight million dollars!*) while others regarded it as priceless. My mind began racing as I thought of all the wines I could have at my fingertips, wines I had previously only read about.

At Harry's, the culture was extremely macho. Wall Street men in gray suits would line the bar, polishing off martinis at lunch like they were cold glasses of water, swinging from market dip to rise. Women were allowed as bartenders only if they showed ample cleavage. The wine sold was from either Burgundy, Bordeaux, Champagne, Italy, or California. Harry's only offered good vintages from classic producers.

The wine list was a fraction of what was actually in stock. Instead, the guests relied on the captains and managers to recommend a bottle. Even those working at the restaurant had no idea what exactly was in the cellar. There was no system, no organization, and only one person knew where everything was—Harry.

Harry knew not only where he'd hidden the 1986 Château Haut-Brion but also when he'd bought it, how much it had cost, and how many bottles had been purchased. His mind had perfectly preserved over forty years of wine buying and selling.

The problem was that it was 2011 and Harry was getting older. When his beloved wife, Adrienne, had died in 2003, he'd shuttered the restaurant. Three years later his son, Peter, had reopened the space with the same name but a different layout. Harry still visited daily, welcoming his customers back with warmth, but something had changed, and he was tired.

Peter had decided it was time to organize the cellar. To do so, he'd brought in Reynard, a former sommelier at other restaurants. However, one man wasn't enough for the reorganization of a priceless collection. He would need help. But who would be up for the impossible task of categorizing four floors' worth of wine?

"I'LL HELP," I told Reynard as he mentioned the cellar renovation that was under way. Although Peter approved the task, Harry wasn't too pleased to see people rummaging through his cellar, moving things from one place to another.

"There is something," Harry said in his thick Greek accent, "I do not trust about this Reynard." Peter reassured his father that Reynard was an encyclopedia of knowledge and, with my help, would be their key to organization. Eventually, Harry gave in.

I had no idea how to organize a wine cellar, but I figured it couldn't be all that difficult. At Lattanzi, I had implemented a monthly inventory system, the first they had ever had. I thought the only skill I needed was the ability to count bottles and read labels.

The first day of the reorganization Reynard asked a couple of friends to join—a wine importer, Paul, and an out-of-work sommelier nicknamed Chip.

While Reynard led us back to the cellar, I asked Chip if one could keep the title of sommelier even if they weren't working as one. He laughed. "It's all bullshit. The title, I mean. A sommelier is someone who sells wine in a restaurant. If you don't do that, you're not a somm. It doesn't matter if you have a pin or became certified." Reynard nodded his head in agreement.

We wound through the well-used kitchen that held the irate chef, around kegs of beer and stacks of boxes. Harry's wasn't Lattanzi. I no longer held the cellar key; I no longer held the power.

I was surprised to find the wine cellar completely empty. Brand-new shelving units lined the walls and gave off an aroma of sawdust. In the middle of the room was a large wood table with a clipboard on it and a stack of papers.

"Where's all the wine?" I asked, dumbfounded.

Reynard turned around and looked at me like I was a complete idiot. His two friends started to chuckle. "Well, that's what you're here for."

First, we would inventory all of the wines in each cellar (there were four floors of storage). Then I would bring these counted wines to the new empty cellar, which would hold, organized by geography, a certain amount of every wine. The other cellars would be used as backups. Since this cellar behind the kitchen was the easiest to get to, it would be stocked with at least one of everything we had. At the end of every dinner service, the "cellar rat" (me) would restock the empty slots here for the next day.

We left the empty wine cellar and followed Reynard upstairs. As soon as I entered the second cellar, I almost ran right into a stack of boxes. The whole room was a maze of teetering bottles. In one corner stood a tower of wooden crates with the words *Domaine de la Romanée-Conti* etched onto their sides.

Paul and Chip bounced back when they saw this. "Whoa! Holy stack of DRC!" Paul exclaimed.

Chip laughed. "That . . . is just absurd."

I made sure to remain utterly silent around these three gentlemen, petrified that anything I said would clue them in to how little I knew about wine. I walked past the wooden boxes of DRC and took a mental note of the name. *This one seems important.*

"Here," Reynard began, "is where a lot of red Bordeaux and Burgundy is."

Chip pointed to a black box that said *Barolo* on the side. "And apparently some Italy."

Reynard nodded his head and said, "Yes, hence the need for reorganization."

Next was a cellar that was so narrow only one person could go in at a time. On each side were cubbies filled with loose bottles. Their labels I had never seen before. Some were ornate, with illustrations of magnificent castles and grounds. Others were much simpler, just a few words scribbled in cursive. There were tiny little bottles the size of my hand and gigantic bottles that came up to my waist.

Another cellar was partially empty—here they had already started to reorganize. Then there was a small cellar behind the manager's office that held random bottles of "loosies," or miscellaneous items that didn't fit into the categories of Bordeaux, Burgundy, Champagne, Italy, and California. These were wines from Chile, still red wines from the Champagne region (which I had no idea even existed), obscure dessert wines from Austria, etc.

"Come on," Reynard instructed us as he popped back into the elevator. Up again we went to the next floor, where past some offices lay a smaller cellar. Here, I recognized champagne bottles (although no Veuve Clicquot or Moët) and lots of squat bottles with wide bases and slim tops. Burgundy, I later learned. Bordeaux bottles were tall with straight sides and high shoulders. Riesling bottles looked like a thin triangle with a long and narrow neck.

Historically, the Burgundy bottle came first, followed by Bordeaux and then Riesling. The last was said to have been designed to fit on the narrow ships that swam through the Rhine and Mosel Rivers in Germany. The tall shoulders on the Bordeaux bottle have been said to catch the sediment before it floods into the neck. Over time, the styles of wine have become associated with their corresponding bottle shapes. This is why, even today, pinot noir, which originated in Burgundy, is usually bottled in a Burgundy bottle.

The last cellars were on the top floor, up a small flight of stairs. This one held some of the oldest and rarest bottles in the collection. Bottles from wineries that no longer existed, formats no longer made, and cuvées (certain house blends) of cult wine.

"How much would this bottle cost?" I asked Reynard, placing my hand on a label that read *Gentaz-Dervieux Côte-Rôtie*. He scoffed and rolled his eyes. I guessed that meant a lot.

He said my question was *vulgar,* that price wasn't the point. "What's most special about the bottle is not the price but that the winery no longer exists." The Gentaz family was one of the first to bottle their wines in Côte-Rôtie, a village in France near Lyon, specifically in the Northern Rhône, where Syrah is king. Marius Gentaz had had some of the best vineyards in the area but retired in 1993.

In 2011, the very year that I first learned about this wine, Marius Gentaz passed away. What few bottles are left are precious because they tell the story of not only a time and place but an extraordinary person. I looked back at the bottle and tried to memorize the label. How could anyone drink the wine? It seemed almost too tragic to do so.

ORGANIZING THE CELLAR WAS physically and mentally exhausting. Reynard would call out inventory items—"Ausone! Angélus!"— and I would run off to find, count, and place them on the appropriate shelves. With each bottle I touched, I tried to memorize the label so I could research it later.

I worked behind the bar Wednesday, Thursday, and Friday. My shift began at ten A.M. and sometimes ended as late as four A.M. All other days I spent locked away in the cellar, fervently organizing and inventorying. Cellar work was, of course, unpaid. I cherished the experience of being able to hold these priceless bottles, see their labels, and learn about each of them. With Reynard in charge we also all drank very well. He would regularly pop bottles of rare and expensive wine for us to taste.

One night, he asked me what wines I liked to drink. I told him that recently I was loving Argentinian malbec. He winced and replied, "I see, your palate is still developing . . ."

He then made it his mission to help me "develop." My supposedly unrefined love for malbec soon evolved into an appropriate

love for Bordeaux and then Burgundy. I wrote down every bottle
we tasted at Harry's, priceless cuvées, and legendary classics. I
didn't want to question Reynard's judgment, but did Harry know
we were drinking (so much of) his wine?

Behind the bar, I was trained by Sean Muldoon, a fiery Irish-
man. He had made quite a name for himself in Dublin, winning
countless awards as a bartender and mixologist. The Poulakakos
family, through one of their investors, caught wind of Muldoon's
talents and brought him over. They promised him his dream—a
bar in New York City.

"Right, then," Muldoon began, "the first thing we'll make
is a Vieux Carré." I took out my notepad and began to scribble
down his recipe: *¾ ounce of rye, ¾ ounce of cognac, ¾ ounce of
Antica Formula sweet vermouth, a teaspoon of Bénédictine, a dash
of Peychaud's Bitters, and a dash of Angostura bitters. Finish with
a lemon twist.*

"The Vieux Carré got its name," Muldoon began, "since it
was invented in the French Quarter in New Orleans." I nodded,
watching him rapidly stir the drink with a long silver spoon.
Oddly, he was holding the round spoon portion with his thumb
and using the twisted handle to stir the drink.

"Isn't that upside down?" I pointed to the spoon. Muldoon,
annoyed, muttered, "Top of the spoon can't stir it up properly.
Never trust a barman that stirs with the head and not the handle."

Muldoon not only taught me the intricacies of vintage cocktails, pre- and post-Prohibition, but how to make a proper drink
in general, one with balance. Unlike at Lattanzi, where I would
free-pour vodka from the bottle into a shaker, at Harry's Muldoon forced me to use a jigger.

"*Precision,*" he repeated, "is the key to making a good drink."

What a relief, I thought. I was sick of "fast means good." I wanted to make better drinks.

Muldoon handed me the little hourglass-shaped jigger. "Well, what are you waiting for? Get on with it, then!" I jumped and nervously began to assemble a Vieux Carré. My hands shook, causing vermouth to overflow from the jigger. I could feel Muldoon flinch whenever a drop missed the shaker. My "dash" of bitters was more like a "dump" of bitters.

I made sure to stir the drink with the handle of the spoon and looked over at him for approval. His stone face remained unimpressed. I concentrated on my stirring. How long did he do this for? Thirty seconds? Was it that long? How long had I been going at it? *Okay, seems like long enough.* I strained the drink into a coupe and garnished with a lemon twist.

"Ta-da!" I presented the Vieux Carré to Muldoon. He sniffed the rim and then tossed it all down the drain. My mouth opened wide in shock. "You didn't even taste it!"

A guest at the bar who was keenly watching us shook his head with sadness. "Damn waste," I caught him whispering.

Muldoon looked at me sternly and in his thick Irish accent said, "You flubbed the ingredients. Now"—he handed me the jigger again—"pay attention." My hands began to shake as I took the measurement tool back from him. My wrist gently flicked a drop of bitters into the shaker, and I panicked as I saw another droplet beginning to form on the lip of the bottle. I quickly retracted the bitters, saving the drink from sure destruction. Then the stirring, fifteen seconds, briskly but surely, followed by a gentle strain into a coupe. I grabbed the lemon peel to twist it onto the drink.

"Stop!" Muldoon pulled my hand away as if I were going to physically abuse the Vieux Carré. "What is the whole point of a twist?" Muldoon asked me, obviously quite serious.

I tried to avoid his eyes. "To garnish?"

As his face stiffened and brows twitched I realized that was *not* the right answer. He breathed in deeply, closed his eyes, and said slowly, "No . . . a garnish is not just a garnish. It is meant to enhance the drink, in this case by imparting aromatics." He grabbed a fresh lemon peel and held it up. "This side"—he pointed to the yellow outside layer, which was bumpy—"has all the oils." Then, with both hands, he held that side of the peel over the drink as if to kiss its surface. He gently squeezed with both hands, and from the skin, a small mist of moisture was released.

"*Whoa!*" I couldn't contain my excitement. How had I not known that a lemon peel could do that? Its skin had given off a burst of aromas. This was called "expressing" the lemon peel. When I looked closely, I saw little reflective spots of oil resting on the top of the cocktail like olive oil in a dressing. The aromas transported my whole body to the lemonade stands of my childhood—crumply dollar bills, hot pavement, and tangy juice.

"Now, that," Muldoon said, holding up the Vieux Carré, "is how you make a drink."

AFTER A MONTH OF working at Harry's, I learned that I could take Muldoon's shifts at the back bar, a small speakeasy-ish spot with a separate entrance. Here, carved away in stone like a cave, there was a wooden bar that could seat six people.

The Poulakakos family started opening more restaurants and needed Muldoon's help building cocktail programs. With Muldoon gone, I jumped at the opportunity to take ownership of something.

"Good luck," one of the girls from the front bar told me. "It would take a whole lotta personality to fill that dead zone." My mind conjured up images of people walking in and asking for Victoria, just like they would ask for Enzo at Lattanzi or Franky at the Plaza Diner. I knew I could make it my own.

At first, the back bar at Harry's was a death sentence. Regulars didn't even know there was a back bar and flocked to the front, where an Amazonian woman and a girl from Long Island ruled. "The tits-and-ass show" was how patrons described it. It was a hard act to go up against.

No other bartender dared work back there, separate from the safety net of the tip pool up front. If you worked in the back bar, you were all alone. Being self-sustaining was fine with me, as I was used to this at Lattanzi and in life in general.

AT FIRST, my only guests were Tom the Pilot and Doug. Tom was as zany as they come, and at sixty-two, haunted by notions of government conspiracy, he should definitely not have still had his pilot's license.

Doug visited daily. He was recently unemployed and lived off a large settlement from his past job. He would arrive around three in the afternoon, right after the lunch crowd, and keep me company over iced tea and a salad. He always brought copies of the *Wall Street Journal* and the *Financial Times'* magazine, *How to Spend It,* for us to read. As the afternoon wore on, he would drink gin and tonics. Then closer to dinner, right as the free popcorn came out at five, Tom would waltz in and say, "Give me the cheapest whiskey you got."

These two men soon became my friends. I lit up as soon as I saw them come down the small side steps from the cobblestone streets. I would laugh along in delight as Doug described a date he had gone on with a girl who he only afterward realized was a hooker. "I thought we had a real connection!"

Soon Tom and Doug started bringing their friends to the back bar. Then their friends brought their friends. Then their friends brought whole crowds from down the street or across the block.

Within a few months, my bar was packed. Just as I had always hoped, people came in and asked for Victoria.

There was something about the world of beverages that re-ignited my passion for hospitality. What Franky from the diner used to tell me was true: "Only happy people can give good hospitality."

REYNARD WASN'T AS PLEASED with my regulars. "You have no friends in this business, Victoria, remember that," he told me, adding that everyone always wants *something*.

The people Reynard hated most were the "washed up" wine salesmen. He was disgusted that they came into the bar begging for appointments. "They are the scum of the earth," he told me. Sometimes, he would agree to a meeting just so he could make the salesmen dance like monkeys, taking great pleasure in their desperation.

Franky's voice would swirl around in my head: "*You gotta love 'em.*" I wouldn't allow Reynard to take away what I enjoyed, which was making others happy. The love cycle was back in full swing.

Luckily, loving the people who came into the back bar at Harry's paid off, literally. The tips I received were far from diner wages. What the Wall Street crowd taught me was how to sell. With my recently acquired knowledge of our wine cellar, I took guests on a journey far beyond the bottle.

Working long days at the back bar helped support not only my unpaid cellar work but also Laura. For the first time in my life, at twenty, I was making real money—enough that I could pay for Laura to go to summer camp and make sure that she never had to wear hand-me-downs. With the help of Timmy, who was now studying finance, we started a savings account and began to squirrel away money for her.

With Timmy now out of the house, too, it was just Laura and baby Angela there. I tried to distract Laura as often as possible with fancy lunches and shopping trips in the city, but there was this pit of sadness in her that seemed to grow bigger and bigger. I had been out of the house for enough time that I had almost forgotten what it was like to live there. "It's only a few more years," I tried to reassure her, "then you can do whatever you want."

AS MY INTEREST IN wine flourished, Reynard began to take more of an interest in me. Every bottle was a story I felt I needed to know. While I exhaustively researched every wine I came across, I struggled to understand its context. Reynard helped fill in the gaps. He would tell me about his days as a sommelier in iconic Michelin-starred restaurants. Although the Michelin guidebook mentions many restaurants, only genuinely exceptional ones are awarded any stars at all. There are thousands of restaurants in New York City, but fewer than seventy-five hold even one star. In these places, they had thousands of wines on their lists, and Reynard had tasted all of them.

"What about this one?" I held up a bottle of Domaine Tempier Bandol. On the label was an ink drawing of a rustic sailboat. This bottle was one of the few wines from the cellar that didn't neatly fit in the Bordeaux, Burgundy, Italy, and California sections. Instead, it came from Provence in the South of France.

Reynard's face lit up with delight when he saw the label. He said that the wine came from a small Mediterranean fishing village and was made by the famous Peyraud family.

I soon learned that in wine there was a pecking order. What Reynard considered famous might not be well-known to others. Over time, things went in and out of vogue. For example, in the 1920s, the white wine Savennières, from the Loire Valley in France, used to command higher price points than Bordeaux.

Now Savennières is rarely seen on wine lists and is cheap in comparison to many Bordeaux bottlings. However, among a few circles of wine geeks, it is still celebrated. If you want something that will last forever and is cheap (for now) buy a case of Savennières.

What the majority of people see of the wine world is a result of fat marketing budgets and "pay to play." Big companies are also the ones with the deep pockets. These groups can spend more money on marketing and sway people to recommend their wines.

I turned around the Tempier bottle to look at the back label. None of what Reynard had just said was on the back. Instead, there was a quote from Thomas Jefferson—"Good wine is a necessity of life for me"—and the words "Kermit Lynch Wine Merchant."

Reynard watched me as I inspected the back label, adding, "That is the importer label." He picked up a bottle of California cabernet that didn't have any label on the back. "Mostly foreign wines need them, since they need an importer. This California wine"—he twirled the bottle in his hand—"doesn't need one."

"If you don't know anything about wine yet, start finding importers you like when exploring foreign wines." He then went on to explain that each importer has a different palate and that I should find one that aligned with mine. "There is Louis Dressner for the funky, natural stuff . . . Terry Theise for acid and sugar. So, a good importer has a certain style to their book. If you like their style, you'll like most of their wines."

"So is Kermit Lynch a good importer, then?" I asked Reynard, who nodded his head.

"What's more, he was one of the first to import wines into the States, before regions like Chinon, Hermitage, and Meursault were famous." Through research I found that he had also written a book, *Adventures on the Wine Route,* that chronicled Kermit's initial journeys around France. It remains, to date, my favorite book on wine.

In addition to teaching me about wine, Reynard also started to take me out to traditional restaurants. At Bouchon Bakery I had my first rillette. When Reynard said it was meat in a jar, I thought he meant it was like Spam. Instead, the meat was so tender it was almost a paste, with a layer of flavorful fat on top.

Next was crudo at the bar at Marea. "Is it like sushi?" I remember asking Reynard, who laughed hysterically. Who knew Italians also did raw fish?

At Gramercy Tavern I ordered sweetbreads, which I thought meant some sort of frosting-covered bun. Instead, one bite filled my mouth with an iron-y and umami flavor. Well, these are certainly not sweet, I told Reynard. He scoffed and said that was because it was calf pancreas.

Even things that seemed familiar to many were new and exciting to me—freshly whipped aioli, parsnips, anchovies, soup dumplings, blue cheese, bagels with lox, ramen, Peking duck, razor clams, cured meats, and kale. I learned that fruits and vegetables had a "season" and that tomatoes should be left out on the counter like the pears my grandma Willie bought.

I had always thought in the world of food there were chefs and everyone else—servers, bartenders, bussers, managers, et al. Reynard showed me a new culture of gourmands and foodies. There were people out there whose food professions ranged from foragers to sommeliers to cheesemongers. My eyes slowly opened to the delights of a world I had never imagined before.

I read about Alice Waters, M. F. K. Fisher, Julia Child, Jacques Pépin, James Beard, and Richard Olney. I learned what a microgreen was, how to roast a chicken, and why caviar is served with a pearl spoon. I started to take my grocery shopping very seriously, would bake my bread, hand-roll my pasta, and grind my coffee.

Much to the dismay of some of my back-bar regulars, Reynard and I had developed a close relationship.

"He is a sociopath," Doug said over his pint glass of Bombay and tonic. "In you, he sees a version of himself he loves—worldly, knowledgeable, a gourmand—it isn't about *you*."

Tom the Pilot was also not pleased. He described Reynard as possessing "superficial charm" and exhibiting "irrational behavior."

Another regular, a loud-mouthed teddy-bear type named Trent, kept repeating, "I just don't trust the man. Girl . . . you be careful!"

I doubt any twenty-year-old has ever listened to the advice "Be careful!" Certainly, I was no exception. I knew there was an ugly side to Reynard—after all, I had seen the sadistic routines he put others through—but I never thought he would hurt me. I thought he respected me, that to him I was a muse, a protégée.

For weeks, I had sensed his advances but managed to deter him. I brushed off his comments and winks by pretending I hadn't noticed them. In so many ways I admired Reynard and loved the wine-and-food world he had shown me. But that didn't mean I wanted to sleep with him. There were quite a few bosses with different titles at Harry's, and Reynard was one of them. He could easily fire me, or worse, destroy my yet-to-blossom sommelier career. The amount of pressure he placed on me was suffocating. I felt like maybe this feeling was a pattern for a reason. Maybe men were supposed to control my body.

I felt owned by Reynard. When the other bosses left, he called me into the office during my shifts. I insisted that I couldn't leave the bar unattended, but he didn't care. Trent and Doug would shake their heads when they saw Reynard drag me away.

I tried to distance myself from him. I ignored offers for dinners and wine tastings even though I really wanted to go. But he wouldn't leave me alone. As he was one of my supervisors, he controlled my work life and schedule. If I gave him the cold shoulder, I suffered. My shifts were cut and invitations to wine tastings revoked. He refused to let me organize the wine cellar unless I would do something for him. Just as he had told me, everyone always wants *something*.

I so desperately wanted to be in that wine cellar, to learn and touch all those rare bottlings. I needed to make a living, too. So, eventually, I gave in.

Reynard was a true fox. On the surface, he was incredibly charming. He was full of witty banter that made me keel over in laughter, and he loved to gorge himself on the pleasures of food and wine. These attributes, along with his intelligence, distracted me to the point where I thought I had fallen in love. When he was kind to me, he was abundantly so, showering me with expensive dinners and wines. I was so insecure that these moments made me grow wholly attached to him. Then, when he was cruel, belittling my youth, I hid my pain.

Reynard abused his power at Harry's and used it to control me. I thought of going to Harry or Peter and telling them everything. Another bartender who had been there for a while told me, "Don't bother. You think you're the first? They would fire you like the rest. He holds the power." Whether that was true or not, I accepted it. To survive, I kept telling myself that it was love, that Reynard cared for me.

I revered Reynard's advice, thinking he was my only ticket into a world I so wanted to be a part of. Sommeliers and fine dining seemed as daunting and as far away as the stars. Reynard provided me with a telescope and a way to get there.

He told me one day that I should work a grape harvest in California, to further understand wine. All of the books I read gave winemaking a rosy hue, but Reynard insisted that I needed to beat those images out of my head. "Winemaking isn't glamorous," he would say.

So I took a plane to California and prepared to be de-romanticized. I so blindly followed all of Reynard's advice that if he had told me to jump off a cliff, I would have backed up for a running start.

MATTER OTHER
THAN GRAPES

FOR SOMMELIERS, WORKING A HARVEST is a rite of passage. I would even describe it as essential to fully understanding and appreciating wine. So off I went to Sonoma to work a harvest at a small winery called Tricycle Wine Company (TWC).

The sunshine warmed my tired New York City bones. It was thrilling to drive past vineyards I recognized from my studies. I followed along on my wine map of California, amazed that I was *in* the region. Californians seemed so relaxed in comparison to New Yorkers. Complete strangers would ask me how my day was going.

For lodging, the winemaker at TWC had a friend who had just renovated a house. He had a second bedroom and kindly offered it to me at no cost. When I arrived, I realized that the "house" was a chicken coop. As in, it was actually a chicken coop before it was renovated. Its history accounted for the smell that seemed infused into the walls and the low ceilings that I crouched below. "Beggars can't be choosers" had never rung so true.

On a Monday morning at the start of October, I biked to TWC for the first time. The sun had not yet risen. I pedaled past fields of cows and over rolling hills, and the aroma of sweet manure and fresh cut grass seeped into my nostrils. There was no litter, no cigarette butts, no horns honking. The only noise for miles must have been my wheels humming against the dirt roads.

TWC was not exactly a grand château but rather a shared warehouse space. It wasn't the romantic setting I'd originally had in mind, but I figured it would do. I biked around a massive parking lot and peeked into the different garagelike wineries. It was like a strip mall of grape juice. Kamen, Enkidu, Talisman, Tin Barn . . . Tricycle Wine Company!

I parked my bike underneath the TWC sign. With all of my strength, I swung open the garage door that separated TWC from the parking lot. A group of faces met mine, startled by the loud *slam* the door made as it hit the ceiling.

"I . . . um . . . I am . . . the harvest intern. Is this Tricycle Wine Company?"

A man with a friendly face and goatee smiled. "Welcome, Victoria. We are excited to have you learn with us." This man was a winemaker named Alex. There was another gentleman named Casey, the cellar manager, who always wore a baseball cap.

Although their relaxed nature should have put me at ease, it made me more nervous. I wasn't sure how to respond to calm; I only knew stress.

Before this, I'd thought I couldn't have possibly found a lowlier job than cellar rat, but here I was as a cellar hand. No longer even a living animal but rather a body part. My job title essentially meant copious amounts of physical labor and mopping. I would spend hours on the sorting table, picking bugs off grapes

as they tried to wiggle up my arms and cleaning out tanks full of
skins and seeds.

There was another intern as well, Ana, from Argentina, and
this was her third harvest internship. *Third!* She had worked
harvests before in Germany and France. I was definitely at the
bottom of the totem pole. Ana just nodded when Casey yelled,
"*Okay, three punch-downs. One on tank two in fifteen minutes, the
other on tank six in an hour, and the last on tank eight in ninety minutes. And hand me three two-inch camlocks, a Perlick valve, and a
cross TC.*" Meanwhile, I would rush to find a notepad, and by the
time I had, it would be too late. Casey would let out an exasperated sigh and then look to Ana, who nodded with understanding.

Safety was another concern. A punch-down was when the
top of the tank, full of juice and grape skins, had to be stirred up
and literally punched down with a big stick. Grape skins naturally
float upward, so many winemakers will push them downward so
all of the juice is continuously in contact with the skins. When I
was asked to do a punch-down, I think Casey forgot I had never
done it before. Scared to confess, I just looked around for a stick
and decided to go ahead with it. Before traveling to Sonoma, I
had read all about winery procedures, and a punch-down seemed
the simplest thing. What could go wrong?

To get to the top of the tank, I climbed up a ladder that led
to a catwalk, an elevated metal platform that ran along the tops
of the tanks. Once on the catwalk with my long stick, I began to
panic. High above the concrete floors, I was sure that even the
slightest misstep would lead to my head cracking open below. I
timidly made my way to the tank that needed punching down.
Then I rested the stick on the catwalk and grabbed the lid of the
container. I unhinged a metal clamp and swung open the top. The
next thing I remember is waking up on the floor of the catwalk,
the stick resting behind my crumpled knees.

If I had paid closer attention during my studies, I would have recalled that carbon dioxide is a by-product of fermentation. The gas was trapped in the tank, with nowhere to go until I lifted the lid. All at once it hit me like a poisonous cloud. I was lucky that I'd only passed out and hadn't fallen to my death.

Casey shouted and asked if I was taking a nap. "And what is that stick for? Use the wine-cap punch-down tool. It's hovering right above you!" He pointed to a metal rod above the tank with a flat and circular bottom, like the base of a lamp. *Ah, that would make more sense*. Absolutely humiliated that I had just huffed an entire tank's worth of CO_2, I shuffled to my feet. I shook away the woozy feeling in my head and grabbed the punch-down tool.

EVERY MORNING I WOULD wake up to an aching body. I thought that working in the restaurant industry was harsh manual labor, but being a cellar hand showed me how spoiled I had been. I barely saw the daylight, trapped in the garage from sunrise until well after sunset. It continued like this for days.

"You think this is hard, try picking grapes." Casey would chuckle. To prove to him that I was tough stuff, I decided to volunteer to pick grapes with their morning crew.

After one row of grapes, my entire back was on fire. The hovering in a crouched position was wreaking havoc on my body. "*Qué chica tan tonta!*" the crew would laugh when I stumbled.

"Get low, girl . . . and get your legs strong!" one worker said, and slapped his thick thigh, glistening with sweat, and flexed his enormous muscles.

Bees would land on the grapes, and my fingers tensed in fear that they would sting me. The worker who had slapped his thigh earlier saw me cower in horror when I came upon a whole cluster covered in bees. In one swift move, he grabbed the bunch with his sausage-like fingers and tossed it into the bucket. This guy was a badass.

I barely lasted the day. The workers ran circles around me, cutting grapes off vines and placing them in bins with such grace and speed, it looked like I was working backward.

After that morning, I swore off grape picking altogether. Instead, I stayed in the winery and stuck to following Casey's orders. Before the grapes arrived, my job was to check tanks and barrels for progress. In a tiny little notebook, I would write down the sugar level of each wine. As the yeast would convert the sugar to alcohol, the Brix (sugar content) reading would lower.

Next was cleaning the hopper (the destemming and grape-crushing machine) to get it ready for use, setting up the sorting table (a conveyor belt not too dissimilar to one found in a grocery store), transferring finished wine from tanks to barrels, cleaning out tanks, hosing out the bladder press, etc.

Essentially, I would get everything ready for new grapes to come into the winery. Once the grapes arrived, chilled and sticky from the vineyards, the clock was ticking. We had to get the grapes sorted, destemmed, and crushed immediately. The grapes could not get too warm.

On the sorting table, my fingers would fly in constant panic. Casey would drive a forklift, grabbing huge containers of grapes and dumping them into the sorting machine. "Don't let any rotten bunches get in the hopper and look out for MOG!" he screamed over the loud machines.

MOG? What is a MOG? I looked over the sorting table at Ana and tried to ask her, but it was too loud. Instead, I just tried to follow her lead. She seemed to pick out anything that wasn't perfect. A moldy grape, a rotten grape, an underripe grape—they all went off the table and into a bucket by her feet. What if I missed one of these? Would I ruin the whole batch of wine? The conveyor belt moved quickly, and my tiny fingers struggled to keep up as the grapes marched into the hopper. Bugs crawled up my arm, and an earwig somehow managed to get under my shirt. I screamed and shook my top until Casey stopped the machines in dread. He was worried I had lost a finger or something.

Instead, Ana just made a buglike gesture to him, and he laughed. "It's just MOG!" Apparently, that stood for "matter other than grapes."

I was quickly kicked off the sorting table and given the lowliest of jobs, raking grape stems. Ashamed, I kept my head down for the rest of the day. Raking stems was easy and not at all scary. This I could manage.

After the grapes had all been sorted and crushed, we transferred them to a tank for fermentation. Throughout the day I ran to fetch hoses, tubes, connecting tools, and fancy-looking wrenches. By the time sunset came around, the winery was sparkling. I had flushed out each pesky grape skin into a compost pile and scrubbed every tank clean.

Casey handed me a beer as a peace offering. I had never enjoyed the taste of beer before. Where was all of the fancy wine we were supposed to be sipping? I popped open the can, not wanting to offend Casey, and took a sip. He watched me as I glugged down the whole beer. It was a mass-produced, generic brand—but it was terrific. There was something about a hard day's work that made the beer taste so much more delicious. It was like the tiny bite of New York strip steak I was afforded as a child if we had balanced our grocery budget cunningly. For the rest of harvest, I drank only beer. And lots of it.

TO MAKE ENDS MEET (the start-up wine biz isn't all that profitable), TWC also made wine for other brands. Since TWC had the facilities, other people would bring their grapes to them and say "Make it taste like this" or "Do this and that." Then the client would pick up their finished product and sell it as their own. This practice is relatively common and not inherently a bad thing. It's like a form of office sharing in a way.

However, there was one particular brand that asked TWC to make their wine. Making this product was how I discovered the seedy underbelly of winemaking. Let's call the owner Joey. Joey's idea was to take shit grapes that were super cheap, add a bunch of chemicals and things to cover up the flavor, then sell the resulting wine for a ton of money. It worked. He didn't even need to waste money investing in a winery or resources since TWC took care of that.

My job was to help create this chemical concoction for Joey. We dumped loads of goopy juice called "mega-purple," bags of powders, and additives into Joey's tank. Yeasts that came in packets labeled "Super Fruity Red Wine" were peppered in.

Joey would justify his winemaking approach with quips such as "Americans, there is something too rustic and honest about real wine for them, they like a little Botox. A little nip and tuck."

Previously I thought wine was made solely from grapes, but rarely is this the case. The United States government has approved over fifty ingredients that are allowed in winemaking, besides just grapes. Most countries have similarly lengthy lists— for example, the European Union authorizes about fifty different ingredients. Egg whites, bentonite (clay), gelatin, granular cork, isinglass (obtained from dried fish bladders), milk products, silica gel (you know, those little packets you sometimes find in dried food with a label that says "THROW AWAY *DO NOT EAT*"), and soy flour are some of the more cheerful ingredients one can add. Some investigations have even found traces of pesticides, fungicides, and other toxic chemicals in wine.

Joey didn't care about sorting grapes, and a ton of MOG found its way into the tanks. I cringed as I saw earwigs drowning in mega-purple syrup. When I brought up my shock to Casey and complained that Joey's recipe shouldn't even be allowed to be called wine, he just shrugged.

"It's really not that bad. I've seen companies do way worse and end up charging way more for their shitty, fake wine." Casey had used to work for one of the most popular "luxury" brands in the United States. Customers would revel in the wine's velvety, silky taste. Their secret ingredient was horse hooves.

ON MY LAST NIGHT at TWC, Ana and the harvest interns from the warehouses nearby threw a mini going-away party. We were all exhausted, but it still felt good to go out in Sonoma Plaza and drink beers until our bodies no longer ached.

Casey said that when he first heard one of his harvest interns was going to be a "sommelier wannabe from New York City," he'd laughed. "We all thought you were going to walk in here with stilettos and a big-city attitude," he said. "But in the end, you proved actually to be of great help."

I would never take a bottle of grape juice for granted again. That wine could hold a sense of place and purpose was magical. I saw firsthand the intense labor that went into the vineyards and winemaking. There were also shortcuts that showed me the composition of poor wine. I promised myself after that harvest that I would only support growers and wineries like TWC, not brands built by people like Joey.

Working harvest showed me that good wine can be affordable, but it should never be cheap. Yes, good cheap beer exists. But good cheap wine doesn't exist.

Unlike beer, wine can only be made once a year. Beer you can continue to make all day and all night. High-quality production techniques in beer aren't affected by quantity. With wine, you only have one opportunity to harvest your grapes. When you do so, you are at the mercy of Mother Nature.

Wine speaks of a sense of place and people. If those things are cut out, it is no longer wine. A good bottle of wine can be $20, but it cannot be $2. If you want to drink cheaply, drink beer.

Back in New York City, I started seeing an acupuncturist for my post-harvest wounds. Her name was Jana, and she began to show me for the first time how the body can hold stress and stories of pain. With an old-school New York accent and tough-broad mentality, Jana offered a sort of therapy. There was so much I was holding in from my childhood and upbringing that I had never told anyone. At the time, I had no one to confide in. Sure, there was Reynard, but he seemed to prefer talking to listening.

When I told Jana about Reynard, she called bullshit. "I don't give a shit if he seems like Romeo, he is bad news. What's he doing with his employee, anyway?! He is supposed to be protecting *you*."

When I returned to Harry's, the back bar seemed much smaller. There was a familiar feeling creeping into my brain again, that sense of wanting *more*. I had felt it when I realized a lemonade stand could be a business, when I saw that the wine world held more than the cellar at Lattanzi, and now, after harvest, I felt that same need to grow and move on. I needed to be a sommelier.

RUMORS BEGAN TO SWIRL about Reynard upon my return to Harry's. One day he wasn't at work. When I asked around, Peter Poulakakos vehemently said that Reynard was never coming back. All of the color left my face. Did Peter know about my relationship with Reynard? Instantly, I thought this had to be my fault.

I dug around a bit more and realized that none of the owners knew about our relationship. When they found out, they apparently just laughed and said, "Well, good for that guy!" It seemed his behavior toward me wasn't exactly frowned upon. I heard that what *did* get him fired was all of the missing wine bottles that had begun to add up.

Apparently, this was a pattern throughout Reynard's career. A captain at Harry's told me the story of Reynard's downfall in the sommelier world. "He took a bottle of old Château d'Yquem, drizzled it all over his dick, and had one of the bussers lick it off. He probably wouldn't have gotten caught if he had chosen a cheaper bottle or done the whole thing off-site. Instead, he chose the priciest bottle he could find and did this shit in the wine cellar! At the epitome of fine dining, a three-Michelin-starred restaurant!"

It all started to make sense. This was why Reynard laughed when I told him I wanted to be a sommelier. He had done this to many before me, most often hostesses or bussers, the bottom of the restaurant class system to him. Reynard would wow them with fancy dinners and wine with hard-to-pronounce names. He probably loved the way they looked at him, the way I had looked at him. He made me feel as if I were a flower in a mud puddle and he, in recognizing my unique beauty, had decided to pluck me for himself. While I thought he was drawn to me because I was "wise beyond my years," it was actually my naïveté that made me a target.

"I told you he was a sociopath," Doug told me on my last night at Harry's. I had found my first sommelier job uptown and would start in a few weeks. I was ready to be taken seriously as a woman and a professional. Well, I was in for a surprise.

PART IV

AGE 21-23

THE CIRCLE OF LIGHT

To BE TAKEN SERIOUSLY, I knew I would need the title. Sommeliers were part of an elite clique I so desperately wanted to be a part of. With their pocket squares, fancy corkscrews, and encyclopedic knowledge, they seemed a world away.

But how does one become a sommelier at twenty-one? The captains, essentially head servers, at Harry's were a band of misfits who slung wine to guests but without an official title. Since one of the captains had once been a sommelier, I asked him how the whole system worked.

He rolled his eyes dramatically. "Oh, honey, *you* don't want to become a sommelier. You're young, you're beautiful, just marry someone rich."

After taking the Wine School's basics class, I had become relatively friendly with the instructor. There were whispers in the class of how he had helped secure sommelier jobs for other students. It was worth a shot, wasn't it?

My hesitation here was the roller-coaster relationship I had observed between him and Reynard. Although the instructor had helped me get the job at Harry's, he seemed to always be in some fight with Reynard.

"Be careful with him," Reynard had once mentioned to me. He was a past student of the WS and described this particular instructor as responsible for "creating a cult, a generation of sommeliers turned buyers whom he guilts into buying his shitty wine."

The instructor—in addition to teaching a few classes at the WS—was associated with an importing company. There were rumors of his "strong-arming" past students, telling them they needed to help him as he'd helped them.

I figured that becoming a buyer was still light-years away, as first I had to become a sommelier. Against Reynard's advice, I asked the instructor for help. "I know some people that are looking," he mentioned with an air of immediate confidence. He told me to send him my CV again.

For a long while, there was little traction. I am sure the instructor sent it off to pals in the industry who had a good laugh.

EVENTUALLY, ONE PLACE DID reach out: Aureole. The name itself was intimidating. An aureole is defined as "a circle of light or brightness surrounding something, especially as depicted in art around the head or body of a person represented as holy."

Most important, the restaurant wasn't just fine dining; it was Michelin starred.

The chef at Aureole was credited with spearheading the "New American" movement in fine dining. Now rarely in the kitchen, the chef's all-American face was plastered on everything from cookbooks to knives to catering companies.

Before my interview, I hoped to prepare by studying the wine list. There was only one problem—I couldn't find one. On the Aureole website, a less-than-helpful paragraph described the selection as "meticulously assembled" and offering "more than 1,700 selections with over 15,000 bottles." No other details, outside of the slew of awards the wine program had received, were provided. I realized that I would have to pitch myself as someone who could sell, without even knowing what I would have to sell.

FOR MY INTERVIEW, I was welcomed by a tall and broad-faced gentleman whose hairline started far back and led to a pile of hair that grew slowly thicker as it reached the nape of his neck. His name was Justin, and he invited me to sit down, extending his hand to an empty chair.

I had carefully curated my outfit for this interview based on videos I had watched of sommeliers. Since there weren't enough female sommeliers to emulate, I hoped a dress would be suitable. Now I realized it might not have been the best choice. The wool of the dress had begun to itch and a pool of nervous sweat was forming underneath my clothes.

Justin was looking for a sommelier who could "be nice to [the restaurant's] guests" and was "eager to learn." Our meeting was brief, but he seemed to approve, passing me on later to his GM for a follow-up meeting.

Under the GM's close-set gray eyes were massive dark circles, as if time had taken its thumbs and pressed deeply, slowly bruising his sockets. The rest of his face was boyish, a little doughy, as if it weren't a part of his taller body. His lips began to move, but just barely, and I had to lean in uncomfortably close to follow his quiet words, slurred together by his French accent.

The GM puckered his lips as if fighting back a smile. I imagined he had learned to hide any sort of merriment over the many years of fine-dining seriousness. I was worried the first question he would ask me would be along the lines of, "How old are you, *exactly?*"

But instead, I recited what I had read about the chef online combined with a general impression I had crafted from customer reviews. I used words like *New American* and *elevated* whenever I didn't know what to say.

With every word he spoke, I felt how far apart our worlds were. He asked me which restaurants in New York I liked to visit (I was mostly surviving on kitchen scraps and ramen at the time but mentioned the places Reynard had taken me to—Gramercy Tavern, Marea, Bouchon), what service meant to me, and which wines I liked to drink in my free time (I had just turned twenty-one two months previously, so I didn't have a lot of experience buying wine for myself, and besides, I couldn't recall any recent free time). Somehow I managed to dodge the land mines in each question, but I still felt there were gaping holes in my responses.

Remembering my casino days, I watched his eyes, mouth movements, and posture. Channeling my grandmothers, I led with positivity, making sure I never spoke ill of anyone or anything. In regard to wine, I mentioned the cellar at Harry's and buzzwords that I had learned working harvest. I assured him that my role would help make the restaurant more profitable, that I was eager to learn and would bring regulars in through hospitality.

As the meeting wound to a close, I thanked him and, suddenly compelled, blurted, "I really, really would love this opportunity, sir." I felt an upwelling of water in my eyes, almost spilling, my warm cheeks turning scarlet. He looked at me and nodded.

LATER THAT WEEK, an email from Justin arrived in my inbox:

As long as your trial goes well for both of us, we'll move forward.

Looking forward to it!

My heart soared. A *trial*? I was almost in! But then, whatever happiness I felt suddenly dissipated as fear entered. I might be a sommelier in a Michelin-starred restaurant in New York City, and I was absolutely terrified.

There were still a few days left between me and my impending career. I committed myself to my computer, wine books, and flash cards. After proofreading my email response to Justin thirty times, I finally hit send. It overall read as excited and cheerful, except for one line that was extremely insistent: *Please send me the wine list to study.*

Within moments, Justin sent me not only the wine list but also a list of after-dinner drinks, Aureole specialty cocktails, wines by the glass, and current liquors in inventory, as well as a glassware chart and a basic wine service guide. There were nineteen steps in the basic wine service and five extra steps if the wine was sparkling!

THINK OF THE EMOTIONS one might feel when handed a wine list in a restaurant. Maybe fear, at first. Then a sureness (*There has to be* something *I know in here*), followed by panic (*Actually, there is nothing I know in here*), then extreme anxiety (*Well what does everyone like? Wait, why is this wine $5,000?*) leading to terror and confusion (*Am I going to have to spend $5,000 on wine?*). Defeated, you decide on the second-cheapest bottle on the list or a name that sounds fun.

Now imagine that scenario replayed *over and over* again. That is what it is like to learn a wine list as a first-time sommelier. Researching the wines, the grapes, the regions, the producers, the rules, and even more rules, and then committing all of this to memory, was incredibly daunting.

My fear would come in gushing waves. At times, I felt

confident that I had mastered the German Riesling section, but then something like Dönnhoff Kreuznacher Krötenpfuhl would jump off the page. *What are you?*

The fear of being called stupid from my homeschooling days drove me to learn more. In public school, I had always been the youngest in my grade. At the diners, I had been the only kid working. At Harry's, I knew, some had assumed that I had gotten the job because Reynard wanted to seduce me. Still, I worked hard to prove my worth. At Aureole, I would have to work much harder than ever before, and I refused to make the same mistakes.

Studying for my first sommelier job wasn't just about memorization. I had to put myself in scenarios that might occur on the floor. For example, what if a guest asks for a cab? Well, I could recommend one from California, for something bigger and more fruit driven. Typically, *bigger* means fuller in body, which means more alcohol. Warm climates like California can lead to elevated levels of alcohol and therefore a "bigger" wine. A "fruitier" wine usually comes from places with more sunshine hours (hello again, California!).

Maybe the guest would then say that they don't like full-bodied wines. So I would quickly hop over to cabernet franc from the Loire Valley for something lighter. Since this region is much farther north, it is a cooler place in general. In colder areas, usually, wines have higher acidity and are lighter in body, meaning less alcohol.

If the guest says that they don't want something *too* tart, I go a bit farther south and west. The birthplace of cabernet is in Bordeaux. Here, cabernet sauvignon is typically the base of blends on the left bank of Bordeaux, as it thrives in the gravelly soils. These wines will be more earth-driven (a.k.a. less fruity than, say, a Napa cab). Bordeaux has more aromas of pencil shavings, pepper, mushrooms, and herbs. The wines will be in between Napa and the Loire Valley in structure (acid, alcohol, body, etc.).

Now I have to figure out if the guest wants something with some age or something more youthful. As a wine ages, the first thing to go is the fruit. Fresh berry smells turn into dried berries and eventually to just a mulchy earth nose. Some people prefer the fruit, some prefer the earth, some in between the two.

The sommelier must also know the nuances of each vintage in each village in each region. When someone says, "Oh! Two thousand nine! What a great year!" what the hell does that mean exactly? A good year for where in the world?

The Northern Hemisphere harvest takes place in September(ish) and in the Southern Hemisphere it's February(ish). The same year could mean completely different things for these hemispheres. Even within the same hemisphere, Napa has very different weather than Bordeaux. A good year in Bordeaux doesn't mean a good year in Napa. Further, a good year in Margaux in Bordeaux doesn't mean a good year in Pauillac in Bordeaux. Plus, sometimes rot and mildew can affect only one parcel of a vineyard in a region. So perhaps one producer was affected and not his neighbors. The sommelier must know *which* winemaker in *each* village had a good/bad year and why. The *why* is what leads to the ultimate flavor of the wine.

Then, after all of these preferences are gathered in a matter of moments, the sommelier still has to figure out how much the guest wants to spend. Most diners are cagey about this, so one has to tread delicately.

Sommeliers train themselves to start studying a guest before they even sit down. The reservationists will most likely Google the guest, stalk their Facebook page, and make notes on where they're from, what they like, etc. Then, when they enter the restaurant, the sommelier immediately scans them for clues. What type of clothes are they wearing? Is their handbag from a famous designer? Do they have a fresh manicure? Did they ask for ice in their water? Are they right- or left-handed? Even the smallest clue could be of use. Think about it; I have to help the guest choose one wine out of 1,700.

The sommelier cannot rely solely on what the guest tells them. Often, what the guest says is not really what they mean. For example, if they say they like dry red wine, that technically means every single red on the Aureole wine list. Most quality red wines have no perceptible residual sugar and are not sweet. However, what the guest probably means is a wine that is drying, that is tannic. Or maybe they just like saying they like dry things because it makes them seem sophisticated. People often think sweet things are lowbrow.

I had never been more nervous. I was playing adult, and I was afraid everyone would be able to tell I was really just a kid.

⚜

I entered Aureole through the "employee entrance," which was way less glamorous than the tall glass doors at the front of the restaurant that opened up to a marble podium. The guests should never see the help outside of the restaurant, and separate entrances ensured this.

I passed by a few Dumpsters and went into a kitchen. Correction, an enormous kitchen. Aureole was a far cry from the greasy diners of my childhood. This was a *Michelin-starred* kitchen. Every surface reflected light, from the stainless-steel knives and the copper pots to the well-scrubbed stoves that lined the walls.

All eyes turned toward me as conversation slowed, then stopped altogether. The kitchen was filled with men in crisp white jackets and little hats. There were no other women. Soon, whispers started while eyes remained fixed on me. They all carried gleaming knives or utensils, frozen upright in their hands like weapons—I thought I was going to die.

I found the GM glued to a computer screen in a tiny office

by the kitchen. He clicked away on his keyboard and ignored me. *Click, click, click.* A small blond woman, the assistant general manager (AGM), got up and briskly shook my hand. Her eyes followed the length of my body. I shifted nervously to hide the holes on the sides of my shoes.

"Today is just a *trial.* You won't be more than a few hours," the AGM said. She seemed tough enough to scare anyone back into line. In a restaurant full of men she was the only woman who held any power. I would soon learn that this would mean very little, as all of the male servers considered themselves above a *girl.*

As I walked through the kitchen and upstairs, I felt everyone sizing me up. *Stand tall,* I told myself, fixing my hopeless posture. The chronic dull ache in my upper back began to pulsate and deepen. I wished I had seen Jana before the trial.

I started behind the bar with an older woman named Regina. The moment she saw me, it was as if her hair stood up and her back curled protectively.

"This job you want, it involves more bartending than sommelier shifts. I've done this job for the past two years, and now I will finally be the head sommelier here." She let that sink in. The current head sommelier, Cedric, was leaving and would become the wine director at Eleven Madison Park. As a result, Regina was being moved up into his position. I would take her previous role, which, she added, was "not fun." "But it will be good for you," she told me.

"Good for me" meant a hybrid job—part bartender and part sommelier. It wasn't exactly what I had imagined when *Michelin-starred sommelier* entered my brain, but as I was twenty-one and extremely underqualified, I didn't have much of a choice. The bad news was that this meant I had to work two jobs for the pay of one. The good news was that I would get a shiny new business card that read *Victoria James, Sommelier, Aureole,* and that was enough for me.

After an uncomfortable trial with Regina behind the bar, I spent time with Justin on the floor. There were rules and corresponding verbiage to fine dining that made my head spin. Movements were supposed to be clockwise, napkin folding was always measured, little cups were called demitasses, and managers constantly reprimanded captains for poor mise en place. The maître d' scolded the waitstaff for using phrases with customers like "No problem" (why would anything ever be a *problem?*) and "Are you still working on that?" (they are here to enjoy their food, don't make them feel as if it is *work*!).

Justin didn't allow me in the fancy dining room, so I trailed behind him as he sold a few "approachable" bottles in the bar room. *Approachable* meant bottles of wine that were under $200 (more money than I had in my bank account).

The worst part about the trial was not knowing where to stand. It was as if everyone else knew the steps to a dance, flowing harmoniously together. "You're in my way," servers would yell. Eyes would roll, and I received a few angry elbow jabs. The bussers would pinch my hips or push me out of the way altogether.

When Justin was serving wine to a table, his movements were hypnotizing. He seemed always to know what to say, and as if on cue, the guests would let out a tiny *tee-hee* or nod their heads with the utmost approval. Tableside, Justin's confidence made him ten times more attractive. His ability to command attention from the room was seductive.

He moved us to a corner by the bar area. From here, we had the best view of the entire room and all of the pantomimes in motion. Justin pointed toward a table with guests. "They're almost to entrées, so we will make sure we get another bottle sale down soon." And then to another table: "We should be nearby to help the servers clear and reset for dessert momentarily"; and then to another table: "Keep an eye on that one, she sometimes tries to take the cutlery 'to go.'"

I remembered what Franky had told me: *"Those bitches will rob you blind every time. And that's a life lesson: watch your sugar."* Even in Michelin-starred restaurants, people stole. Our Aesop soap dispensers were ripped from the bathroom wall. I once saw a woman put all of the wineglasses from the table in her handbag.

On and on Justin went until we'd discussed the happenings of every customer in the restaurant in under thirty seconds. "This is crucial," he said, turning to me. "The sommelier should always be the smartest person in the room."

JUST AS THE AGM had promised, I wasn't there long that night. Within a few hours, the staff was fed up with my roadblock of a body and invited me to leave for the evening. As soon as I left, I felt disheartened. I knew Justin could tell I didn't understand what he meant by "open-hand movements" or "synchronized service."

What I did know was how to work hard and not ask questions. I made sure that I looked incredibly crisp and clean, without falling into the pitfalls of female presentation that had been ingrained in me. I couldn't look too slutty, or—possibly even worse—too masculine.

A week later, I began my official training. At the beginning of the week, I would tend bar, in uniform with an atrocious bright orange tie, a boxy black vest, and matching pants. Then I would have one day off to lie in bed and study.

I came back to work as a different beast, a wine steward. As a sommelier, I dressed in my own clothing, a suit (which I had gone into debt to buy) and a cheap blouse. I felt invincible against all the uniformed employees. After all, I was a *sommelier*.

It seemed no one else shared my illusion of grandeur. To everyone else who worked there, I was the new girl (and very much just a girl). They either ignored me completely, showed their disdain in very obvious ways, or played tricks on me.

When I first started at Aureole, it didn't occur to me that I was the youngest sommelier in the country. After all, there wasn't some national database that listed all wine professionals. In fact, I used an ambiguous old student ID to fill out paperwork, and whenever someone asked how old I was, I usually made up a number. I was ashamed of my youth.

AUREOLE FOLLOWED AN OLD-SCHOOL fine-dining caste system. At the top was the mysterious owner and his circle of associates. These persons only interacted with the next in line, the corporate team and management. Next were the captains, sommeliers, and maître d', who reported to management and only ever interacted with the top if they were serving their coffee. Last were the servers, SAs (server assistants, a more modern name for bussers), food runners, and finally, the hostesses. In this system, it takes years to move from one level to another. Everyone at Aureole saw me as skipping the line.

The captains gave me plenty of coats to check. "Back to your class," they would mutter. A young girl belonged in the coat check of a Michelin-starred restaurant, not on the floor, and definitely not selling wine.

The captains often sent me to the kitchen to check on their dishes. They knew the chef was terrifying and would laugh when he would scream at me in his thick British accent, "You're about as useful as a chocolate teapot!" When I asked how much longer an entrée would take, he would angrily retort, "How long is a piece of string!?" I would then report back with this useless information. The captains found my discomfort delightful.

In addition to torturing the new girl, the staff found pleasure in drinking—a lot. After a shift, everyone would gather within their class and go to a local dive bar. These binges would mostly occur before a day off—rarely would one risk not being on their

A-game before a shift. The GM could smell stale booze on breaths a mile away and would swiftly crack down.

I was only invited to these outings after two years of working at Aureole. The first time I went, I watched money made only moments earlier being handed over at the bar. There was a hostess passed out in the corner. One of the cooks kept screaming about his dick getting hard. A bartender and a maître d' were having sex in the bathroom. Cocaine was passed around on the tip of keys. A couple of servers stared blankly at a pint they were nursing.

I looked around the dark bar and in so many faces kept seeing my father.

One day when I was behind the bar, my father visited. Since moving out of his house, I had mostly kept conversations between us cordial. Although Timmy, Laura, and I spoke every week, my father and I were distant. We would text each other on birthdays and holidays and keep talk light. For me, it was easier to forgive from a distance. Visits meant being reminded of the demons my parents were battling, and often, not battling well. To see them in this state would send me to a place of frustration and sadness.

I flinched as I saw my father at my new Michelin-starred restaurant. He couldn't get drunk *here*! I was petrified that he would talk to my guests or coworkers. No one knew much about me; I purposely kept quiet about my background.

He ordered a double vodka with the smallest splash of pineapple juice. I tried to water it down without his noticing. While I made his drink, he introduced himself to anyone who would listen—guests, the AGM, a few bussers, servers.

He talked loudly, especially after a few more drinks. "MY DAUGHTER HERE IS A TWENTY-ONE-YEAR-OLD

SOMMELIER!" My cheeks turned red, and I shook with embarrassment.

Then he screamed to a random guest, "I AM SO PROUD OF HER."

Proud? My embarrassment dissolved and turned into confusion. I had never heard him use that word before, especially toward his children. I looked into his watery eyes, which were slightly red from the alcohol, and saw someone who was hurting. Just like me, just like everyone, he was looking to be loved.

When I gave him his tab of $200, I worried that he might not be able to pay. Surprisingly, he didn't bat an eye. He remarked that things were "going well" for him. I hoped it was true, for Angela's and Laura's sake. Before he left, he took out a wad of cash and generously left $60 on the bill.

"As a tip," he said, smiling, and added, getting louder, "I know that it's ALWAYS BETTER IN CASH."

I wanted to tell him that this was a *Michelin-starred* restaurant. All team-member tips were put into a pool and then divided. His contribution would barely affect me. I thought of how much I'd needed that money as a child, when it would have paid for a field trip, school lunches, or new clothes.

He waited for me to accept his tip. I took the cash and smiled. He smiled back and then in a whisper said, "Thank you."

⚜

When I was behind the bar, I would work from ten in the morning until closing. There would be a meal served to the whole staff at around three in the afternoon (called "family meal" in the industry). It wasn't free, as a mandatory amount came out of your paycheck every week to cover the cost.

At Aureole, the notion of the "family meal" was a bit depressing. Mostly because the group was the furthest thing from a family. Unlike the staff at the diners of my childhood, fine-dining characters were less outwardly eccentric and much more uniform in appearance. Underneath, however, there was still a wandering-soul mentality, a brokenness. The captains gossiped about happenings at the pub the night before, who was sleeping with whom, over a dish of almost-expired food. The kitchen was on a tight budget (as was Justin for the beverage program), and the majority of these family meals were hard to swallow.

Still, I was happy with anything. By the time three in the afternoon snuck around, I was ravenous, not having eaten for hours. Due to Department of Health regulations, none of the staff were permitted to bring in outside food. We could be docked points during an inspection for unlabeled lunches. Therefore, the whole team relied on the family meal. However, bartenders got the worst deal. Although Aureole was closed between lunch and dinner service, the bar was not. I was forbidden to abandon my post, which meant a long shift without food and fighting back the impulse to faint.

At these times, I would ask the closing bartender to watch the bar while I ran to the restroom. Along the way, I would steal bread and hide under the stairs to frantically cram it into my mouth. If Regina wasn't watching me closely, I would sip briny olive juice behind the bar and be taken back to my childhood, when I would drink pickle juice for sustenance.

By the end of my tenure at Aureole, I had lost thirty pounds off my already small frame. I was all elbows and knobby knees, just like when I was a child, scavenging for food in an empty cupboard.

I had thought that once I entered the upper echelon of society, the Michelin-starred restaurant, and as a sommelier no less, I would experience better treatment. Instead, I found that the diners of my youth and Lattanzi were more civilized. At those places, I was allowed to take a break, have a meal that the cooks all too happily prepared for me, and go to the restroom whenever I pleased.

At Aureole, if I went to the restroom more than once a shift, Regina was furious. I purposely dehydrated myself to avoid this. Captains associated multiple bathroom trips with feminine weakness, cracking jokes with punch lines about "small bladders," "that time of the month," and "heavy flows." A captain once stated that this was the very reason women shouldn't work in fine dining. Life at Aureole, the circle of light, was incredibly dark.

WINE IS A BLOOD SPORT

IN ADDITION TO WORKING EIGHTY-PLUS hours a week, I also continued taking classes at the Wine School. By now I had memorized all of the 585 premier crus of Burgundy, their historical origins, and their land delineations. All of the 61 Médoc châteaux mentioned in the 1855 classification of Bordeaux, and the 26 Sauternes châteaux, were now old hat.

Every week in the WS class, we had a quiz (though no one else took it quite as seriously as I did). I always arrived fifteen minutes early. One week, I was running behind because of train delays. I sprinted a mile through the sweaty New York streets, my wineglasses clinking in their bag, and arrived two minutes before the quiz began.

I held myself to an unusually high standard. A score below 95 percent only happened once. I could hear my father's words in my head—*You will never excel like this*. The region we were focusing on was particularly challenging because of its expansive size and constant changes in regulations and categories.

The Languedoc-Roussillon is in the South of France just west of Provence. Known as the world's largest wine region, the Languedoc is plagued by swaths of bulk wine production and a slew of confusing classifications.

We had one week to learn about the Languedoc and all of its intricacies. Imagine having to memorize the complete history of a region about the size of Hawaii—each city, how many people lived in each town, the significant resources of each village, the microclimates, the soil types by city, the average temperature in each area by month, etc. I furiously dedicated myself to textbooks and flash cards, but it all seemed too scattered to stick. On the quiz, I received not only below 95 percent but a fail—*a fail*.

After class, with my tail between my legs, I talked to the instructor. I apologized about my quiz grade. It would *never* happen again, I promised. "Is there any way," I began nervously, "you would let me retake it?" I even offered to write a report instead of the quiz, something lengthy and punishing.

The instructor smiled. "There is one thing you can do, and if you do it well . . . I will give you a pass on that quiz." *Please don't ask for anything sexual,* was all I could think.

EVERY YEAR A COMPETITION is held called the Sud de France Sommelier Challenge. The instructor wanted me to enroll. I was absolutely terrified. Up until now, I had flown under the radar in the sommelier community. I kept to myself and worked tirelessly at a restaurant mostly tourists and old people visited. I had no friends in the industry, and when I was around other sommeliers at tastings I made sure not to speak or make eye contact. The competition would ruin everything. Suddenly, I would be flung into the spotlight and would surely humiliate myself in front of everyone.

"Competing shows your peers that you have balls," the instructor said, trying to convince me. "You want to be taken seriously? Put yourself out there. Keeping quiet won't do any favors for your career. No other student studies as hard as you do—you could win this." If I competed, he promised to drop the failing quiz grade. I couldn't just accept the shameful score. So I enrolled.

Sommeliers from all over the United States signed up. The winner would receive a free trip to the South of France—the land of wine, bread, and cheese. Of course, I was dying to visit Paris and explore historic vineyards around the country. Since becoming a sommelier, I had even learned basic French.

With only one month to study, I overcaffeinated, never slept, and barely ate. I studied flash cards on the subway, in bed, and even when walking on the street. I recorded myself reading statistics and played the tape on a loop while I slept, hoping somehow the information would seep into my brain. All of the obscure soil types and ancient laws started to blend together. *Does Malepère have more marl or calcareous clay in the soil? Did Minervois–La Livinière receive its appellation in 1999 or 1998 for red wines? What is the minimum amount of mauzac required in blanquette de Limoux? What is the difference between* vin doux naturel *and* vin de liqueur?

One evening, I felt woozy. The next thing I knew I was waking up on the floor. I spent the weekend in the hospital. For a moment, there was the scary talk of a heart murmur or epilepsy, but in the end, it turned out that I was just exhausted.

Even though I had a doctor's note and a weekend's worth of paperwork, the GM saw my absence at Aureole as a big black mark on my record.

"Ridiculous," he muttered as I handed in my paperwork.

He wasn't alone in his feelings. No one seemed particularly pleased with my weekend away. Justin looked as if he had been physically beaten, dark navy blue circles lining his eyes. Regina was convinced I had made the whole thing up. I was sure the hospital visit made me something pathetic in their eyes—human.

The hospital bills were astronomical. Like many restaurant workers, I had health insurance that was essentially useless or nonexistent. Losing a weekend of work also didn't help my bank account. I calculated that it would take me seven months to pay off the bills if I only spent $40 a week on food and expenses. Luckily, my acupuncturist, Jana, worked with whatever I could pay.

"That's a crock of shit!" Jana said after I told her about the hospital visit. "You need to get out of there. You're going to kill yourself, I feel it in your body." She poked needles into the spot on my back that was always sore. Now that soreness had spread. It was everywhere. My whole body was worn and ached.

I CHUGGED ALONG GRUDGINGLY, studying in every free moment. By the time the competition rolled around, I'd barely slept for a week.

When I entered the room, I looked around for a friendly face. No one from my WS class was there. I learned that the other competitors were almost all twice my age, buyers at some of the top restaurants in New York, and mostly men. One was wearing a three-piece suit! Another had on so many accreditation pins he looked like an Eagle Scout. I immediately felt self-conscious in my drab outfit.

Then, a Frenchwoman, Marianne Fabre-Lanvin, the director of the Sud de France group, welcomed all of the sommeliers with a cheery speech. She seemed so full of life, so chic! Her presence calmed me down just enough to let me focus on my exam.

Suddenly, I was racing through the stacks of paper. *Why are there so many pages?* A map of the Languedoc was in there, completely blank—they expected us to fill it out with every single tiny village. Questions referenced obscure dates, a random architect who'd built a bridge in a small town, the soil structure of a specific vineyard, what laws were set in place and then destroyed and then rewritten. I imagined the judges reading my responses later and laughing at how horribly wrong I was.

After the exam was a blind-tasting portion with one white and two reds. Competitors had to smell, taste, and guess what was in the glass. What's more, we had to describe the aromas and structure accurately.

The white was zippy, fresh, but with some weight in the mid-palate. It tasted like yellow flowers, or were those white flowers? Definitely some beeswax and honey. Maybe spices like ginger and clove? Did this mean there was new oak on the wine? I wrote down my guess: 2012 bourboulenc, roussanne, and marsanne blend from La Clape. In the Languedoc, there is less consistency per region, which makes it incredibly difficult to be sure of a guess. As I wrote down La Clape my hand kept shaking; maybe it was Minervois instead? Or perhaps from Pic Saint-Loup?

Ripe black fruit, purple flowers, black pepper, potting soil, damp leaves. I raced to write down descriptors for the red wines. Moderate plus acidity, high alcohol, no residual sugar, moderate tannins (or was it just dry extract!?), balanced, long finish—the structure of each wine whizzed through my mouth so quickly I could barely think. Based on all of the clues I was picking up, I wrote down: a 2010 carignan and grenache blend from Fitou and a 2011 grenache, Syrah, and mourvèdre blend from Corbières. The varying blends of the region made it even trickier to hone in on specific characteristics of each grape. Was I picking up black fruit from Syrah or a Malepère cabernet blend? Every time I went back to the glass I second-guessed my answers.

While the judges graded our exams, the competitors had a

break. Everyone seemed to be friends with one another, quickly falling into little circles of chatter. "I can't believe he called the first wine mauzac, ballsy move!" one somm blurted out to another, who laughed and patted him on the back.

The sommelier scoffed, "It had to be a bourboulenc-roussanne-marsanne blend . . . I mean, the waxy and oily palate alone . . ." My insides flipped. He'd called the same wine as I had! If he was right, maybe I was right, too. He was tall with glasses and had a self-assured posture. He looked like the type of sommelier who knew all of the answers.

I struggled to talk to my competitors. People kept asking me where the bathroom was. *I don't work here,* I wanted to say, *I am a competitor, too!* Occasionally I would walk over to a circle to overhear, "Then this lady comes in and asks me for a Sancerre, and I'm like, *basic bitch*!" The ring erupted in laughter. Why were they making fun of guests who liked Sancerre? I thought back to the first glass I'd had at Lattanzi with the goat cheese salad. Sancerre was what had first gotten me excited about pairing food and wine.

"I hate when chicks try to swirl a wine, and they can't even do it. I mean, she looks like she can grab a dick and give it a yank, if you know what I mean. It's not that hard!" Their eyes would then flick toward me.

The rest of the afternoon, I pretended to review notes while trying to block out nearby conversations. Occasionally I heard "Who invited Barbie?" or "Is she supposed to be some effort at diversification?" They spent most of their time complaining about guests at their restaurants and trading notes on PITA (pain in the ass) customers and "whales" (big spenders).

The best thing about that afternoon was meeting Marianne. She was an absolute delight, a breath of fresh air in a stifling room of self-important men. She praised my courage and remarked that it would be amazing if a woman could *finally* win this thing! Her overwhelming positivity gave me the guts to stay until the finalists were announced.

ONE OF THE FINALISTS was the tall man who seemed to know all the answers. The other was a man who'd laughed at the dick-yanking anecdote. Last was a Frenchman who was actually from the Languedoc. My stomach sank with sadness. *Why did I even try? I knew I wouldn't win!*

Still, I stayed until the end and watched as the finalists were whittled to one. The competitors had to stand in front of the whole room and answer a series of tough-as-nails questions, followed by a pairing challenge, a mock wine-service demo, and finally the task of pouring sparkling wine into ten flute glasses without stopping or returning to the previous glass. The sommelier had to do quick math and pour precisely 2.5 ounces of wine in each glass. It was also a race; there were points in it for whoever finished first. Of course, if there was any wine left in your bottle at the end, you lost. The whole performance seemed terrifying.

The instructor pulled me aside. "You didn't go to the finals," he said, "but . . . you came close." My exam was one point away from the third finalist. "I'll give you a pass on your Languedoc quiz in class so long as you promise me one thing . . ." I quickly nodded yes; whatever he wanted, I would promise. "Compete again next year."

A Frenchman overheard the instructor and scoffed, "Don't fill her head with dreams. Competitions aren't a game, they're a blood sport."

THE FOLLOWING YEAR, AS promised, I competed. This time I made it to the finals. During the last round, I looked around the room in a panic. It was the same group of competitors as last year, and the guy who'd complained, "Who invited Barbie?" wore a deep frown.

The last question the judges asked me, in front of the whole room, was, "How would you sell the wines of the Languedoc to a guest?"

I could feel tears welling up in my eyes. This last question seemed like a trick, and I was exhausted. The group of sommeliers who had laughed about Sancerre and dick-yanking all had their arms crossed furiously. I don't think a single person in the room wanted me to win.

That is, until I saw Marianne. She was beaming, and she gave me a little thumbs-up. To know that at least one person was rooting for me made all the difference. I forced the tears to subside.

"The wines of the Languedoc are not just about the grapes, the laws . . ." I knew that the judges didn't want a rote answer; they wanted a sales pitch. I smiled at Marianne and decided that instead of flaunting my knowledge I would give them passion. "The beauty of these wines is that they capture that French joie de vivre; they possess effortless charm. Wines from the Languedoc are about the Mediterranean lifestyle. They are about enjoying life."

When I finished my sales pitch, the panel of judges all smiled. Much to everyone else's dismay, I won. The only American female sommelier, to this day, to ever take home the title. I could barely contain my excitement—I was going to France!

THE YOUNGEST SOMMELIER

"THE MOST IMPORTANT THING a sommelier can do is remain humble," Justin told me one day. He said we should never forget what it was like when we first started drinking wine, that feeling of fear and incompetence; it could be a scary thing. "Make your guests feel comfortable; their knowledge is enough," he said. A good sommelier will not only fetch a great bottle of wine for a guest, at the price point they requested, but also make them feel incredibly special.

"Every guest that is coming in tonight"—Justin outstretched his hand and gestured around the width of Aureole—"around three hundred people, they all are coming in for an experience." For some of these people it was just another meal—they wanted noninvasive service, good food, and good wine. For most of our diners, however, Aureole was a "destination" restaurant. It was near the theater district, so a lot of our guests were eating a special meal before a show. For many, this was one of the few times a year they went out for a fancy dinner. The average that a guest at Aureole spent started at around $125 *per person,* and it went up, drastically, from there. That is a lot of money for one dinner! At Aureole our job was to figure out what *kind* of experience the guest wanted and make it even better than they could have imagined.

It seemed few at Aureole shared that sentiment besides Justin, who did thrive on others' happiness—service is what calmed his various neuroses. Then there was Sean, the bartender. Sean was from upstate New York and embodied an old-school hospitality few others could rival. He was the type of bartender who shook your hand when you left, kept quiet at all the right times, gave an ear to the lonely drinker, and was quick to provide a chuckle to those who needed it most. His drinks were stunningly accurate, and he was always coming up with ways to make systems better.

ON THE FIRST OF every month, the beverage team got together for inventory—a grueling task that plagues restaurants around the country. Every bottle of wine, spirits, and beer must be counted.

"Grand Marnier," Sean would scream from behind the bar while I recorded the numbers on a laptop, "zero point one!" That meant one-tenth of a bottle was left of the liqueur. Extreme accuracy! If our count was off by even a tenth, Justin would have a conniption.

One month, I paired with Regina for inventory, since Justin was away. With every bottle I counted came a stinging comment: "You're mumbling!" or "That is *not* how you pronounce Vosne-Romanée!" I was convinced that Regina despised every bone in my body. She constantly found ways to break me down in service. Simple duties such as polishing silver coasters or cleaning decanters became enormously nerve-wracking.

I spent hours before service scrubbing coasters with silver

polish, really putting my full weight into the process. Bullets of sweat would shoot down from my scalp and dot my forehead. Afterward, Regina would thumb through each coaster, all fifty of them, and scoff. "Do you think this is a joke?" Her eyes would roll as she held up a coaster that was undoubtedly 100 percent polished, shiny and glistening. Even perfection wasn't good enough for her. So over and over again I would polish the coasters, until her scoffs became tight-lipped nods.

During service, Regina would track my movements like a hunter, carefully calculating each decision I made. "You didn't move counterclockwise around table eleven," or "Why would you clear the man's plate first!?"

One night, after I'd gotten pummeled at the bar with an especially insane pretheater crowd, Regina popped up like a weed. She drummed her fingernails on the zinc bar until I finally turned to see her there. Sean and I were running through restock items, murmuring to ourselves.

"Is there a particular reason," Regina began as I walked over, "that you have left these filthy trays here?" She pointed to two round trays that each held a couple of glasses—some highballs with leftover ice, a couple of coupes with untouched olives in them. Before I could begin to explain that our bar back was off fetching ice, and Sean and I were reviewing stock items, Regina cut me off. "Stop, Victoria, just stop," she snapped so loudly that a server, Corey, got closer to listen in on the commotion. "There is no excuse for your behavior. Every guest in this restaurant can see this *filth* here, and you are just standing there, not doing your job."

Fat, frustrated tears started to inch down my cheeks. Nothing I ever did was up to her standards, and everyone else in the restaurant just turned their heads when Regina yelled at me, grateful they weren't her target.

"Hey, baby girl." Corey came closer and whispered, "Don't ever let them see you cry." I nodded and ran to the restroom.

I looked in the mirror and was ashamed. My eyes were red and my face was puffy. Two years of Regina's torturous nitpicking had begun to decay my spirit. I had to tell someone. The next morning I spoke to Justin in the wine cellar. Unable to control myself, I burst into tears again. I felt so silly, crying to my boss about a bully. Why couldn't I stand up for myself?

Justin listened, and in his most tender voice, the one he usually reserved for little old ladies who needed help getting to the restroom, he said, "I'm so sorry." And he genuinely was.

The problem was that there was no solution. A culture of fear festered at Aureole. This mentality trickled down from the top. Even Justin constantly panicked over his job security. If his beverage costs weren't at an unrealistically low 16 percent of sales (the New York City fine-dining average is usually closer to between 22 and 30 percent), his head would be on the chopping block.

In a way, Regina's nitpicking did come in handy. She would watch, like a hawk, to see if servers might try to give away a free coffee or if bartenders would attempt to "top off" a glass of wine. Everyone was scared of her, but for some reason, I was her favorite target.

NOT ONLY WAS REGINA constantly tripping me up around every corner, but Justin was also unraveling. The instructor from the WS who had gotten me my job and claimed to be friends with Justin would come in regularly and sit at the bar. There he would push wines on Justin. If, after all, they were friends, Justin had to buy wines from him.

One of the most sought-after spots on a menu for a distributor to snag is "wine by the glass." This page is the first a guest sees,

and often the only section they will look at. The buyer will have
to order this wine often to keep up with demand, providing the
distributor with a steady cash flow. Also, the distributor's wine
receives free advertising on the wine list. Who wouldn't want to
gloat that their wine is poured at a Michelin-starred restaurant
for the rich and powerful? I thought that once the instructor secured this coveted spot, his pressuring Justin would have to stop.

Instead, it was just the beginning. Once he secured one glass
pour, he went after a second. Then a third. Soon, he was pressuring Justin for placements throughout the list. On a particularly
heated night, after I served the instructor multiple glasses of wine
at the bar, he pulled Justin outside. With the sounds of Times
Square in the background, I could barely make out Justin crying,
"You are supposed to be my *friend*!"

Justin was exhausted. Service, which he had always excelled
in, was now his weak spot. He was like a ghost in the dining
room, often forgetting to refill wineglasses or fetch bottles.

At the time I was taking a third course with the WS, having passed their theory classes with the highest grade on record.
This next class was Tasting. Instead of poring over flash cards I
was spending all of my extra money on wine, relentlessly tasting.
There was a grid we had to memorize, and I would repeat the
boxes in my head (gas, intensity, color, rim variation, viscosity,
staining of the tears, sediment, etc.) all day and night.

When the instructor would teach these classes, it was torturous. He would also put pressure on me, asking, "So why hasn't
Justin bought my Cali cab yet?"

I would always try to change the subject, but he wasn't de-
terred. "After everything I have done for you, you won't just
simply talk to Justin for me?" He stood over me and would pick
on me throughout the class.

At least here I was reunited with Marianne, from the Sud de
France group, who was also taking the Tasting class. We had

become friends, and I looked up to her as a mentor. In such a boys' club, she was fearless but also effortlessly charming. I tried to always sit next to her to boost my confidence, and she would ask me for advice. "Is this one a little salty to you, *non?* I get like a salted meats and charcuterie type of thing. *Et vous?*" Without Marianne, I don't think I would have survived that class. Never underestimate the relief that charm can provide. When I find myself in an uncomfortable situation tableside, I still think of Marianne and try to channel her lighthearted spirit.

During one of the last classes, the instructor called on me to taste the first wine, so I quietly began, only to be interrupted. "Oh, ass and a pair of tits here wants to tell us how to taste," he began, mocking me. "You're just a kid, a kid . . . Here, I'll do it." He grabbed the glass from my hands, smelled, and smiled. "Easy, chardonnay, right?" The class continued like this for another hour. Marianne wasn't there that day to protect me, and everyone else kept quiet.

I put up with the instructor's behavior because I didn't know any better and I was still a pushover. I trusted people who were actually taking advantage of my naïveté.

By the time our final tasting exam rolled around, I was so sick and tired of the instructor's games. The test was six unknown wines. In twenty-four minutes you had to dissect the nuance of each wine precisely—every aroma and the exact structure—and finally, name the vintage, region, and grapes. So, for example, cabernet franc, Chinon, Loire Valley, France, 2010. No one passed the exam. Everyone failed.

After much back-and-forth I finally met with the instructor. "I failed you because I thought it would be good for you," he told me. "No one likes a know-it-all."

It was as if he had hit me with a swift blow to the stomach. All of the air from my body left, and I thought I was going to faint. "You have two options," he said, "re-enroll, and you can take the exam again"—he paused—"or keep the fail."

I hated that word—*fail*. I was filled with insecurity and doubted myself completely. I couldn't have a *fail* on my record! So I swallowed my bitterness, coughed up the cash, and retook the exam.

This time, it was even more ludicrous. The instructor proctored the exam and poured a bunch of random samples from his office. There was no other teacher there, no accountability. The wines were not traditionally testable. Chilean sauvignon blanc, for example, or high-octane central-Spain whites. These wines would never be on a sommelier exam because they are considered atypical. The point of a sommelier tasting exam is not to trick the student but rather to assess their training. It's like telling someone they will be tested in French, but then a few Chinese words are thrown in. Still, I believe the instructor passed me just because I had come back groveling.

I cried when I left the WS office. I now had a shiny gold pin, but I didn't feel accomplished. I felt instead like a pawn in a game much, much bigger than me. *There has to be another way,* I thought. I had worked too hard to be under someone else's control, again.

I started to research other programs. Unfortunately, the whole sommelier certification industry is unregulated, and therefore there is incredible potential for abuse. Young women like me are especially easy targets, since we are desperate to fit in. The WS wasn't alone in the world of handing out pins and certificates that meant little. It is something not often discussed because those who go through all the work and spend all the money don't want to admit that their pin might be pointless. And if their pin isn't real, are they a *real* sommelier?

I thought back to what Chip had said in the cellar at Harry's, that being a sommelier meant selling wine in a restaurant. Nothing more. In a way, he was right. A pin and a piece of paper didn't make me a sommelier. Aureole's hiring me as one had made me a sommelier.

"I DON'T UNDERSTAND WHY you need to be a *certified* sommelier if you're already a sommelier," my little sister Laura said. I had learned of another community of sommeliers, one different from the WS. It was called the Court of Master Sommeliers and had been around since 1977. Instead of offering courses, it was more of an examining body. You studied on your own, then showed up for a test.

A movie had just come out on a recent phenomenon, "master sommeliers" like Finn Ferguson. Everyone I asked about the system said it was like one big fraternity. When I did more research I found that there were at least a few female master sommeliers. Maybe this meant it wasn't *completely* a boys' club?

"It's just an accreditation I can show people, so they take me seriously," I told Laura.

"People do take you seriously! You work at a fancy Michelin-starred restaurant!" Laura was, of course, extremely biased. I was sure that everyone else saw me as just a girl.

At work, older men constantly berated me tableside, before I even opened my mouth. "Oh, looks like they sent the *wine girl* over today. I guess they only bring the real sommelier out when you spend some serious money," they would say.

Or worse, "Hey, *wine girl,* you want to come over and see my private cellar? I got so many bottles I bet you haven't seen. If you're good, I might pour you a taste."

I thought that a shiny CERTIFIED SOMMELIER pin would put an end to all of this, so I signed up for the Court of Master Sommeliers' "introductory level" exam, which was being held in just

a few months in Washington, DC. Financially, this meant months
of saving.

First, I would have to request time off from work, which
meant exasperated sighs from the GM and fury from Regina.
Then I would have to make up for the time away and expenses of
the trip by penny-pinching. The exam itself was also a whopping
thousand dollars! For a test! At that price, I had no choice but to
pass, which I did.

Two months later, I signed up for the certified sommelier
exam. This test was, luckily, held in New York and I could take
it before my shift. Unfortunately, it was six hundred dollars, and
I had to ask a friend for a loan. It was the first time in my life I
had ever borrowed money from someone, and I hated every moment of it.

Prep for the certification exam seemed completely silly. Why
did I have to know the *tête de cuvée* (usually considered the best
label from a producer) for every Champagne house in existence?
Also, who cared about the ingredients in a godmother cocktail? I
had never even heard of anyone who drank it. (Eight years later
and counting, I still haven't.) To be ready for the exam, I had to
know all of the grapes, places, soils, weather, histories, and laws
and what they all meant.

There were three portions to the exam: theory, tasting, and
service. The theory portion is where I excelled, essentially re-
gurgitating information that was far from relevant. Next was the
blind-tasting portion, which was much simpler than what the
WS had put me through. For the Court of Master Sommeliers
program, it was a couple of wines—white and red—and we had
ample time to fill out grids on each.

Last was service. Everyone else in the room had infinitely
more experience than I did. It's not that I thought I was a lousy
sommelier, but I was intensely aware that I was green. Every night
at Aureole I was humbled. Some guests had been drinking wine

for over fifty years! Perhaps they didn't know exactly *what* they were drinking, but they knew wine in a way I didn't (and wouldn't, for quite some time). Moments like these made me feel guilty. How dare I, as a kid, try to tell them what to drink? What right did I have?

ONE EVENING AT AUREOLE I felt particularly run-down, so Justin pulled me to the side. A few tables had scoffed at my very presence before I was even able to say two words. Instead, they requested "the real sommelier," and Justin came down from the office upstairs to help. Away from the tables, he tried to cheer me up.

"Don't worry about people like that," he said, and offered me a glass of Puligny-Montrachet at the bar, a treat he usually reserved only for himself.

I gratefully accepted the wine and mumbled, "I just want to make these people happy . . . Why won't they let me make them happy?"

Justin chuckled. "Some people don't want to be happy. Let them be unhappy!" He helped himself to a glass of wine as well. "You know, they say it takes ten thousand hours of doing something before you're an expert. Let's say you work here eighty hours a week. It'll only take you a couple of years until you're an expert sommelier. Until then, be okay with not being an expert. Learn from these people, let them humble you. It's good for the ego."

I kept repeating this over and over to myself. *Be okay with not being an expert.* I couldn't begin to pretend that I was the most qualified person in the room, so I didn't. Instead, I offered what I could: good energy and a positive spirit. If I didn't know the answer to something or messed up in any way, I would recover and try again.

I was lucky I had Justin, who taught me that I wouldn't and

couldn't know it all at only twenty-one. This humility is a hard thing to accept at a young age when you want to prove your worth. Staying quiet, speaking only when I should, and calmly trying to learn from my mistakes were the best things I ever did for my career—that, and trying to work harder than everyone else around me.

WHEN I WALKED INTO the service exam, a mock dining room with one master sommelier sitting at a separate table, I tried to channel this strength. The first task was welcoming the MS and listening to instructions. I was supposed to pretend that there was one man at the table and two other women. According to the rules of sommelier service, I was supposed to serve women first, then men, then the host, moving clockwise around the table.

I first tasted the wine on the MS host (the only real person at the table), who approved, and then I passed a fake man to serve two fake women, passed the host again to serve the fake man, then went around the two fake women to finally pour for the host. I thought of how ridiculous this was. Carnival music should have been playing. All of the seconds wasted on this pouring merry-go-round would never fly in the real world, where Regina would scold me for squandering so much time on one table.

While serving wine to the table and checking off all of the obscure boxes—two coasters, place foil in my pocket, three serviettes, two pens—the MS tried to distract me with questions.

"So I had this wine at the bar," he began, obviously meaning a fake wine at a nonexistent bar, "and they said it was a Manzanilla. Can you tell me what that is?"

I took a deep breath and calmly explained sherry. Next, they asked me about a Singapore sling. The cocktail has so many different ingredients! Okay, so I knew I'd lost one point there . . . *Remember, be okay with not being an expert.*

Hours later, they announced the names of the small percentage of people who had passed. My palms began to perspire, and I froze in anticipation. One by one, they called out names and handed out official CERTIFIED SOMMELIER pins. I started to shake with nerves.

I couldn't remember if I'd held the champagne bottle at the proper angle or if I remembered to call a cru classification on one of the blind wines. I wondered how many points I'd lost on the Singapore sling question. All of my answers on the theory exam I began to doubt.

Suddenly I heard "Victoria James." Phew.

After the exam, I thanked the proctors. One of the master sommeliers furrowed his brow and asked, "And how old are *you* exactly?" My cheeks became warm, and I sheepishly told him my age. "*Twenty-one!?*" he exclaimed. "Wow. That definitely makes you the youngest sommelier in the country!" Still embarrassed by my youth, I kept this fact a secret for years.

After nine months of being a sommelier at Aureole, I became *official*.

THE UNDOCUMENTED
SOMMELIER

I HAD HOPED THAT AFTER I became certified, my nickname of "wine girl" would fall by the wayside. Instead, it caught on like wildfire. I made the horrible mistake of wearing the pin to work the first week after I earned it. Captains, especially the older men, would stare at the pin (and, of course, all pins for women rest just above their breasts) and laugh wickedly. "You have such great . . . I mean, what a nice *pin*." After a week of pin-staring, a.k.a. breast gazing, which led to breast grazing, I took it off forever. Maybe the pin didn't mean anything after all, but I was thankful I'd gone through the steps to get it anyway.

When I asked a captain to stop calling me wine girl, he laughed. "What's the big deal?" I went on to say, what if someone called him *wine boy*, how would he feel? My idea seemed absurd to him. "It's different for men."

A PAIR OF OLDER FRENCHMEN, friends of the GM, would occasionally visit when I was bartending. They gorged themselves on multiple courses and bottles of wine for lunch. Since they were friends with the GM, I had to make sure to give them extra attention, lest they report any missteps to my boss.

This wouldn't have been an issue if they had behaved. Of course, they never did. As soon as the GM would walk away, the two men would dig into me like a sharp knife.

"We are thirsty, wine girl, come over here and give us a big glass of something delicious," one started, licking his lips as if parched. With each wine they sampled came a revolting description, their illustrations escalating the drunker they became.

"This one tastes like a sloppy wet pussy, just ready to get rammed," one said with a laugh, and swirled around an assyrtiko from Santorini.

Next, a godello from Spain would taste like "a little girl's pubic hair," and a Volnay from France would feel as good as "blowing a load on a chick's tits." I winced at each horrifying account and flinched when they tried to make eye contact with me. When the GM came over to check up on them, they were suddenly prim and proper.

"And, Victoria, she is taking such great care of us, thank you . . ." They would point to me, and the GM's face would light up with pride. I was too scared to tell him that his friends were actually creeps.

"Wine girl," they would say, beckoning me from the other end of the bar where they sat. "Come over here and keep us company." I always tried to stay as far away as possible, but sadly, I was trapped. When I would bend over to get into the low refrigerators, I could feel their eyes burning a hole through my backside.

The worst was when I had to shake a drink. I am naturally well endowed, and no matter how hard I tried to keep my upper torso from moving when I shook a cocktail, I always ended up jiggling. When an order came through for a gin martini, *extra cold and shaken*, I would build the drink in the shaker and then turn my back to the two men at the bar. I desperately hoped they wouldn't see me flailing. Of course, they did.

"Shake your titties for us again, wine girl," they whispered, bursting into laughter. My cheeks would turn scarlet, and I could feel tears welling in my eyes, though I refused to give them the satisfaction of seeing me cry.

One day, one of them moaned while trying a grenache blend I had poured for them. "Oof . . ." His eyes closed and he mumbled, "I could just pour this in your pussy and lick it out."

I began to tremble and screwed up countless drink orders. I knew that, finally, I had to say something to the GM. I wrote down every word his friends said and planned to present it as evidence.

The GM came to the bar after his friends left with a big smile. They had a great time, he said. I knew this was my chance to speak up. "Uh, sir, I think I need to talk to you about your friends." Suddenly, the smile left the GM's face. "It's just that . . . ," I started, and then tried to collect my words in a way that made sense. "Sometimes, they are maybe a little *graphic* with their words, and it makes me uncomfortable."

Judi, one of the servers, had said she'd once seen the GM stand up for another female server when a guest screamed at her and began to threaten her. My hope was that he would show that same strength here, for me.

The GM's lips curled downward into a frown, and I could tell he was thinking as the silence between us elongated. I suddenly felt a sort of camaraderie with the GM. I was trapped behind the bar, and he was trapped between the owner and his guests.

He said that if I wasn't comfortable to try to stay away from them. Then he walked away. I kept their words that I had written down instead of handing them in. I knew that whatever a guest said, it wouldn't matter, not here.

This mentality is not unusual in restaurants. If there was ever a "problem" guest, management told me to just "try to stay away." If I complained about a coworker who had called me a "little bitch" and another who had sent me a graphic message about how he wanted to "stuff his dick in my ass," they put me in a different section of the restaurant. Anytime I mentioned something uncomfortable, it created an annoyance. "Wine girl is so sensitive"—one server laughed when I requested to not wait on a man who had just pinched my ass. Eventually, I stopped complaining.

After work, I would head straight home. I kept looking over my shoulder, in fear that a customer or staff member would follow me. The recurring nightmare of my late-night diner rape kept playing in my head. I was sure that it would happen again.

The rotting environment at Aureole began to stink, from the head down. As exhausting as it was, I hoped that my time there would make me stronger. I thought of my little brother, Timmy, and when my father put him in the mental institution.

"You can do anything for two years," Timmy always told me. I had spent two years at Aureole.

Only later did Timmy confide this to me: "I feel like whatever I am today is not what went into that psych ward. Something didn't survive. Something is lost forever. And for better or worse, I'm what came out."

When news broke that Justin was leaving for a better job elsewhere, I took this as an exit cue. There was no way I was going to stay there without him (and alone with Regina). But now what?

For two years I had kept my head down (literally pointed downward at books and hovering over tables) and I had few connections in the industry.

I printed out fresh copies of my CV. Then I made a list of all the Michelin-starred restaurants in New York and started asking around. For a month I lined up a tiresome series of interviews all around the city.

Some of these were eye-opening, as I crept into restaurants I had only ever read about and never had the time (or money) to visit. By the end of the month, I felt like a professional interviewee.

Still, out of all the places I was considering, few excited me. Most disheartening was that nowhere seemed focused on hospitality. I lamented this to Justin, who listened carefully and after a bit of silence said, "I have an idea."

Justin's best friend, Hristo, worked for the Altamarea Group (which had more than ten restaurants, including Ai Fiori and Marea). He introduced us via email and Hristo responded right away:

> Here's the plan.
>
> I want you to be at Marea at 1:30pm to meet with Richard Anderson.
>
> Richard is going to be the head somm at our new restaurant we are opening this fall. Then I will meet and interview you afterward.
>
> Does that work?

Of course, it worked. Marea had not one but *two* Michelin stars on display. The Dover sole might have cost you a few hundred dollars, but your waistline would remain intact! It was a mecca for waifish socialites and celebrities who wanted to be seen in a beautiful room with other beautiful people, drinking champagne and snacking on tiny fish eggs.

What Marea possessed was a relevance Aureole had never seen. The food was some of the best in the city, and people from multiple generations were scattered throughout the dining room. Aureole had only two types of clientele: the old folks who always bitched that the restaurant hadn't been the same since it moved to a new location (it had quadrupled in size and become a corporation) and tourists.

For my trial, just as Hristo said, I followed around Richard, their head sommelier. A Louisianan turned New Yorker; his accent sounded like Foghorn Leghorn meets the big city. As soon as I met him, I knew I wanted to work with him. He had long since passed ten thousand hours of expertise and was able to offer a perspective on guests of a certain caliber that few others could. Every night at Marea, they juggled celebrities, politicians, and royalty. As their sommelier, Richard was unfazed. Whenever a guest would try to ask for his credentials (after all, where was his pin!?), he would look them dead in the eye and say, "I am an undocumented sommelier."

What made Richard great was that he had worked his way up in the industry. He was methodical and precise. So precise that he always made sure to pencil in "downtime" to taste wine and offer up jokes at the sommelier station. By the end of the shift, my sides were aching from all of the laughter; I barely noticed my body was exhausted.

Richard wore thick-rimmed glasses and a navy blue suit that hugged his broad shoulders and tapered in at his waist like an upside-down triangle. The job that was open, he explained to me, was not at Marea. Instead, with Hristo, he was opening another location uptown. It would be a promotion for Richard, as he would go from sommelier to wine buyer. He cocked his head and added, with a purposeful twang, "Once you start buying shit, you got power."

By the end of the night, the whole experience felt bittersweet. I wanted to be in the energy that pulsated throughout Marea, but I was so keen to work alongside Richard. I had never opened a restaurant before, and I thought it would be a good learning experience. In an email to Hristo the next day, I accepted the position, adding: *I think a lot of my admiration for the place stemmed from Richard.*

WE WERE A TEAM of three: Richard, myself, and a skyscraper-tall redhead named Jane. Unlike both Richard and me, she had deep roots in the sommelier community and everyone I spoke to about the new project, Ristorante Morini, would exclaim, "Oh! You'll be working with Jane! We love her!"

I wasn't supposed to meet Jane until training, but the opening of the restaurant continued to face delays. During the downtime, Jane organized her birthday into an industry bonanza. Richard and I were invited, along with just about every other sommelier in New York. Not yet having met Jane, I was so nervous about what to bring. It had to double as a cool sommelier gift *and* birthday present. She was only five years older than me but seemed infinitely more impressive.

I walked into her party just as she was crouched over a big tub of water, a bottle of sparkling wine upside down in it. Curls of her red hair bounced in front of her cherubic face. Her height alone was enough to make anyone feel inferior; she towered above most of the other sommeliers in the room. I found Richard in the crowd and asked, "What's she doing?" pointing to the bottle of wine in the tub of water.

Richard greeted me and added, "That's some serious sommelier shit, there. She's disgorging Movia Puro Rosé, this sparkling wine from Slovenia." *Disgorging* means removing the sediment from sparkling wine before serving. The best way to do it without causing a mess is to pop the cork underwater, so the deposit is captured without spraying everywhere.

I looked over and saw her pop open the cork while it was submerged, a stream of cloudy pink juice exiting into the water. Swiftly, she lifted the bottle upward, and like a killer blowing on the tip of a gun, she let out a small puff, her head and pronounced cheekbones tilted upward. The wine stopped flowing from the top of the bottle. *Holy shit,* was all I could think. *She is so cool!*

Jane then came over and offered me a glass. "You're Victoria, right?" A genuine smile lit up her face.

"Yes, hi, nice to meet you." I shook her hand and passed along her birthday present, a bottle of Olga Raffault Les Picasses Chinon from her birth year, 1985. I was so happy when her eyes became brighter as she held the bottle up gently.

"Thank you," she said, looking me in the eye. I could tell she meant it.

PART V

AGE 23-24

WATCH OUT FOR THE WIVES

I KNEW THAT OPENING A RESTAURANT was a foolish endeavor and that the odds were against us. Most restaurants fail within their first two years, and even if they do live past that, usually they never turn a profit, let alone thrive. In New York City, sustaining a restaurant is especially tricky. Rents are skyrocketing, labor costs are exorbitant, and there is only so much you can charge people for a plate of pasta and glass of wine.

When Richard, Jane, and I set out to open Ristorante Morini with the Altamarea Group, we had no idea what to expect, mainly since it was on the Upper East Side, a neighborhood in New York that particularly eats restaurants of any substance alive. "A wing of a nursing home," is how it was described, "but drenched in diamonds."

The owners of the Altamarea Group saw the void of high-quality restaurants in this neighborhood as an opportunity. Surely these wealthy and older persons wanted a nice local place where they could grab a solid plate of pasta? Wrong.

Before the opening, however, we didn't know this. Richard put together a mini version of the Marea wine list. The chef created a remarkable series of dishes. The company had been planning this venture for years. The director of operations (DOP) had scouted locations with the owners, negotiated deals with the landlord and the city, and interviewed hundreds of people for the staff.

Every day it was two steps forward and one step back. Mountains of paperwork grew as things were incorrectly installed, improperly ordered, or delayed. Procedures were set into place to ensure that things would go according to plan. Which, of course, they didn't. So new systems were created. Those didn't work out either.

A company installed security cameras before staff came in for training. Still, we couldn't figure out who had stolen an expensive bottle of brandy off the bar. A first-aid kit was ordered after someone managed to fall up the stairs. Because of this, management also frantically reviewed our liability insurance. Towers of wine boxes began to arrive. Richard, Jane, and I spent days inventorying, organizing, and putting them away.

Opening a restaurant was like working a harvest. In theory, it was romantic, but in reality it was quite tiresome. What made things worse was that when guests finally did start to trickle in, they seemed indifferent to our struggles. The wine wasn't cold enough (Americans, in general, make the mistake of drinking their white wines too cold and their red wines too warm), the linens had too much starch, pasta dishes were salty, the bathrooms didn't have good lighting, our reservationist had too strong an accent, and the list went on.

Many who worked at the restaurant described our Upper East Side patrons as "without a soul," "evil to the bone," "cruel and unusual," etc. There was some truth in this. Even I found Franky's love cycle completely useless here. Mostly I saw our guests as hilarious. At a certain point in life, age and money can turn someone into a caricature of themselves.

Our secret weapons for the worst guests were two of our team members: Philip "the Ritz" Dizard (Ritz was his actual middle name) and Mireille "Mimi" Downen.

Mimi pronounced Philip's name as Fee-leeeep. He was a sizable man both physically and in presence but, impossibly, able to move about like a nimble *ballerino*. Whenever an old bird would squawk, Philip would run to her side and spellbind her with words such as, "Well, this simply won't do! I will personally see to this, madame . . . ," adding a flashy smile and a heart-lifting wink. He always wore a well-tailored dinner jacket and rarely was seen without a coupe of champagne or Hemingway daiquiri in hand.

Much like Philip, Mimi was full of joie de vivre. From Paris via Hollis, Queens, and New Jersey, she was a brassy broad, the perfect mixture of crass and class. Once when a wrinkled man berated her for not having a table, calling her the most horrid names, she remained firm. "Sir, with all due respect, I am a human being. I would demand, at the very least, recognition as such." As the maître d', she pored over seating charts for hours, riddled with guilt if she had to seat long-standing nemeses Henrietta Katz and Martha Bass near each other. Once when Mimi was training a new hostess who was also a student in physics, I overheard her saying, "Girl, you might know science but this is some serious shit, this is *OpenTable*!" Honestly, the seating chart at RM mattered more than anything else.

I don't know how Mimi did it, as I only once was the recipient of seating anger and found it hard to keep my composure. "How dare you seat us at the worst table in the house?" an older socialite known for organizing celebrity pet weddings exclaimed to me on opening week.

"I am sorry, I don't quite understand, this is one of the best tables we have. It's in the corner, great view of the restaurant—"

She quickly cut me off. "A great view! *Ha!* Well, look at my view!" She stretched out her hand in front of her, each finger knobby and jewel encrusted.

"I don't think I am following, how may I be of assistance here?" I struggled to identify her problem.

"How can I enjoy my meal with a view of these *immigrants?*" She pointed directly at a busser going into a nearby service station to get a teacup. He looked at her and smiled warmly. "Ugh, disgusting. If I wanted this view, I would visit the ghetto."

While Mimi and Philip calmed our guests down, Richard calmed me down. I couldn't understand why guests would be so cruel to us. I thought of my granny and how even though she was a countess, she still treated everyone as an equal.

"These type of rich folk operate under an old-school misconception," Richard would tell me, "that wealth always goes to the most deserving in society. Their behavior is justified in their heads because they feel as if it is a reward."

At RM, I distracted myself from this unpleasantness through friendships. Jane and Richard became integral to my happiness, and I loved everything they taught me. Suddenly, I was no longer alone in the wine world. Their friendship transformed me, and it gave me confidence.

There was a supreme softness to Jane that made her look almost angelic tableside, and I longed to float the way she did around guests. But it was Richard's tight grasp on reality that kept me grounded. He had the innate ability to separate himself from those he served.

Unlike Richard, many sommeliers I came into contact with tended to misunderstand their position. They became accustomed to the habits and conversations of the rich and started to think of themselves as on their level.

I remember distinctly the first time I waited on a sommelier. Bottles of rare wine were ordered and chatted about incessantly, and guffaws marked by flying foie gras spittle jetted out. A sense of importance prevailed until the check was dropped. Nervously, the sommelier held his breath while I swiped his credit card—was he worried that it would be declined?

It wasn't an absurd worry. Although sommeliers are constantly surrounded by wealth, most are barely making ends meet. At the time, I was certainly struggling. According to a 2016 Guild of Sommeliers salary survey, a male floor sommelier makes around $65,000 a year, and a female $58,000. For an eighty-hour workweek, this is roughly $14 or $15 an hour.

My rent in a cubby of a New York City apartment was $1,800 a month. Paying for health insurance was out of the question, and like many in the restaurant industry, I went without. To make ends meet, I had to take in roommates, write articles on the side, and start maxing out credit cards.

The only thing I never cut was saving a bit of money for Laura. Even if it was only $20 a week, I still put it aside in a bank account for her. Timmy was now managing investment portfolios and helped us funnel saved money into a conservative low-risk mutual fund. Still, I know that he went without many luxuries for a very long time to be able to save up for Laura. Together we hoped that our struggling would mean she wouldn't have to. Through all of this, I wondered how anyone could support a family on a sommelier's salary, let alone find the time to start one.

In comparison to other restaurant workers, my financial woes were laughable. Although I felt I was barely scraping by, my paycheck was double that of many of my colleagues. Servers and server assistants, cooks, and porters were often earning well below minimum wage. To complain about my single-workplace-paycheck seemed selfish. Many by my side were struggling with two or three jobs to feed their families.

On such a tight budget, how do sommeliers afford all the fancy wine and expensive dinners they advertise on their Instagrams?

They don't. Often, they're posting a picture of a bottle that isn't their own but instead was served to a guest. Meals out are sponsored by large wineries who hope to influence their palates.

When sommeliers do open up their wallets, many buy what they cannot afford. Since they are surrounded by guests who spend $200 on a bottle of wine like it's nothing, they start to think this is the norm. An obsession with trying more wine and a fascination with luxury become ingrained into the culture. I certainly was not immune. It wasn't until I became a wine buyer, years later, that I was finally able to crawl out of debt and start a savings account. Many in the service industry, however, become stuck in low-paying jobs because their wages are too low to allow for savings, and they don't have enough time to train for another position.

⚜

I received my first guest complaint at RM. The DOP warned me that, especially in this neighborhood, I had to "watch out for the wives."

It happened one evening, about a month after we opened. An older couple was seated at a banquette. The husband had the wine list open, so I eagerly skipped over, hoping to chat about wine with him. As I approached the table, I noticed the wife flinch ever so slightly. I asked if he needed any assistance or if there was a bottle that I might fetch for them.

Quickly, his wife cut me off. "*You* stay away from us, just stay away!" I jumped at her words and shrill tone, completely caught off guard. What did I do wrong? Frightened, I backed away from the table and ran to find Richard.

"What did we tell you?" When Richard saw that I was drawing a blank, he elaborated: "Watch out for those damn wives!

They gonna think this young hussy is up in here to steal their man *and* all his money. Nuh-uh! I am sure she was not having it."

She gave the DOP an earful about me and complained about my "sexual behavior" tableside. She even took to the Internet. In a review of my performance she wrote, *Women like that only get ahead by lying on their backs.*

I decided to make myself appear as homely as possible. I cut off my waist-length brown hair and took to wearing multiple layers underneath my suit, hiding any sense of a curve in my body. Tableside, I made sure I made contact with the woman first, always directing my body language toward her, leaving the man as an afterthought.

In a world so male dominated, I never thought that women would be the ones who made things difficult for me.

THE EAGLE HAS LANDED

ASIDE FROM THE UPPER EAST Side clientele, our biggest worry was the critics. In New York City dining culture, everyone is a critic. Even Yelp reviewers think they hold a level of importance (though I have yet to meet a restaurateur who agrees with this sentiment).

There are only a few who can make or break a restaurant: Adam Platt from *New York* magazine, Ryan Sutton from Eater, and the godfather of all New York City critics—Pete Wells from the *New York Times*. One could argue that Pete Wells is the only critic who matters. The reach the *Times* has is undeniable, and a bad review can mean a restaurant closes by the end of the month. All of the hard work, money, and time spent—it would all be a waste.

Our team at RM was trained to spot critics. Underneath the hostess stand were photos of every writer, reviewer, and influential person in New York. Mimi would scan the book for common aliases used for critics and would Google every person who came into the restaurant. This practice is common in New York City, and many restaurants share a database of information on their guests.

For example, let's say you once ate at Ai Fiori (a sister restaurant in the Altamarea Group) and made a mess in the bathroom, hoping no one would notice. Well, when the hostesses did their routine hourly bathroom checks and found the mess, they informed their maître d', who then scanned the security cameras to see who'd last gone into the bathroom. The maître d' then wrote a firmly passive-aggressive note in your reservation profile: *January 2014, mussed up Ai Fiori bathroom, HWC, PITA.* The last two acronyms stand for "handle with care" and "pain in the ass." A security camera photo might even have been attached to the reservation profile.

If you are rude to the team, it is recorded. If you steal the mother-of-pearl caviar spoons because you think they're super cute, it is recorded. If you don't tip well, it is recorded. If you spend too long at your table, it is recorded. Having trouble getting a reservation somewhere? It might not be because the restaurant is full—you might have been blacklisted.

Guest information is incredibly valuable, and restaurants trade it back and forth like currency. Hostesses continuously scan the room for clues on people and record accordingly. When you walk into a Michelin-starred restaurant, extensive research has already been done on you—your name has been checked against an in-depth database compiled from other restaurants and industry friends. Unless you use an alias, which they can check through their online reservation systems and compare with your phone number, email, credit card, and public records, restaurants know more about you than you would probably be comfortable with.

Don't worry, though, restaurants don't do this to be nosy. Information is, quite simply, power. Since they only have one to two hours to give you the best possible experience, restaurants need a few clues beforehand.

With critics, the staff prepares by studying an extensive booklet of what the critics look like, what they have ordered before in other restaurants, corresponding reviews, things that annoy them, things they like, who they regularly dine with, common aliases, previous outfits and disguises, etc. Many restaurants even give their hostesses quizzes and will fire them if they do not pass with flying colors. By the time Pete Wells walked into Ristorante Morini, we were on red alert.

According to our notes, he came in twice. He traditionally will visit a restaurant two or three times before reviewing it. On his first visit, just as the booklet had said, Pete Wells joined an already seated party, fifteen minutes late. His late arrival is meant to draw attention away from him but usually (thankfully) has the opposite effect. Wells himself is almost unrecognizable. On the night he came in, he was wearing a gray sweater and kept his head downward. He looked like any other dude.

As soon as he was seated, however, panic buzzed around the restaurant like electric shocks. Mimi grabbed the telephone and in her brassy French accent called the DOP and said, "This is *not* a drill! The eagle has landed! Get here *now!*" She slammed down the receiver and gave Philip the *look*.

Philip, who was leaning against the bar, Hemingway daiquiri in hand, complimenting a seventy-year-old woman on her mink stole, complete with heads and feet, stood up straight. For the first time, I saw him spill a few drops of his drink. He ran his hands down the front of his jacket nervously and excused himself from the fur-clad woman. This paperweight of a man delicately danced over to Mimi and asked, "Are you sure?"

Mimi clenched her jaw and nodded to Philip. "Go get that fucker."

PHILIP RACED UP THE STAIRS, and I followed, stopping by the wine cellar to grab Jane and Richard. I opened the door to the cellar and found Richard dancing to a Theo Parrish mix and shouting, "Hot damn!" When he saw my flushed face, he knew it was time to stop dancing.

Jane was already on the case. I watched her float around Wells's table with such ease and beauty that it made me want to cry. Not a single drop of wine was spilled.

Richard told me that beverage service is tricky with Wells. "He doesn't know shit about wine and judges a list by how many thirty-dollar bottles they have. When you don't know anything about wine, you only judge based on price point." I later scanned hundreds of Wells reviews and found Richard's comments to hold some truth. Wells rarely mentioned a wine program or wine director, and if he did it was usually in passing or to criticize an expensive list. Luckily, Richard had prepared for this and made sure that at least thirty percent of the wine list was under $100.

Then came the food. Chef had banned everyone from the kitchen except for the DOP and personally ran every dish to the Wells table. Philip's job was to appease all of the angry guests in the dining room who weren't getting their food because of Pete Wells. I poured so much free prosecco, and Mimi, with the strength of the Hoover Dam, held back guests eager to be seated.

When the pasta course landed on the table, we all watched with curiosity as Wells took a scoop of each type of pasta and ladled it onto his small share plate, creating a sort of gluten trough.

"Why is he mixing it all together!? How can he taste the pasta like that!?" I asked Richard in amazement. Richard ventured to guess that he did it for speed and efficiency. I imagined how much pressure he must have felt as a reviewer who could destroy entire careers. Who would want that sort of power? Especially over something as simple and charming as food?

Many legends swirl around the world's first restaurant. Some claim that the first was started in Paris in the mid-eighteenth century by a Monsieur Boulanger. He served a "restorative" broth that nourished guests and gave birth to the name *restaurant*.

Think of how far restaurants have come since then, with tablecloths, sommeliers, tiny spoons, and databases of information. What was once restorative is now much more, an elaborate performance. Wells dug through the fuss and cut to the center. His job was to determine *what* the purpose of a restaurant was in the grand scheme of things and *if* it was any good at executing that purpose. For example, if he identified a place as a French bistro but they couldn't make a good steak frites, then the review might not be that great. Further, he analyzed how the owners, concept, history, execution, and design were relevant in today's market.

The worst-case scenario was if he determined that a restaurant held no purpose at all. Which unfortunately was the case with Ristorante Morini.

When our review came out, I was puzzled at first. I found that the first half of the article was not dedicated to RM but instead to a sushi place downtown. All the way at the bottom was the start of *our* review.

He had combined our review with that of another restaurant, finding that the concept at RM did not even deserve a full column. It was one of the shortest reviews in the history of the *New York Times*.

Inside Ristorante Morini's split-level space, the chandeliers look like grotesque experiments in stretched skin, and the artwork is the type that speaks eloquently of corporate tax write-offs.

Ristorante Morini hasn't bestirred itself to become a unique destination; it seems to want nothing more than a piece of the action in a neighborhood whose residents proved long ago that they don't mind overpaying for pasta.

"That motherfucker!" Mimi exclaimed, holding back tears at our preshift meeting. Our reservations for the evening had dropped from two hundred to sixty.

Overnight, everything changed at RM. Business slowed down to a crippling trickle. Our sommelier shifts were cut. I was barely taking home $300 a week. Philip was let go. The chef was eventually let go, too. People were redistributed throughout the company. Mimi went back to Marea. The naive excitement that had once banded us all together had disappeared. What was the point of it all?

SINCE MY SOMMELIER CAREER was stagnant at RM, I decided to use all of my free time to study for additional exams. Jane belonged to an inner circle of wine professionals who were all studying for their master sommelier (MS) exam. They held a weekly tasting group at Eleven Madison Park, a three-Michelin-starred restaurant. The whole thing seemed daunting and impressive, so, of course, I wanted in.

Jane prepared me for the tasting group with practices beforehand. At RM during quiet lunches (they were all quiet these days), she would "blind" me on wines and have me run through "the grid." For each glass of wine, I would have to identify the vintage, grape(s), country, region, subregion, classification level, and defining characteristics. This method is called deductive tasting.

Naturally, I was a good taster. I say this not with arrogance but recognition after winning multiple competitions and zipping through many blind tastings. To be a good sommelier one has to have a bit of natural talent and a lot of learned skill. For example, if you can't taste the difference between chicken and turkey, a wine career might not be for you. Most important, if you don't care about the unique flavors of the two, a wine career is *definitely* not for you. The best sommeliers care about the details and have a never-ending curiosity.

However, as a twenty-three-year-old, I was also very nervous. Everyone at the Eleven Madison Park tasting group seemed way smarter than me. I was the least experienced in the room by far. Conversations among the other sommeliers flooded me with waves of insecurity: "Is this a rotundone-driven wine?" or "Don't mistake pyrazines for terpenes"—what were they saying?

All of the tasters led me to question why people became sommeliers in the first place. Many of the members of the group were like Jane, full of love and respect for hospitality. Others had no interest in service and instead worshipped pure knowledge, collecting obscure knowledge to pad their own egos. "Can you believe it, this woman the other day kept asking for more *champagne* but was just drinking *prosecco*! It's like slapping a Mercedes-Benz marque on a Saturn!"

Some sommeliers were obsessed with memorizing esoteric wine laws, the thousands of subregions and vineyards that fell within a large area, and the percentage requirements of certain grape varieties in blends. I once was given an unabashed eye-roll when one of these sommeliers learned I'd mixed up the percentages in Cerasuolo di Vittoria. "Thirty to fifty percent frappato is allowed with fifty to seventy percent nero d'Avola . . . not the other way around! I don't know *how* she expects to last as a sommelier without knowing the percentage requirements of Cerasuolo di Vittoria," I heard the sommelier mumble to another academic.

There were others in the group who were instead motivated by the glitz and glam of the job. To the outside world, sommeliers have the best career in existence. We get to hang out in restaurants, taste the world's finest wine, travel to the most enchanting places on the planet, and eat like royalty. Part of this is true, but good sommeliers will make sure to focus more on work than on perk. Sadly, with free trips, meals, and alcohol on the table, few take the higher road.

To some in this heralded tasting group, achieving the title of MS would mean more of the glitz and less of the drab. A pin would mean never again checking coats, cleaning bathrooms, or even working in restaurants. The hope was that a big company would scoop them up and parade them around like Miss America.

Regardless of their intentions, everyone in the group was blindly chasing this MS goal. For a while, I thought this meant that I should, too. Master sommelier was a title (and even bigger pin) that lay two tests above the one I had taken to become certified. But I thought of Franky and his lesson on becoming "burned up and washed out." If you don't go into the business for the right reasons, you'll never succeed.

DRIVEN TO PROVE MYSELF among my peers, I continued to enter competitions. I won the Chilean wine challenge, the Ruinart Sommeliers Champagne Challenge, and a Guild of Sommeliers enrichment trip to Switzerland.

I also participated in wine festivals around the country and saw what sommelier life is like in other markets. I realized how lucky I was to live in New York, where I could taste fifty to one hundred wines every day. In other, smaller cities, some sommeliers rarely have the opportunity to taste five to ten wines in a shift.

While working at an annual sommelier conference in Dallas, I realized that I was the only one from New York. "You come all the way down from the big fancy city just to polish glasses?" one sommelier asked with a southern twang. There was an aura around New York sommeliers. New York City is a high-volume international market with infinite resources—we were both worshipped and hated at the same time.

In New York, I was also beginning to see more minorities

and women as sommeliers, whereas other markets were almost completely male dominated. Even more rare was anyone of color, let alone women of color. In the whole room of hundreds of wine professionals, I spotted only one black person. The sommelier pool was a sea of older white men. At this same wine conference in Texas, one of these older white men, an MS seen as the godfather of the masters, slapped me on the ass and congratulated me. "You pretty young thing, love seeing girl sommeliers!"

The ass slap was also when reality slapped me—I didn't want to belong in this homogenized MS fraternity.

AS I TRAVELED MORE and my career grew, I began to notice much more alcoholism in corners of the industry. Drinking a bottle of wine (or more) in a day seemed normal. For a while, I didn't notice that my drinking had become excessive. My acupuncturist, Jana, warned me to cut down on my drinking, seeing the effects on my body. I started to notice that at many events I was the only one spitting.

There was so much pressure always to taste more—the newest vintages, recent releases, etc.—that I quickly found myself going to an event almost every day. Wine tastings are held for the trade usually from morning until the afternoon, before many sommeliers' workdays begin. Then there are the late-night parties. In New York City, in the sommelier industry, it is possible to drink hundreds of wines for free almost every week. The accessibility alone can drive someone to alcoholism.

Since all of the sommeliers who go to these events chronicle them on their social media, the "FOMO" factor is also huge. Fear of missing out, of not tasting the right wines with the right people, drives the whole community. There is an unspoken contest to see who can Instagram the coolest wine. The more you can drink, the cooler you look.

Many don't realize that wine is a drug and that these big companies are not their friends. The companies don't care about their health, well-being, or future. Instead, wine is used as a tool to gain better placements on wine lists and a foothold in the industry. Wine reps are expected to befriend every famous sommelier in the city and rub elbows with needle-moving players. Sometimes, to sweeten deals, cash handshakes or free product is traded. This "pay to play" system is used in every industry in the world. However, the difference in the wine world is that a drug is being used to sell more drugs.

Over time, this drug starts to take hold of people's lives. Promising sommeliers begin to dwindle and burn out, just like Franky told me they would. Time seems to slip through their fingers. I promised myself that I'd treat beverages with respect and not abuse them as I'd seen done in my childhood. Expensive wine doesn't make one's drunken stupor more elegant.

At sommelier parties it was as if I were a lamb in a den of wolves. Hands wandered, people stepped in closer and closer, and sleepover invitations were handed out like business cards. When I denied these men, I was suddenly a "prude," "no fun," a "stuck-up bitch," or "not that hot anyway." And at times when I gave in, I was a "whore," or my favorite, a "somm slut."

I once made the mistake of sleeping with a man I actually liked after one of these parties. The next week, I heard that he had told everyone, "She was full-bodied but with a short finish."

After that, I stopped going to events after work. Instead, I spent all of my money buying wines to practice tasting at home. Blind tasting and studying theory became an obsession. I felt that I needed to work twice as hard as others to prove myself.

All of the studying did get me somewhere. It got me out of books and into the world.

THE FACTORY AND THE FARM

I HAD A LONG LIST OF trips lined up from winning contests. As a result of winning the Chilean wine challenge, my first trip would be to this South American country. Traveling with me would be winners from four other major U.S. cities. Our leader would be none other than Finn Ferguson, the master sommelier I'd met at my inaugural wine tasting. Finn just so happened to be the brand ambassador of Wines of Chile.

When I met the other sommeliers, I was shocked to see that two of the other winners were also women! One was from Baltimore, the other from San Francisco. I wondered aloud if we would all share a hotel room. They laughed. "Oh, this must be your first wine trip!" Apparently, we would each get our own hotel room, a luxury I had never had before in my life. In *my* room, I spent the whole afternoon dancing on the bed and raiding the mini fridge.

Within a day, I had the nickname of the "baby" of the group, and everyone went *awwwww* when I acknowledged that yes, it was my first wine trip. The all-inclusive trip involved visiting four or

five wineries *a day*. "The secret to wine trips," a sommelier from
Miami told me, "is to drink as much water as possible, take two
Advil in the morning, an antacid tablet after every meal, try not
to eat spicy or hot foods that will mess up your palate, and take
naps." When I started to write down his advice carefully in my
notebook, he couldn't stop laughing.

His advice was not all that helpful. No amount of Advil or
water would save me. By the end of the week, I thought I might
die. From New York City wine tastings and late-night partying,
I *thought* I had seen sommeliers at their rowdiest. Not even close.

Wine trips are when sommeliers unleash their true selves, far
away from their jobs and obligations. And here, Finn Ferguson
was the ringleader. All of the sommeliers looked up to him with
boundless admiration. It was similar to the way students of the
Wine School would look up to the instructor, or how I might
have looked initially at Reynard. All of the sommeliers wanted to
become a master, and to do so, they thought they needed to keep
up with Finn. I thought I had won the challenge and the trip was
my reward. Instead, the trip proved to be the challenge.

EVERY DAY WAS a death march. At first, I enjoyed visiting the
gorgeous wineries that looked like tropical resorts mixed with
laboratories. Then it became too much. We sometimes visited
six wineries a day, and by the last one, all of our teeth were dark
purple, black even, from all the carménère. At one dinner, I took
a tiny bite of soft bread and was shocked to find that the bread was
soaked in my blood. My gums had started furiously bleeding,
irritated by the copious acidity and tannin from the wine.

Sometime in midafternoon, everyone would stop spitting the
wine. By dinner, we must have all been close to blackout drunk.
After supper was when Finn let us know that we would *really* start
partying. I'd begin to panic and chug any bottled water I could

find. Eager to impress, I drank pisco when everyone else did and danced at the late-night *discotecas* alongside them until we were all sticky with sweat. The later it became, the blurrier the memories of what waited at home became, and the more drugs were offered. In the bathroom, a tall and handsome Chilean man offered me lines of chunky, yellowed heroin on a silver platter. I managed to slur a polite "*No, gracias,*" while others seemed much keener. As if the clubs weren't enough, we would all end the night in Finn's hotel room, drinking more wines until the sun rose.

Each morning of the trip I would wake up and puke.

MOST OF THE WINERIES assumed I was a "girlfriend." One winery representative even went as far as to joke, "Who did you sleep with to get on this trip?"

All week long Finn kept laughing at our exhaustion, adding, "Wait until Friday night! That is when we will really party. Last night of the trip will be at Grant's pad!" He was referring to the other man I had met at my inaugural wine tasting, the winemaker. He had been so kind as to make me feel comfortable in a room full of suits, and I looked forward to seeing him again.

Grant lived in Valparaíso, the vibrant port city known for its eclectic street art. In Valparaíso, the ocean sparkles against the grunge of the cliff city. It looks like San Francisco meets the Amalfi Coast. The wondrous town was our last stop on the trip, and its energy seemed to awaken our tired bodies.

The salty air clung to us as we climbed the hills that led to Grant's home. By nightfall, all of Valparaíso was a twinkling crescent of stars. Stray cats rubbed up against our legs, and I couldn't resist petting them even though I knew they probably had fleas. By the time we reached Grant's house, a parade of cats was following us.

The door was flung open, and Grant clapped his hands in

delight. "Ah, yes, summ-uhl-yeers from America! Come, come in. Get ready to be destroyed." He was wearing a tight gray T-shirt, and his red hair was spiked up at the front. In one of his hands was a whole salmon, and in the other a bottle of pinot noir. He brought us to his terrace, where we began to grill the fish. I tried to contain my awe as I caught sight of the view, a sea of black with spots of tiny lights below, and then the ocean underneath it all.

Grant remarked when he saw me, "You've come a long way from that 'fish out of water'–looking girl I met all those years ago at the Wines of Chile tasting . . ."

A FEW MONTHS LATER, I took my very first trip to France, a result of winning the Sud de France competition. I was scheduled to travel southwest from Montpellier to Carcassonne. As the winner from the United States, I was joined by corresponding winners from Brazil, France, and England.

Now, with the Chilean wine trip and a second trip to Portugal under my belt, I thought I knew the routine—up early, multiple wineries a day, vineyard visits, barrel tastings, large lunches, long dinners, and late-night partying.

I was the only female sommelier on the trip, as well as the youngest, and many winemakers refused to believe I had won fairly. At one of the first wineries we visited, the director used every moment to poke fun at me. "No, are you sure you're a sommelier?" He laughed and went on, while the rest of the group pretended to ignore him.

When he began to pour the red wines, he skipped my glasses. Thinking he'd forgotten, I reminded him.

"Well, most women find the red wines too powerful. They like only white and rosé."

My cheeks flushed the color of the wines he hadn't poured me. I was furious. I had spent countless sleepless *years* studying for this stupid competition. I had gone to the hospital, unable to sleep or eat, sick with worry. I'd paraded myself in front of all of my peers, for what? To be humiliated like this by some French winemaker? No one else at the table came to my rescue, so I had to stand up for myself. My voice shook, but the message was firm: "Just pour me the fucking reds."

Throughout the trip, I was either coddled like a child or shunned as an imposter. A large *négociant,* someone who purchases fruit from growers to make their own wine, attempted to seduce me with a story about a sunset. During his long, winding story I couldn't help but think, *He can't be serious.* I tried instead to ask about his wines, which were factory-made products with a healthy marketing budget. Perhaps he could elaborate on those instead of telling me a contrived story about a sunset? Not surprisingly, he was tight-lipped about his winemaking practices. He asked if I wanted to hear more about the sunset. I decided to pass.

I had hoped my trip in France would be similar to the journey Kermit Lynch had written about in his book. I expected to meet oddball winemakers with eccentric charm and taste wines that would give me goose bumps. Instead, I felt like I was paraded from one large factory to another. It didn't feel like France; it didn't feel like anywhere. The wines also reflected this. They all seemed generic and soulless. Where was the France I had dreamed of?

On many wine trips sponsored by big companies, it is hard to find the good stuff. I was naive in thinking that my won trips were only a prize for my hard work. Instead, they were a way for the organization paying for it to further their cause, charging wineries (who are desperate to sell their products) for visits. Top sommeliers bringing exposure helps the region and bolsters sales.

The trip culminated with a rural celebration called Toques et Clochers. I looked forward to it; perhaps here I would find some authenticity. In the morning we went to an auction of barrels of local Limoux chardonnay. Men in funny hats paraded around playing trumpets and stringed instruments. The combination felt more like Disneyland than rural France.

The next morning I tried to sleep on the long drive east back to Montpellier while one of the other sommeliers puked up Limoux chardonnay all over the car.

I decided that I'd had enough of this fast-and-furious lifestyle. Maybe other sommeliers are just fine with partying all night, but I was exhausted and failed to see the purpose in all of it. I extended my trip for a few days and rented a car. There was something I knew I hadn't yet experienced on the trip—the real France.

I KNEW THERE HAD to be something beyond the large conglomerates in the wine world. There were the growers, the *vignerons*, I had read about in Kermit's book. Instead of factories, these are farmers. They tend to their grapes and produce wines with terroir. The notion of terroir is often hard to grasp, but essentially it means a sense of place. It is the weather, the year, the slope of the hills, the soils, the pruning methods, the history, and the tradition. Wine is one of the few products in the world that represents all of these things.

From Montpellier, I drove up to the Rhône Valley. The valley follows the curve of the Rhône River from its headwaters in the Swiss Alps to the Mediterranean Sea. I stayed in the north of the region, in Côte-Rôtie, or the "roasted slope," which in reality was more of a cliff.

I had only tried the inky Syrah wines from Domaine Jamet a couple of times, but I had promised myself that I'd visit one day. The winery was tiny, run by the husband-and-wife team of Corinne and Jean-Paul Jamet. My knuckles turned white as I clenched the steering wheel, praying that my car wouldn't tumble over the edge.

After a week of laboratory-like wineries, I was pleasantly sur-prised to find that theirs was a humble home, almost a garage like TWC. As we prepared to taste wine, Jean-Paul placed a bottle in between his legs for grip and plunged his corkscrew confidently into the cork. With a few swift turns and a loud yank followed by a *pop*, the cork was out of the bottle. Without thinking, I began to laugh.

I thought of all the time I'd spent performing proper wine service (nineteen steps!). Slicing the foil capsule, the precise two flicks, followed by wiping off the cork with a serviette, carefully cradling the bottle as I twisted my corkscrew, gently removing the cork, and wiping down the lip of the bottle again.

Now here was Jamet, popping his priceless bottle of wine open between his legs with one swift pull. His milky-blue eyes were the same color as the Rhône River, and they sparkled when my laugh hit him. Corinne cracked a smile. *"Très propre, non?"*

Yes, it was very correct.

Jean-Paul's hands were leathered and caked in what looked like a permanent layer of soil and red wine stains. Little cuts, I assumed from being a true *bêcheur* ("dirt worker"), were scattered around his fingers and palms. As he poured the wine for me, his hands fought to remain steady. The delicate movement of pouring wine seemed too precious for his rugged nature. I watched as a bit of dirt (possibly mold) fell from the lip of the wine bottle and into my glass. *Terroir!* Far behind me were the sterile wineries filled with chemicals.

At this moment I decided that Jamet's wine, mold or no mold, was the best I had ever had.

MIRAGE OF
A MAGICAL KINGDOM

RISTORANTE MORINI, MY ENTRANCE TO the Altamarea Group, did not hold the glitz and glam that shimmered throughout Marea. Just a few months after we opened on the Upper East Side, the chef had to start dumbing down dishes because of our lousy review. A beautiful *lumaca* dish, loaded with earthy and creamy snails, was replaced with bruschetta. Wine sales did not justify three sommeliers on the floor.

A twist of opportunity wiggled its way into our lives. Two sommeliers mysteriously left Marea. To save a bit of money, Marea would only replace one of them and ask the rest of the wine team to work more. In the meantime, they needed shifts covered. Enter team Ristorante Morini.

Richard had worked at Marea for five years before the opening of RM and could easily slip back in as needed. Although Richard was now a wine director and equipped with more power and leverage in the business, Ristorante Morini was no Marea. He missed the intensity, the crazy volume of unicorn bottles popped and constant flow of guests who were happy to be there. He would lament, "This place, the Upper East Side . . . it's crushing my goddamn soul!"

Jane, I assumed, would be offered the permanent job at Marea. She was way more knowledgeable than I was, wore her shiny green advanced sommelier pin like a medal, and towered over us all. With her broad smile and air of ease, I cannot imagine there was a guest who ever disliked her.

The cover period at Marea lasted only a month. The manager sent us three at RM the available shifts, about two or three a week, and let us agree on dispersion. Richard picked up one or two, and Jane picked up one. I chose eight.

"You ain't takin' a day off in all of May?" Richard looked bewildered. "Are you crazy?! Marea ain't like here. Those are *long* shifts. Huh-uh. You're gonna need a day off."

I was stubborn. To me, the cover period was a monthlong interview. Yes, Richard had more experience, and Jane was the better candidate on paper. But I had grit. The GM at Marea was skeptical—who was this crazy girl who wanted all the shifts? He made one thing clear to me before I committed: "You had better not *get tired* in my two-Michelin-starred dining room."

AFTER A SIX-MONTH LULL at RM, Marea hit me like a cracking whip. There was a fury upon entering—bussers moving at the speed of light, runners skating around with Dover sole resting on silver-encrusted china, the polishers whizzing through glassware and steam like robots, the cooks shouting and clattering away ferociously, the sommeliers darting down a flight of steps and into dark cellars jammed with bottles. Marea was a beast.

The restaurant was the perfect breeding ground for the one percent. Prices were listed in a microscopic font on the menu— "If you have to look closely, you don't belong here," a server reminded me. It was a jewel in the crown that was billionaires' row, the corner of Central Park West that I'd heard was home to the densest population of billionaires anywhere in the world. One Michelin star would have meant that the wealthy were slumming it. Three stars would be too much show, involving elongated tasting menus geared more toward tourists and the nouveaux riches. Instead, Marea was just right. It was somewhere the one percent could go to dinner a few times a week. Which they did.

Thankfully, a *temporary* flag seemed pinned atop my head. Therefore, the sommeliers didn't worry about training me or even how I would affect their lives and future schedules. To them, I was merely their bitch. A fill-in. What a dream!

My job was to only speak to the tables that the other sommeliers were too busy to attend to. That meant no celebrities, politicians, big spenders, regulars, socialites, or folks in the industry, which was just fine with me. I figured it was best to start with the low-pressure guests.

What I quickly learned was that even the low-pressure guests at Marea were the equivalent of the high-pressure guests at RM. "Can you help table fifty-four?" a tight-lipped server asked— commanded—me. "They're cheapskates."

All too happy to accommodate the penny-pinchers, I strolled over with a wine list clenched firmly to my chest. At the table, two couples were seated. When I approached the table, they glowed. *They were happy to see me!* I suppressed my excitement and coolly asked if there was a wine they were looking for that evening. The list unfolded as one of the gentlemen asked for a Brunello. "It is our absolute favorite, I know it doesn't go all that well with fish, but . . ." I could tell he was a bit self-conscious about his preference.

Brunello, after all, is a big wine with tannin and acid, not typically the ideal pairing with delicate fish that costs a fortune.

"The best pairing is the wine you like best," I said, and recommended some options in the low, medium, and high ranges.

To my utter shock he pointed to the high option and said, "Great, we'll take this." I stumbled for a moment, pointing to the wine and then across the page to the price, to confirm. It was $300! He nodded and then went back to holding hands with his wife.

I pressed the wine list close to my chest and skipped away from the table. When I got back to the wine station, I practically screamed to the tight-lipped server, "They got the Biondi Santi Tenuta Greppo! It's three hundred dollars!" My squeals seemed to hit him and ricochet, hitting me back in the face with a slap.

He rolled his eyes again. "*Cheapskates*," he mumbled before walking away.

Here, among the .01 percent of the one percent, $300 for a bottle was chump change. And I, the sommelier selling the $300 bottle, was no more than a stand-in. The server rushed along the Brunello table, shoveling pasta onto their plates and clearing dishes with graceful swoops of grandeur that left the guests too mesmerized to remember that they had yet to finish eating what was being taken from them. The environment was intoxicating, and they glugged down their wine, which was rapidly topped off. They were done before they knew it. An hour and a half. The perfect turn time for those "not spending."

"Service is like sex," the tight-lipped server told me. "Yeah, sure, some people say they want to make love all night, but then you get sore, and the magic wears off." He crossed his arms and nodded over to a table that had left within the ideal hour-and-a-half turn time. "See, that is the perfect experience. It is a whirlwind, satisfying, not just some in-and-out—but for God's sake, let's not allow it to drag on!"

FOR THE REMAINDER OF my eight shifts, I strove for sheer perfection. I memorized the name of every busser, dishwasher, barista, cook, and runner. I treated a busser with the same respect as a sommelier but still made the sommeliers feel as if they were gods among men. Which, at Marea, they were. Here, they each carefully counted the amount of money they brought in nightly from wine sales. As the night progressed, you could almost see numbers above their heads, skyrocketing into the thousands of dollars.

Much to Jane's and my surprise, I was offered the full-time sommelier position at Marea. As soon as the GM told me the news, in a monotone, I turned white. What would Jane think? Would she still be my friend? The guilt seemed to sink deep into my stomach. I asked the GM if he was sure; why not choose Jane, who was so much more qualified? The GM shrugged. "We want a worker, not a queen bee."

My eyes widened at his description of Jane and myself. Did I want to be a workhorse?

"Besides," the GM added, "the bussers keep annoying me. They want to know when you're coming back."

I PUSHED DOWN MY guilt and said goodbye to Richard and Jane, who were genuinely close friends of mine by this point. I wouldn't miss the stretched-skin lamps and corporate-tax-write-off paintings of RM, nor would I miss the clientele who refused happiness. But what I would miss was the disco ball that Richard had installed in the wine cellar and the times Jane would help me practice blind tasting. Without Jane and Richard, I didn't know what would happen to me.

The two previous sommeliers who'd mysteriously disappeared from Marea warned me about the role: "Get in and get out." They lamented that there was no growth, that my role would be at the bottom of the sommelier totem pole. "You get the worst shifts, the worst schedule, and they expect you to kiss their feet." Another class system with trivial rules, where hospitality was all a lie.

"Then when you're all burned out and need a hand, they are disgusted and turn their backs. And you, *especially*, will be gone within three months." They even described the GM as an "evil robot."

I tried to consider the source. Perhaps the ex-sommeliers were just bitter. Besides, I was too in love with the glitz that Marea held and eager to build my career in a two-Michelin-starred dining room. Not long after I left RM, Jane was offered a job at Eleven Madison Park, a restaurant that soon became "the best restaurant in the world." She was at home among her tasting-group friends. It had all worked out, and she finally was working somewhere that fully appreciated her.

LIKE RICHARD, THE SOMMELIERS at Marea were there because of apprenticeships rather than exams. All of them had gotten to where they were by working their way up in restaurants.

However, there was only one true star there. One person who shone so brightly that the rest of us all bowed down. George, the maître d', was the glittering gold that made the restaurant a treasure.

Mimi, who had come back to Marea as a server, had trained under George before the opening of RM. She introduced him to me as "a New York icon" and said, "He was a maître d' at Bouley in the eighties and has kissed every politician's ass and every princess's cheek! They don't make them like him anymore."

It was true; George was one of a kind. He was the best parts of Mimi and Philip "the Ritz" combined. George ruled the reservations book with an iron fist but was always able to loosen things up, making room for the likes of Mercedes Bass or Bono, whom

George called Paul. "I address people by their *real* names," he insisted. Whenever Sting and his wife would stop by, my head would spin as George welcomed them with, "Good evening, Gordon and Trudie."

Even on the busiest of nights, George would find time to schmooze. He was even better than Franky from my diner days or Enzo from Lattanzi. George had mingled with the .001 percent for so long that he knew their every wish and all of the dirt.

Every time a particular celebrity chef came in, he would say, "It's a chore to find *anywhere* to seat him. The man has slept with half of New York!" he might be heard saying one day, and the next, "Oh, the Rockefeller child is coming in. We should seat her next to the Kennedy kid. They will absolutely hate (and really *love*) it."

He "dressed" the dining room—attractive, young, and fashionable persons always were seated near the windows, while people who were slovenly, chubby, or had had botched plastic surgery went far in the back.

I asked him once if he studied the gossip columns every day to stay in the know and he scoffed, "Honey, I *am* Page Six." Once, when I was completely in the weeds, with bullets of sweat jetting down my back, I looked across the dining room to see George holding a baby. "No, darlings, let me take care of the little one here. You focus on your plates." He made silly faces at the baby and clasped the thick wad of cash one of the guests slipped into his hand.

On another night, a wealthy but incontinent woman in her late eighties made the whole dining room smell like urine. "Poor darling. Well, we cannot have this," George whispered to me before he went over to chat her up, nonchalantly spraying deodorizer around her table's perimeter. "There, much better."

When movie director Mike Nichols came in with untied shoelaces, George didn't even hesitate. Within moments he was on his knees, tying Nichols's shoelaces for him. Months later, when he heard the director had died, he cried and gave a speech in his honor during our preshift meeting. To George, all guests were his friends.

I tried to learn how George was able to seduce the most important people in the world but eventually realized that his secret was experience. *Be okay with not being an expert,* I told myself. It would take me years to get to George's level. He was a god because he had worked the door for decades.

To the DOP and the owner, however, George was a liability. There were some slight slips, and they wondered if he was "losing it" to old age. I would overhear whispered arguments between George and management, only to have him dismiss it with, "Oh, that? 'Twas just a little row. Not to worry." The truth, however, was quite worrisome. They were trying to push him out.

MAREA FELT LIKE A world that was too magical to exist. I watched as George welcomed in "regulars" who were presidents and princesses, celebrities and socialites. On Valentine's Day, two blockbuster couples came in: Miley Cyrus with Patrick Schwarzenegger and Beyoncé with Jay-Z. George was in a panic to make sure they didn't see one another—after all, we wanted both couples to feel like their special date night was wholly unique.

In an unfortunate turn of events, that same night a cockroach found a home on one of the walls in the dining room, just across the way from Miley Cyrus. Everyone on the staff was in hysterics. Would Miley see the cockroach? Would all of our guests scream and leave? Instead, it remained frozen on the wall for all of the dinner service. It was *so* frozen in fact that after a while it became less disgusting and more endearing. A server and I even gave it a pet name, Zamboni. When guests started to leave, a busser nonchalantly stood on a chair and, as George had instructed, "pretend[ed] to clean the wall." *Smoosh*.

During some services at Marea, I was a complete fangirl. One night Wes Anderson, who adores obscure Italian whites made from grapes like pigato, called me over to his table. I assumed he wanted more wine; instead, he and Frances McDormand held up an oyster shell where, crawling inside, there was a tiny crab. "Look," he said, holding it up to my eyes as the little critter wriggled around. I profusely apologized and offered another platter of fresh oysters. "No," they said. They wanted a plastic bag with water so they could take the crab home.

On another night, Mick Fleetwood came in for white Burgundy after a show. Then I accidentally splattered Tina Fey with olive oil. She was (luckily) incredibly gracious about the spill and (thankfully) the GM never found out. Pouring Chassagne-Montrachet for Hillary and Bill Clinton was exhilarating.

The week before Christmas, myself and a few of the staff members organized a holiday party at a local pub. Marea, of course, never threw any celebrations for their staff. The evening of the party, the GM informed us that he had just taken a "last-minute PPX guest." "PPX" meant *personne plus extraordinaire* (industry jargon for *VIP*). The PPX in question was Mariah Carey, who showed up hours late for her reservation, causing us all to have to cancel our festivities. "Mariah loves prosecco," she kept repeating as she forced us to play her Christmas album on repeat for the entirety of the evening.

Mariah Carey's visit, which led to our Christmas party's being ruined, reminded us all that we were servants. I realized that waiting on important people did not make me important.

Then there were the socialites. One regular suffered from a severe eating disorder, and in between each tiny morsel of fish, she would excuse herself to the restroom to throw up. For wine, she would always order an expensive bottle of something that was "low acid," so it wouldn't burn when it came up later. Her tab was probably around $500 on each visit, and it all went down the toilet.

The children of socialites were also a delight. One pimply-faced teenager with braces often dined with his mother. She always ordered a $600 bottle of white Burgundy, which was mostly for her son. After two or three glasses she would try to cut him off. Politely but timidly she'd begin, "Now, now, son . . . let's not forget you have school in the morning."

"*Fuck you, Mom!*" he'd reply while gulping from her wineglass. Sometimes he would even order a second bottle.

Another little girl, maybe around seven years old, must have been dying for her parents' attention. Since they refused to acknowledge her presence, instead focusing on their tower of caviar and blinis, she began masturbating at the table. At first, a server and I weren't sure. Was she *actually* touching herself? We looked closer. Soon the seven-year-old was gently moaning, her hand moving faster in her pants, her mouth wide open. She *definitely* was masturbating at Marea. Within a couple of minutes, she passed out and slept for the duration of the meal. The parents remained unmoved.

Another crowd of regulars we often saw were tourists from China. They came in waves, with lots of new money they were eager to spend in a glitzy place. One of these was the "Asian Taylor Swift," her nickname given by the servers, since she kept coming to Marea after hearing rumors that the real Taylor Swift dined here. She had spent thousands of dollars trying to restructure her face to look just like the celebrity singer. Eyelid surgery, cheekbone implants, shaving off half of her jaw, and of course, platinum blond hair. She even coordinated her outfits to reflect new styles that Taylor Swift had recently worn. Whenever I served her wine, she would ask, "Is this what Taylor Swift drank when she was here?"

As the staff, we were unable to ever discuss those who dined in the restaurants. When one busser snuck a picture with David Beckham as he was on his way back from the bathroom, he was suspended and later let go. "My kids love soccer," he cried. "I just wanted to show them the picture." We all had to pretend we didn't see one politician there for lunch with his wife and then back for dinner with his mistress. Or a prostitute. I gritted my teeth when one wealthy businessman screamed at me, "Bitch, I *bought* you!" after I refused to serve him his $1,200 bottle of wine while sitting on his lap.

And then there were the "corkage cowboys," who crept into the restaurant like a swarm of flies. They swung their big bottles from their private cellars around at Marea like they were performing an unwelcome mating call. It was always a clique of three or five cowboys and at least one hooker. They often didn't allow the women they dined with to eat, only drink. A prostitute once grabbed for a bread roll, ravenous, only to have it slapped out of her hand by a cowboy. "*No!*" he screamed. "*No! You* do not get to eat!"

I always refused the "tastes" the corkage cowboys offered me, knowing that most of their wine was fake or stored improperly, as the other sommeliers warned me. I looked up to the other sommeliers immensely, both had way more experience than I did. Lizzy Jo, the only other female on the team, with a Betty Boop haircut and a no-nonsense attitude, once laughed as Alexander, who was closest in age to me among the sommeliers, passed her a sip of a wine that was supposed to be *white* Burgundy and instead was very much *brown*.

One evening, when Lizzy Jo and Alexander were long gone, one of the corkage cowboys lingered with his friends. I wished that I weren't alone, but as the newbie sommelier, I was always the last to leave. The "bitch shifts" had started to add up to a hundred hours some weeks, and eventually, I was worn down.

The cowboy insisted I try his "priceless bottle." I figured drinking their wine would help speed along the cowboys' progress out the door, and I was just so tired. As soon as I began to swirl the wine around my mouth, I felt something was off. The cowboys looked expectantly at my face. My legs wobbled, and the whole room became foggy. The rest of the night I can't remember. They had put something in the wine.

The next day when I asked my coworkers what happened most of them just shrugged. "You did seem a bit off," one server mentioned, another adding that I looked "just really sleepy." But no one at Marea had thought to help. I have no idea how I got home that night.

It wasn't just date-rape drugs that made the corkage cowboys feel like gods. Corners of the wine world were created just for them. On Saturday mornings, about once a month, an auction was held at Marea by a private company. In addition to purchasing more wine, the cowboys would use this opportunity to bring in big bottles and show off. The auctions began bright and early but went on into the late afternoon, leaving us in a pinch, as we had to scrape out the last stragglers, drunk and teetering, from all corners of the restaurant before we opened for dinner service. The auctions weren't so much a chance to collect more wine but rather an opportunity for the cowboys to plunge into their already existing collections. The cowboys hoped their bottles would top everyone else's. It was as if they were pleading, *Look at me, look at me!*

It had to have been the world's booziest brunch—a petri dish of mass quantities of fake wine, bathroom puke, and cocaine. The cowboys would wave bottles around the room at their friends, who would then wave the bottles they'd brought back and forth, a dick-swinging contest of epic proportions.

When I asked a man if he could use help opening his wine, he responded with, "You wanna open my wine?" He stuck the bottle in between his thighs and pushed it up and down, up and down, the bottle peeping out between his legs. "Come and get it, wine girl!" He winked and handed me a corkscrew. I walked away.

A barely drunk Domaine de la Romanée-Conti (DRC) La Tâche was abandoned as soon as the DRC Romanée-Conti was brought out. Meaning a $2,000 bottle was dismissed for a $25,000 bottle. A woman wanted a glass of rosé wine but was upset to see that there weren't any expensive rosé options, so she instructed us to mix the DRC Montrachet white wine with a Lafite Rothschild red wine. The result was a $5,000 glass of pink wine.

When I did a last-minute bathroom check one evening before dinner service after one of these auctions, I found a corkage cowboy in the *ladies'* restroom, bent over the sink, red puke oozing out of his mouth. He looked over at me and, shocked, screamed, "G-g-g-get out! This is the l-l-little boys' room!"

PART VI

AGE 24-26

LIKE PIGS FOR SLAUGHTER

O NE DAY, MY FATHER WALKED into Marea. I hadn't seen him much since his visit to Aureole. Only occasionally would I visit New Jersey with the objective of seeing Angela and Laura. Mostly, I brought Laura into the city to visit me. She was nearing the end of high school, and we planned her future over roast chicken dinners and trips to the farmers' market. I loved showing her the world of food that I had discovered.

I wanted it to be me who showed her these things. I didn't want her to make the mistake I had, of letting someone like Reynard seduce me with the simple wonders of life.

Our father had mellowed over the years, at least a bit, Laura reported. But still, his presence at my two-Michelin-starred job frightened me. At Marea, I couldn't monitor him at the bar. I was too busy running around the floor, pouring wine for the rich and infamous.

When I told the bartender to water down his drinks, he said to me that that would be difficult, since my father had ordered vodka with "really just a *suggestion* of pineapple juice."

What's more, I was horrified when I looked over and saw my father talking to the DOP. Their laughter could be heard ringing out from the bar and funneling into the dining room. I was struck by how similar they were, two men who yelled a lot but really liked to laugh. The DOP then walked over to me and remarked that my father was so *jolly*!

Was this how others viewed him? I noticed his high-pitched giggles and how his belly shook—maybe my father was no longer the man of my childhood.

Then the DOP made a cutting remark about my father's necktie, a bright and loud relic from the past. I pretended to chuckle but began to feel self-conscious. My own clothing was undoubtedly unfashionable; it was cheap fabric from a bargain store, made to look expensive. Whether or not the DOP realized it, he was insulting not just my father but my upbringing and, ultimately, me.

MONTHS AT MAREA FLEW by. I barely had time to breathe, let alone think. On an average day, the restaurant would seat three hundred to five hundred guests. Compare this with Aureole (around one hundred to two hundred) or RM (less than one hundred). Although Marea had two Michelin stars, it was more like working in a club. The hours were long, the guests were demanding. There seemed no time for hospitality, and any time I tried to take the extra step to form a relationship with a guest, I could hear the GM whispering behind me to *hurry up*. So I stopped trying.

The final straw for me was Princess Alexandra of Denmark. All day long she called the restaurant and asked to speak with me. "Victoria, the princess is calling *again*. Be a dear and take it downstairs," George would remark. I spent forever on the phone with her, editing her wine selections for her dinner that night. Then again, George would tap my shoulder as I was racing off to another table and say, "Not so fast, the princess wants to speak with you again." Then I would run back downstairs to take her next request. Lunch service went on, then came dinner.

That evening, I was the closing "manager." I technically wasn't a manager, but I still was responsible for closing the restaurant once a week, as were all the sommeliers. Closing meant that everyone else left while I was in charge of watching the dwindling guests. If they stayed too late, I was to turn up the lights just a *bit*, turn down the music ever so slowly, and blast the air-conditioning. On nights where guests stayed well into the morning hours, the servers all egged me on: "Come on, just maybe turn the lights up a *little* bit more." Exhausted, I all too happily obliged.

That evening, the princess stayed so late that the sun was about to come up. She was downstairs in the private dining room with her guests, not able to see that the sky was brightening outside. In only a few hours I had to be back at Marea for my lunch and dinner shifts. I turned up the lights in the restaurant and turned off the music, and still, she didn't leave.

THE WHOLE RESTAURANT LIFE had broken me. After twelve years of working in diners and fine dining, I finally felt defeated. The long hours started to get to me. Every time I walked into Marea, my body would tense up.

About a month later, I spilled a drop of red wine on a tablecloth, and the guests complained vehemently to the GM. They even wrote a horrible review of the restaurant and sent it directly to the DOP. The next day, the DOP flew in like a hurricane. "The GM should be fired for this!"

This was a side of the DOP I had heard of but never seen. Sure, he held so much power that he was frightening, but with me, it seemed he always had time for a quick joke and some witty banter. I saw the GM leave his meeting with the DOP fuming.

I was next. The GM did not give me the privacy of an office.

He reamed me out in front of anyone who cared to listen (which was, of course, everyone). My eyes began to well up. I apologized and told him that it was a *mistake*, that it was just a *drop* of wine.

The GM's head almost exploded when I said the word *mistake*. "There is no such thing as a two-Michelin-starred *mistake*. This is Marea. We cannot afford the luxury of *mistakes!*" Whenever the GM said the M-word, I flinched. After that, my hands began to shake whenever I would pour a bottle of wine. I thought of Jamet's shaking hands in Côte-Rôtie. Whereas he trembled from years of doing what he loved, I trembled from years of living in fear. One more mistake, and I would be pushed out.

When I wasn't working, I was sleeping. That was it. I longed to pick up a hobby. At the restaurant we worked with a forager, a profession I found captivating. I spent occasional days off with him, learning to find wild edible plants in the woods. Sadly, after a few trips, we both realized I didn't have any time or strength left. Others at the restaurant couldn't make it to their daughter's recital, an AA meeting, a book club, a grandmother's funeral, or a vacation with family.

I began to skip the weekly tasting group at Eleven Madison Park and rarely saw Jane or Richard anymore. Never before had I felt more insecure and washed up. Nothing appeared to hold purpose. At this point, it seemed I was in too deep. After all, where else could I go?

I began to recognize this same fear and exhaustion in other staff members. Then they were gone. Rumors started to swirl of another "cleanse." Right before I had arrived, a similar sweep had happened, a round of layoffs. I thought of the sommeliers who had previously held my position and their words of advice. *Get in and get out!*

I told myself that I was "used to" the environment, but really, it had instilled in me a false sense of security. Since I was surviving as a sommelier, I thought I was fulfilled, but I had just grown complacent. The restaurant business counts on complacency to stay alive. Since we were all too tired to look elsewhere, we forgot about the ordinary pleasures of everyday life. Free time, a family, a personal life—I had unknowingly sacrificed these things when I signed on.

Restaurants fetishize long hours of manual labor. Marea could have easily hired another sommelier to lighten the burden on all of us. Instead, we were told to take pride in our extended shifts, that it was a trophy to hold up for others to see. The sommeliers and captains almost bragged about who worked more, unable to admit that much of our work was superfluous. The manual labor of Marea, the sheer exhaustion, the insane pressure, all stripped me of my humanity.

AS I HAD AT Aureole, I became hungrier as a shift wore on. There was a difference between the family meals at Marea and Aureole, however. At the two-Michelin-starred level, the cooks at Marea used the meal as an opportunity to show off their skills. Even the pastry department participated. In the early afternoon, everyone gorged themselves as if they would never eat again—because they wouldn't, at least not for a while. Any food was forbidden during the rest of the shift. The GM once caught me eating a granola bar in the wine cellar and lost his mind. This was *service*, not snack-time. I hadn't eaten in ten hours.

In a twelve-hour (although it was usually longer) shift at Marea, I would walk well over twenty thousand steps. In comparison, the average American walks around three to five thousand steps a day. I would also have to jet down and up flights of stairs every few minutes to grab wine from the cellar downstairs. I averaged around seventy-five to eighty floors a day, the equivalent of hiking up the Chrysler Building daily.

This intense physical exercise burned thousands of calories, and by the time midnight crept closer, I was ravenous. While others were better at sneaking food, I always found myself getting caught.

"This is how they fatten up pigs for slaughter," a server told us one day as we ate together. I went on to listen as he described the process of stuffing pigs with a huge meal, starving them for hours, then giving them another large serving. "It's the quickest way to fatten them up. That is what Marea is doing to us—fattening us up like pigs for slaughter."

ALEXANDER AND I EXPRESSED our weariness to the wine director, begging him to bring on another team member, as there had been four sommeliers initially and now there were only three. As the newbie, even after a couple of years, I had the absolute worst schedule. He quickly shushed us, looking over his shoulder, and said in an understanding yet firm tone, "The management and owners already think there should be one *less* of you. Don't let them hear any complaints."

Alexander and I looked worriedly at each other. We had heard whispers about budget cuts, since the other restaurants in the group weren't doing well, but now the wine director had confirmed our fears—one of us was getting the boot.

I HAD JUST WON a spot on the annual Zagat "30 under 30" list, the youngest person on it that year, for my work as a sommelier at Marea and for winning so many competitions. The list was released on my one day off that week. I had closed Marea the night before and hadn't gotten home until close to four in the morning. I imagined that the next day, when I went back into Marea, there would be a whole fanfare. The company, via my name, had made it to the Zagat list! I was sure that this would mean a crack of a smile from the GM, and perhaps the DOP would even swing by to congratulate me.

When I arrived, the GM immediately told me to follow him. He led me down the back hallways and into the private dining room, where the DOP was seated. He was sitting in the same chair that the princess of Denmark had parked herself in only months earlier. Were they going to give me a bonus for my achievements? Or perhaps a promotion? No, something seemed off. Neither of them smiled, and when they formally *invited* me to sit down, I knew I was in trouble. A piece of paper sat in front of them.

I was exiled from the kingdom.

HOW COULD THIS HAPPEN to me? With all of the hours I had put in, no prior marks on my record, never calling in sick even once, working every single holiday, and now the award—I'd thought I was untouchable. In reality, I had let them make me a lousy sommelier. It would have been easy for me to blame Marea, but I knew they wanted a worker bee, like the GM said, and work me they did. I'd sacrificed my sense of self in the hope that somehow it would pay off, but in the cutthroat world of fine dining, what did I expect?

Although their rejection hurt me, it was for the best; it was my time to go. I had grown complacent and had completely forgotten what I loved most about my job—the people.

Even with the pressure, the long hours, I put up with Marea because I was so enthralled with the magic. It wasn't intangible magic but rather a carefully curated sense of magic elaborated with pressed tablecloths, pinched pasta, air-shipped fish from Japan, shiny marble, and those two Michelin stars that hung on the wall.

As the previous sommelier in my role had warned me, this is what big companies did. They had fattened me up for slaughter.

I have been told this feeling is not exclusive to Marea. Many sommeliers in high-pressure, Michelin-starred corporate restaurants share my sentiments. This one restaurant wasn't the problem; it was the whole goddamn industry.

I SPENT THE EVENING crying as Richard comforted me. The timing could not have been worse, as I was about to hand over all of the money I had saved up over the years to Laura for college. She was starting her freshman year in just a month. I couldn't take this from her. I felt like such a failure—Laura and I had been planning her escape for years. If she didn't have this money, how could she have independence?

"You'll figure somethin' out," Richard reassured me as I bawled into his shoulder, "you're all resourceful and shit. It's all gunna be okay, now. Don't worry."

Many urged me to take another sommelier job, but it all seemed lateral. For the first time in years, I was forced to stop and think. What was my purpose?

I grew up in a household of manipulation and neglect, left to fend for myself. From this, I found independence but also became too reliant on it. For many years, I thought of myself as an island and let no one else in. Then I was raped, assaulted, and abused. I was sucked into a cultlike wine school. I let peers and guests bully me. I thought that being a young woman was a weakness, and I grew increasingly insecure.

This is why I kept quiet for years about one of the most traumatic incidents that happened during my growing career. A man who was my boss trapped me in a wine cellar, and I realized that I didn't have a choice.

In an instant, his hands pressed my body against a wine rack, and my heart broke. Was this all I was worth to him?

With no one else there and the cellar locked, I didn't know what to do. My boss was the only one with a key to the cellar. I was trapped. Worse yet, I knew that even if I screamed at the top of my lungs, no one would be able to hear.

If I fought him off, where would that leave me? He was my boss and could fire me, or worse, destroy my yet-to-blossom sommelier career. Ever since I'd lost my virginity to a rapist, I'd placed little value on sex. *What is happening doesn't matter,* I told myself as my boss pushed me up onto a stack of boxes and penetrated me. I begged him to at least use a condom, and he laughed.

I deserve this, I thought, *for leading him on with my curiosity.* I was too nice to the regular at the diner, who then locked me in a car, and I was too nice to my boss, who was now locking me in the wine cellar. Just like in the car, I froze. After, as his semen leaked onto boxes of wine, I felt shame.

When I went home that night, I cried like never before. I heaved until my chest hurt and my limbs went numb. *Better that way,* I remember thinking. *Better to feel numb.*

This was just the beginning. For months, my boss would call me into the office or wine cellar for "meetings." Sometimes this meant sex. Other times it was to show me videos and photos of his past escapades. There was a photo series of him having sex with a youthful man, including graphic images of his penis covered with blood. Then lots of girls, around my age, bent over with their still-budding breasts hanging out. His favorite video was one he would repeatedly show me or reenact: him masturbating in front of a mirror. The finale, as one might guess, was his milky semen shooting out all over the reflective surface. This filled him with a voracious delight.

My whole body was a prisoner. For further control, he took naked photos of me to add to his "collection." Whenever I tried to break away from him, he would threaten, "I'll show everyone in the wine industry just how big of a slut you are."

Then one day, he had me meet him out for dinner. When I walked into the restaurant, I saw him laughing from across the room and showing his friend something on his phone.

By the time I was next to my boss and his friend, I realized that they were laughing at me—pictures of me. Sprawled across his cell phone screen was my bare flesh, all of the bumps and lumps one is supposed to keep hidden. My body felt weak, and I thought I was going to throw up. He had seduced me for his own vanity, and for the pleasure of twisting my life with torment.

"Don't worry," his friend said, "we will forget all about these pictures as soon as we get photos of your little sister." Laura was still in high school at the time.

I was finally done. To hold me hostage was one thing, but to threaten my sister was unacceptable. My living in fear of what he might do was giving him power over me. At that moment I realized it was time for me to take control. I never let another boss touch me, even if they tried.

Losing my job at Marea was devastating, but I realized it was a lesson. In the world of wine, earth-shattering events can produce good things. For example, the incurable phylloxera, a root louse, has destroyed grapevines around the world. A recent outbreak of this pest occurred in the 1980s in California, when whole vineyards were wiped out and many businesses destroyed.

From this devastation came something positive: an opportunity to focus on quality. Growers could now reassess their land and see which grape varieties were best suited for their areas, and plant for quality instead of quantity. This event was similar to the opportunity I had been given. I could now focus on a new, quality experience, something with meaning. I no longer wanted to sling wine like a robot for hundreds of people a night.

Now it was time to do things I loved but hadn't had the energy to invest in before. I spent the rest of the summer foraging in the woods. Like I had in my childhood, I escaped into the forest, this time in upstate New York, and learned all about medicinal herbs, roots, and barks. I hadn't realized how much I needed this time in nature, far away from the unnatural world of fine dining.

In restaurants, there is a disconnect from the natural world. Sommeliers are expected to talk about the complex soil types of far-off vineyards, but when we ask for time off to take trips to these places, management scoffs. By learning to forage, I found not an escape from the "real" world but an ability to cultivate a sense of wonder, an appreciation for the simple, untarnished bits of the universe.

The ability to appreciate the natural world eventually set me apart from my peers.

I DECIDED NOT TO rush into another job. I wanted to take time to accept my mistakes, heal, and learn how to become a better person and sommelier. I taught wine classes, worked private tastings, and started to pour all of my emotions into writing. While foraging, I rented my apartment out to friends.

Slowly, I started to round myself out. I decided that I would subscribe to the *New Yorker* and read a non-wine book for the first time in five years. I ignored a tinge of guilt (*You could be memorizing obscure rules governing canopy management in vineyards!*) and one afternoon cracked open *The Baron in the Trees* by Italo Calvino. My mind soared as the text brought me around treetops in Liguria. I almost expected to read about the local wines, maybe pigato, rossese, or cruvin . . . but instead tumbled into a story about fierce independence.

Wine is part of a broader picture; like music and art, it only has a purpose if it fits into a bigger world. I realized that my career as a sommelier had so far been frivolous. I had no idea what was happening in the world around me because I had become obsessed with obscure information and working tirelessly. Memorizing vineyard laws didn't make me a better sommelier, but using my knowledge as a tool to bring joy to guests would.

Carefully, I started to interview and search for a place that was not just a business but, rather, a home. I went on over forty interviews. They were horrifying—the perverted male owners, greasy business dealings, and places void of soul. Every restaurant seemed to propagate a toxic culture. Was there nowhere in New York City I could work and be proud to do so?

TO BLOSSOM
피다

THEN, MONTHS LATER IN OCTOBER 2015, I met Simon Kim, the proprietor of Piora. Piora was a small Michelin-starred restaurant in the West Village that looked like a garden mixed with a tatami room. An air of tranquility and peace floated around the space. One of the managers, who had also been exiled from Marea, was now the GM of Piora. A hostess from Marea ran the door there. They called me and asked if I was interested in "getting back into the Michelin-starred world."

I hesitated and asked them about Piora. "The exact opposite of Marea," the GM said, "and I need a wine director. I can't think of anyone better than you."

The first step was meeting the owner, Simon. The GM said that I shouldn't worry, that Simon was very nice. Still, I was incredibly nervous. I had only met the owner of Marea twice in all of my years with the company and had seen the owner of Aureole

one or two times. Owners seemed to live far away from their restaurants, counting their money and checking boxes. I asked what
I should wear. "Simon likes collars. Make sure to wear something
with a good collar."

Piora was a jewel box of a restaurant and walking into the space
put me at ease. There was something very natural about Piora—
the worn wooden floors, the lush green garden in the back.

Simon Kim was wearing a well-tailored gray suit with a white
button-down shirt. I nervously played with my collar, trying to
make it stand stiffly, the way his did. Of course, I had researched
Simon extensively before the interview, but I was shocked by how
striking he was in person. His good looks were defined by his
powerful jaw juxtaposed with a head of jet-black hair. Was he
the *owner*? Simon looked maybe five or ten years older than me,
remarkably young to own a Michelin-starred restaurant, and then
I realized that this was what people probably thought when they
saw me.

Simon possessed an air of confidence, sitting upright with his
legs calmly crossed in front of him. As soon as we began speaking, I knew he was different. My résumé was in front of him, but
Simon barely looked at it. Instead, he made eye contact with me
and asked me *who* I wanted to be. We spoke about foraging, the
natural world, finding happiness by making others happy, and
what I liked to eat. Simon and I enjoyed the same restaurants
and shared a philosophy on hospitality—that restaurants were
all about people. The food, the wine, the fancy silverware—it
was all there for the guests. If we don't use these tools to give the
guest the best experience they've ever had, all of it is meaningless.

"Not just guests," Simon further explained, "but also the
people that work for me are important. Piora is a small place,
and every person we have on the team is crucial. There is me, the
chef, the GM, and the wine director. We need to work cohesively
together, inspiring and leading everyone around us. Do you think

you can do that?" I looked around the table at the GM and Simon. I *really* wanted to do that.

Before I was given the key to the wine cellar and officially handed the title of wine director, Simon and I met once more. This time, we walked from Piora to a small park. Before arriving at the park, we stopped for tea. I watched as Simon greeted the man at the bodega by his first name, high-fiving him and stuffing a generous tip in the jar by the register. When we walked together on the street, Simon nodded at people, occasionally smiling and saying hello. What kind of New Yorker *acknowledges* another stranger's presence!? He genuinely seemed happy to see every person who passed him.

The park he brought us to looked like a *clos* in Burgundy, closed off to the street by a high set of stone walls. Inside, summer still lingered, even though it was September. Jasmine wrapped itself around trees, and birds chirped as they hopped from one branch to another. I wanted to laugh, thinking of how beautiful this interview already was, and how it was worlds away from anything I'd ever experienced. Simon and I sipped our bodega teas and sat across from each other on wooden benches. There was something about him that put me at ease but also made me want to win his approval. His concept of a restaurant aligned with its historic purpose—to restore.

"This is a big role," Simon began, "and a lot of responsibility. Do you think you are ready for it?"

I thought of how little I knew about purchasing wine, balancing budgets, and directing my own program. Being a wine director was a step above being a sommelier, as it meant that not only would I be selling the wine, I would also be purchasing it for the restaurant. I would be responsible for hundreds of thousands of dollars.

On paper, I was extremely underqualified for the position, which I admitted. But what I saw in Simon was the same thing I saw in myself—grit. I thought back to my childhood, when I'd balanced grocery budgets and gone Dumpster diving for coupons to clip. I knew that I was scrappy enough to learn the role and do it well. Most of all, I wanted to make this magically kind man proud. I hoped to help him make others happy. Just like when I'd first met Richard, I knew that this was someone I wanted to work for.

"Yes," I said to Simon. "I am ready for this." Saying yes to Simon turned out to be the best decision I ever made in my career.

IN KOREAN, *PIORA* MEANS "to blossom." What Simon Kim wanted for his restaurant, and for everyone who worked there, was exactly that. He found ambitious talent, gave them resources, and allowed them to blossom into something so much bigger than they could have imagined. His youthful enthusiasm for life and the industry is what filled the seats at Piora.

"I knew, as an immigrant, what I could offer is that I can work harder than anyone else around me," he once told me.

Simon put his whole life and soul into Piora. Growing up in a traditional family in South Korea, he always struggled to win his father's approval. His father had polio as a child and was never able to run around like the other kids. Instead, he turned inward and gained pleasure from the world of food and drink. By the time Simon was born, his father had dined at all of the best restaurants in the country. Simon soon learned that the way to his father's heart was through food and hospitality. Eager to gain his acceptance, Simon dedicated his life to being a restaurateur.

"My father was worse than even a Michelin inspector," Simon would tell me. "If I would make a dish and it was too salty or not cooked well, he would not eat it. Not in a mean way, just in a *No thank you, why would I want to eat this if it isn't perfect?* sort of way. This made me always want to be better." Simon had gone on to work for prestigious chefs such as Thomas Keller and Jean-Georges Vongerichten, all the time learning, taking notes for when it was time to open up his restaurant.

Simon's restaurant was also a home where we could all grow and learn. "When you take a young, ambitious person"—he paused and looked at me—"like you and me, for example, we are wild things . . . right? Some restaurants will take this wild thing and put it in a cage. They beat the animal and say, 'Behave! Do this and do that!' But then what happens? The animal behaves for a while, but you take away what originally made it so special, that *wild* ambition. Then the cage becomes too confining, and it kills them. So instead I take the animal, I give it a cage—but I leave the door open. I say, 'This is your home, come and go as you please, find things out there in the wild and bring them back to your home. Make your cage your own.' Then soon, the cage is not just a set of walls for them to rest in and build themselves, it is a home. The wild thing keeps their fury but has also been groomed."

Simon took the "blossom" meaning of Piora very seriously. As if tending a small spring bud, he would check in daily, constantly watering me and ensuring that I had enough sunlight. Most important, he never tried to pluck me while I was still growing. Amateur foragers will see a patch of wildflowers and, charmed, pick them all. Then when they return later, they're shocked to see that the flowers never grew back. It is because they were too greedy—they took too much and killed the natural beauty.

At Piora, I practiced the lessons I'd learned from Franky (to find ways to genuinely love everyone), from Enzo (that good service is a bit of seduction), from Justin (the sommelier should always be the smartest and humblest person in the room), from Richard (use your goddamn head!), and from all the inspiring women I'd met, like Jane and Marianne (float with ease, ooze charm through confidence). Additionally, there was so much to learn from Simon.

Unlike other owners I had worked for, he was in the restaurant all the time. He truly loved people. During service, he would spend the first half of the night watching me calmly, then later stand next to me and offer tidbits of advice.

He treated me with a level of respect I had never before received. Never did he say, "Why the hell did you put the wineglasses down on the table like *that*!?" Instead, he would ask, "Table thirty-two, the glasses are to the right of the water glasses, do you prefer them that way or do you think they should be to the left of the water glasses?" As he asked me I realized that he was bringing something to my attention—inconsistency. I looked around the room and saw that on some tables I'd put the wineglasses to the right of the water glasses and other times to the left. I admitted that I hadn't before thought of where the wineglass should go.

He nodded. "Well, let's decide now, then. What do you think looks best?" Then he went on to illustrate both examples for me, to the right and to the left. We paused to think. Finally, we both agreed that wineglasses should go to the left of the water glasses. "The tiniest details matter. It is our way of subliminally telling the guest we care about them, that we care about even your wine and water glass. Subliminal hospitality is just as important as overt hospitality."

Also, at Piora, I had free time, a first for my career. In the mornings I would go foraging to unwind, read long books, and work on the wine program for the restaurant, all before service at night. A healthy work schedule of forty to fifty hours a week is unheard of in the industry. Simon knew that if he took care of his staff, they would take care of his guests.

While I was learning, I was also teaching. I hated that when I was growing up in the sommelier world, few wanted to take the time to mentor me. It seemed selfish, to hold all of this knowledge and not give back in some way.

A Korean man in his midtwenties named Wesley reached out

to Simon for career advice, and Simon, in turn, offered him a job at Piora. Naturally, Simon started him in a beginner's role, that of a food runner. At first, I hesitated when Wesley asked for wine lessons. He had no hands-on experience, having studied economics in college followed by a brief stint at a culinary school. I was sure that after a couple of weeks Wesley would lose interest, make up some excuse about a grandparent dying, and neglect the rest of the lessons.

Before Wesley, a few other servers at Marea and Aureole had approached me for wine classes, and I had eagerly jumped to buy books and make lesson plans. I would always find myself disappointed, as their interest would wane. Studying wine was a lot of work; it took a tremendous amount of discipline. Wesley wasn't even a server; I was worried he'd be one of those culinary school students who think they're a gift to mankind.

But perhaps what made him such a good student was his love of serving others. Wesley wanted to learn about wine, not because he had a specific passion for it, as I did, but because he viewed it as a necessary tool in hospitality. Like Simon and me, Wesley genuinely loved making people happy, and I watched as he took pride in even the smallest details of his job. When Wesley would run food to tables, he gave translations in both Korean and English, always ensuring that the plate rested at the perfect twelve o'clock position, protein facing the guest. Wesley polished wineglasses as if each one were a holy chalice, never breaking a single piece of stemware. He wanted to know why things were done a certain way and how he could make a system better.

Every week, Wesley showed up to our wine class fifteen minutes early. Often, he would come in an hour early to review. I would enter the dining room at Piora and find a row of perfectly lined-up glasses, water for us both, and notepads. When he didn't understand what I was saying, he asked, but mostly he listened. Months passed, and he never missed a class. Soon, he was promoted to server assistant, then bar back, and eventually server. Wesley was friends with everyone in the restaurant, from Sidy, the dishwasher, to Chef, to Simon. There was no class system at Piora—the owner and the dishwasher were equals.

PIORA WAS HIGHBROW MEETS lowbrow in all of the best ways. The Talking Heads would softly dance out of the speakers while white truffles were shaved over $100 bowls of pasta. Simon wanted the beverage program to have a similar vibe. He wanted approachable yet cool, refined but not stuffy. I began purchasing grand cru white Burgundy and favorites like Jamet Côte-Rôtie alongside quaffable Bandol rosé and budget-friendly Beaujolais. I instituted a policy where a guest could order *any* bottle on the list and only commit to drinking half of it, hence paying half price. It was a considerable risk from a cost perspective because it potentially meant that I would lose half of my revenue and waste half of my inventory. The reward, I thought, outweighed the danger— guests would be able to try cool, sometimes pricey things that they otherwise wouldn't be able to.

Guests loved the concept. Because Piora was so tiny, and it was me working the floor as both the sommelier and wine director, I was able to sell the remaining half bottles that same night by the glass. I would text regulars of mine from Marea or Aureole saying, "TWO GLASSES OF GRAND CRU WHITE BUR-GUNDY $50 EACH! COME AND GET IT!" Moments later, they would be at the bar, crushing the last glasses.

As a buyer, a sommelier starts to hold power. After years of working in wine, I was now able to vote with my dollars and put my money where my mouth was. I wanted to highlight the small and honest producers that I'd first fallen in love with at Harry's after reading *Adventures on the Wine Route*. It took me years to go from sommelier to buyer, but I am thankful I took the time to learn how to do the job properly.

Now, as I started to climb to the higher rungs of the wine industry, I noticed fewer and fewer women by my side. In the restaurant world, women are found in many entry-level positions. However, few women hold real power. Female managers, general managers, beverage directors, and restaurant owners are a rarity. As in many industries, at the top, men still dominate.

Before Piora, when I was interviewing, a manager said to me, "Well, women are good at *spending* money but not saving it! I can't even let my wife have more than a hundred dollars in her pocketbook, or she'll blow it. Now, why would I put a *girl* in charge of my restaurant's pocketbook?"

To combat sexism, I hoped to align myself with other women in power. A couple of women in the industry were receptive and did help support my growing career (Laura Maniec, Rita Jammet, Aileen Robbins). However, too often women were less helpful than men. They viewed me as their competition, following the "eat or be eaten" mentality.

Around men, so many women feel the need to put on this tough-girl demeanor to survive. Softness and femininity are considered weaknesses. There are so few jobs at the top, and many women know the chances of a woman's holding these coveted positions are incredibly slim. Therefore, they claw their way upward and use the fallen women by their side as step stools.

AS A NEW BUYER, I had a lot to learn. What I had not prepared for was the level of corruption in the business. At Aureole and Marea, how to buy wines was kept a secret. Since there are very few good wine director roles, those who hold them keep quiet about how they run their programs successfully. I had no idea who to contact if I wanted to buy a specific bottle of Brunello or how to price it on the wine list. It was a very steep learning curve.

From little things I had picked up here and there, I started piecing the role together. I created spreadsheets for everything, and soon the Piora wine budget looked like a more detailed version of my childhood grocery lists. I worked closely with our accountant, who taught me how to balance costs, and soon I learned the "art of the markup." Sommeliers from all over New York gave me advice in this category.

"Make sure the basic-bitch pours—pinot grigio, Cali cab, Sancerre, prosecco—are marked way the hell up, and the somm stuff—cru Beauj, sherry, grower champagne—you can basically give away for free. As a *reward* for those in the *know*."

In New York City fine dining, a standard restaurant markup is between three and four times the wholesale cost. My job was to make sure Piora was profitable. However, I wanted to do something different from just a thoughtless markup. If I put a wine on the list for 3.5 times wholesale, I might sell one bottle of it a night. But if I put the wine on the list for 2.9 times, then I might sell two bottles a night. And by the end of the month, I would sell more because guests would recognize the value in the buy.

AS SOON AS THE announcement went out that I was buying for Piora, the sharks started circling. My email inbox jumped from thirty emails a day to three hundred. Eager to secure their placements on the list, distributors would come to Piora and sit at the bar, harassing me and trying to influence my decisions. The tough thing about working in a restaurant is that it is a very public office. Imagine if, at any time, someone could barge into your cubicle and bombard you with bribes, threats, or seductions. Many thought that I would be easy to convince.

"You must be so overwhelmed, *sweetie*, let me make it simple for you. You should buy X and Y and Z from us. Don't worry your pretty head," distributors would tell me, attempting to secure my purchasing dollars. When I would request tastings, the distributors would often treat me like a complete imbecile, barely allowing me to speak. "Now, so this is Bordeaux. It is a *red* wine. It is mostly cabernet . . . *sauvignon*. It is from *France* . . ."

A salesman once told me, "So this is from the Corbières, which is in Provence." When I corrected him gently, reminding him that Corbières was west of Provence, in the Languedoc, he said that I was mistaken. I shook my head, bemused. I had been to the Languedoc when I won best sommelier of the Languedoc-Roussillon competition.

Being belittled because of my age and gender was one thing, but pure corruption was even trickier to stomach. Offers of direct monetary payments sent to my home, free trips to wineries, and quid pro quo deals started to crowd the restaurant. Was this being a buyer? I wanted to purchase wines because I believed in them, not because someone was paying me to buy into their company. When I let Simon know what was happening, he reassured me, "You are stronger than them. Eventually, the sharks get tired of circling."

Piora was a huge pay cut from Marea. It was such a small place, and Simon instead offered me something that was priceless—reasonable hours, time off, and unwavering support. He knew it was important that I visit wine regions and allowed me to take four weeks of wine travel a year. His only request in return was that I come back even more inspired, teach the team what I'd learned, and crush wine sales.

Although the restaurant was technically fancy, there was a relaxed downtown energy. My regulars from Lattanzi, Harry's, Aureole, and Marea followed me there and slowly started to fill up the small space.

THE WINE SALESMAN

BETWEEN MY TIME AT MAREA and Piora, I met Lyle Railsback. After I was ousted from Marea, Lizzy Jo took me out one night to reconnect. We ended up with friends at Marta, Danny Meyer's Roman-style pizza place. There I introduced myself to a wine salesman who promptly invited me over for dinner. Lyle has described this meeting:

> We've reminisced many times about that first dinner, the one I invited you to, and you said you were dating someone else. On the second invite you were still dating this someone so I suggested you bring him along and that we'd make it a dinner party. As luck would have it, you wrote the day before saying that you'd broken up and would be coming solo, which worked out for me, as I'd been too busy traveling and hadn't invited anyone else, so it would just be you and me for dinner.
>
> I knew within moments that we were meant for each

other, like Rumi's idea that "Lovers don't finally meet somewhere, they're in each other all along."

There were two things I first noticed about Lyle: his eyes and his voice. His eyes were like the sea. Sometimes they were bright blue and sparkling, as if the warm Mediterranean sun were beating down on him. Other times they were gray, as if an upcoming storm were rolling in with clouds and thunder. There were even moments, like when we were foraging in the woods or lying next to each other in bed, that tiny flecks of green would appear in his eyes like sea glass.

He had a voice that drew one in, both powerful and gentle. Hearing his voice was like adding fresh cream to a cup of coffee, the richness softening the acidic and bitter drink. When we first started dating, he would read poetry to me on the subway on our way to work. I would close my eyes and let the vibrations of his gravelly voice hum through me. Maybe this is what made him so good at selling wine. He could wrap his voice around a story like a warm blanket.

Lyle came from a family of farmers. His grandma Jane and grandpa Bob were cotton pickers, just like my grandma Willie. They lived in California and grew all kinds of things on their land, like plums, cherries, watermelons, and huckleberries. I imagined Lyle as a little boy, poking his fingers into huckleberries and sucking out their juices. Like me, he held an appreciation for the natural world in a way not often seen in the industry.

Lyle's family moved around a lot, just like mine. By the time I met Lyle, he had lived in Colorado, Kansas, Oregon, California, and Washington, DC. His fascination with food also began when he was a young child, and one of his first jobs was at a McDonald's in Kansas. From there, he went on to wash dishes, and in college, he studied Japanese pottery.

To make ends meet, at twenty, he started to apply for restaurant jobs in the Willamette Valley in Oregon. At one place, he mentioned he could cook, and the owner said, "Well, we don't need a cook, but we do need a sommelier!" which is how Lyle got into the wine business. At twenty he was (under the radar) the youngest sommelier in the country, eleven years before I started at Aureole.

His grandma Roxie often said to him, "My, you are a resourceful little brat!"

Years later, he would interview with Kermit Lynch, the importer I had long been obsessed with. He listened as Kermit went on to say, "I hate when you read a tasting note and it says something like '*This wine tastes like huckleberry*'—what does that even mean? Who even has had a huckleberry?!" Lyle proudly responded that he had, in fact, had a huckleberry. As soon as Lyle got home from the interview, he overnight-shipped some fresh huckleberries to Kermit and thanked him for his time. To this day, Lyle says he thinks this is why he got a job in national sales with Kermit Lynch Wine Merchant.

NOT ALL WINE SALESMEN were washed up, as Reynard had told me they were years before. During our first dinner together, I was so nervous that Lyle would pull out impressive wines from the Kermit Lynch portfolio. Instead, he brought out one of his favorite wines, a simple rustic red from La Tour Vieille in Collioure, France. He believed, as I did, that there can be just as much pleasure in a $20 bottle as there can be in a $2,000 bottle. We drank the juicy wine alongside anchovies and his rendition of Zuni's chicken salad while he read poetry by Jim Harrison, who had been close friends with the winemaker from La Tour Vieille. Lyle lived in a romantic and circular world, where everything was connected, and that night I forever became a part of it.

He traveled weekly, heading to markets around the United

States and coming back with reports on who was drinking what and where. When he was in New York, we were always together. After my shift at Piora, he welcomed me home with a three-course meal.

It seemed that Lyle bought a new cookbook daily. He experimented with ancient Ligurian recipes from Colman Andrews, Provençal fish stews from Richard Olney, or Japanese farm food from Nancy Hachisu. His love of food and wine was rooted in the age-old belief *What grows together goes together.* So, with *torta di verdura* from Liguria, we would sip on crunchy rossese di Dolceacqua. With bitter greens and dashi, it was *sobacha*. It was never about finding the most expensive or obscure bottle, but rather about taking a moment to celebrate the history and tradition of a region fully. The connecting power of good food and wine seemed boundless.

Lyle's love and respect are what finally helped me heal after years of abuse. He gave me the confidence to believe in myself and embrace who I am. This, coupled with Simon's belief in me professionally, transformed my life. Soon, I barely recognized the scared girl whose hands had shaken when she poured a bottle of wine. I no longer so desperately sought the approval of my peers.

I knew that I'd always possessed a sort of strength and resilience. It was something that seemed to run in my blood. Laura also had it. I watched her grow into a dynamic woman with a ferocious appetite for good deeds. She pushed me to stand up for myself and invest in mentoring other women. She also had an insatiable curiosity—together we discovered the English seaside and hitchhiked our way across the Amalfi Coast. Although we loved to create adventures together, I didn't have her bravery. She jumped off cliffs into Spuyten Duyvil Creek, the "devil's whirlpool"; traveled alone in Greece for months; urged me to skydive; and made reservations for one at restaurants.

Timmy had a certain courage, too. His was the ability to forgive. Although he could have harbored a rotting bitterness toward
our father, he never allowed those feelings to fester. Instead, he
poured his energy into his wife and career. He was able to keep this
tender sort of kindness, something usually found only in children,
while adults too often harden over time like stones.

While Timmy and Laura strengthened me, Lyle and Simon
gave me a platform to let this strength shine. Before I'd needed it
only for survival—it was all I had. Now, in a safe environment,
I felt that there was nothing I couldn't do.

PART VII

AGE 26-28

THE REAL WORLD

I T HAD BEEN THREE YEARS since my first trip to Chile. I had won
another trip in a competition and would return to the country
with a group of sommeliers. But this time, I was the leader.

With my assembled group of sommelier friends—Luke Bo-
land from Del Posto, Ida Rae from Le Bernardin (who had previously been my boss, a manager at Harry's), and Mike Noah from
Marc Forgione—we competed against other teams in New York.
At the last minute, Luke had to drop out of the trip. Instead, Tony,
a sommelier from another team, joined.

I didn't know Tony that well, but it was a small industry. Almost everyone who met him seemed to like him instantly. There
was, however, something unsettling about him, something that
reminded me of Reynard. He would never hold eye contact for
long and sometimes would trail off into another world.

As the leader, I was eager to show off the Chile that had
shaped me. I channeled my inner Finn Ferguson and took the
team out as soon as we landed, first to a wine bar called Bocanáriz

for dinner, then to the Clinic, a leftist bar run by local hipsters. We drank warm lagers and sipped on a range of piscos until we were all fuzzy and ready to head back to the hotel. Still, it was the first day of the trip, and although we were tired, our bodies were not yet ready for the night to end.

I did as Finn had done years earlier and offered my hotel room as a place to unwind. We sipped on pisco and made plans for the week. Mike eventually went to bed, leaving just Ida Rae, Tony, and me.

Soon, we ran out of ice, and Ida Rae offered to refill the bucket. I got up and opened the door for her. The door had not yet swung closed when I felt my body being pulled backward.

With a *thud*, the door slammed shut; I was thrown against the rear wall and pinned tightly. Tony pressed his body against mine and used his hand to pull open my mouth, pushing his tongue inside. His other hand was pressed so hard against my breasts that I could barely breathe. As he exhaled, aromas of the pisco we had both just drunk leaped out, except now it was stale and the smell stung my nose. It had been almost ten years, but instantly I was brought back to the diner attack. I felt like a frightened little girl, reeking of French fry grease and trapped inside a car. That shame, of not being able to move, of weakness drenching my body, all came flooding back. Was this like before? Had I been too nice to him? Why did I agree to host drinks in my room?

I felt his teeth sinking into my lips. He began to chew on my skin like it was a snack. A jolt of pain shook me, and I pushed back against his cinder-block arms. Unpinned now from the wall and my mouth free from his, I started to scream, "*NO! Stop*—"

Tony pushed out his strong arms, and I fell back onto the bed like a rag doll. "It's just a release," he kept saying over and over again in a drunken slur. "It's just a release."

Had it been only a few seconds? I was sobbing and screaming while Tony's hands thrust up my dress and into my underwear.

A series of pounding knocks landed on the door. Tony sat up, and I was free from his weight, trying to breathe as he shouted, "Just a minute." The pounding knocks kept coming, and I kicked Tony off me, running for the door. Ida Rae was back.

Although small, Ida Rae was ferocious. She held some sort of tae kwon do belt, and as my old boss, she was a protector. We both waited in the doorway. "Get out!" I kept screaming at him. Ida Rae looked at me; I can't even imagine how I must have appeared. Eventually, she managed to persuade him, even in his drunken stupor, to leave the room.

"Are you going to be okay?" she asked before leaving.

"Of course, it was nothing, I am fine." I forced a smile. Even then, I thought that I had to be strong, the leader of the trip.

My hotel phone kept ringing and ringing. Soon Tony was back, knocking at my door. He kept banging until he tired, eventually crawling back to his room. Alcohol had the power to unleash the ugly side of a person. I had seen this with my father, who gambled away his earnings. Now I realized that as a young woman, being alone with someone like an inebriated Tony was dangerous. I didn't have the luxury of entertaining people in my room that Finn had as a male leader.

After the first night, I just wanted to go home. Instead, I had to keep up the charade. In private, I iced the dark bruises that encircled my breasts. These marks reminded me that even as the leader, I held no power.

In the restaurant industry, women are expected not to make a scene. Those who harass us are often our bosses, colleagues, or guests. By calling these people out, we are seen as a nuisance or liability. In this particular case, I was sure that if I said something, everyone would hate me. What kind of leader ruins the trip by causing a big scene after the first night? Who would even care how I felt? In retrospect, I should have reported Tony right away to the program directors and gone home. I should have verbalized what he did to me and realized that doing so would have been a sign of strength, not weakness. But instead, I kept quiet, punishing myself for someone else's crime.

When I returned home, I promised never to let myself be in such a vulnerable state again. I realized that alcohol could turn hidden intentions into public actions. Booze weakened me and made me an easy target. That was a dangerous place for a young woman.

⚜

After that, I traveled only with Lyle. Together, we visited France, Spain, Italy, Switzerland, and Morocco, and jetted all over the United States. My apartment used to be for just me and my dog, Rocco. Now Laura had gotten a full ride to Macaulay Honors College in New York and moved in. Then Lyle moved in, too. For so long I had felt alone, and now, finally, I had a family. Together the three of us (and Rocco) started our own home.

The first trip Lyle and I took together was to Collioure, where the Pyrenees Mountains fall into the Mediterranean Sea. The first wine we had drunk together was from here, and it was a place Lyle loved. The small fishing village, nestled on the Spanish border, once attracted artists such as Pablo Picasso, Tsuguharu Fujita, and Salvador Dalí. Because of the rare quality of its natural light, Collioure became the birthplace of the Fauvist movement. Notable poets such as Jim Harrison and Antonio Machado, whose grave is in the town center, found shelter and inspiration here.

There was something about seaside towns that drew me in, like Valparaíso had years earlier. The colors of the village: turquoise-painted shutters on stone houses, mustard-yellow and aqua-blue boats bobbing on the sea, the rose-pink and ivory

buildings. A small and stony crescent beach was squeezed in between two jetties, large piles of rocks that stretched like fingers
into the sea.

Sometimes it is the company that makes the place. Lyle had
found a spot in the world that spoke to him but never quite the
right person to share it with, until now. A restaurant, a house, a
vineyard—the people we choose to share these things with can
change the whole experience.

IN COLLIOURE, WE VISITED Lyle's friend Christine from La Tour
Vieille, the domaine that produced the wine Lyle and I shared on
our first date. A longtime friend of Lyle and the poet Jim Harrison, Christine was a rustic woman who spoke quietly with an
accent that seemed not entirely Spanish nor French.

She clapped her hands in delight when she saw Lyle and later
told me, "I think that Lyle is the best kind of gourmand . . . the
one who likes good things, simply, with good people." For dinner, we tested this notion. Christine instructed us to meet her at
a place called Le Cabaret and added, "Be ready—the owner . . .
he is a bit mad."

We were almost an hour late to dinner, which drove Lyle
and me both crazy. Although the map easily illustrated where Le
Cabaret was, just by Perpignan, it was not as easy to find. Lyle
and I drove around in circles, myself in tears from hunger and
frustration. We called Christine, and she seemed nonplussed by
our delay, speaking in the same light and mystical tone.

"Oh-kay, well, let's see, where are you now? . . . Ah, no . . .
That doesn't sound right. Well, it is just to the left a bit . . ."
After a while, she passed along the phone to Antoine Delmas,
the owner of the restaurant. I thought, *At last, we will receive some
clear direction!*

Instead, Antoine gruffed on the telephone: "*Dépêchez-vous . . .
Ou je vais boire tout votre vin!*" (Hurry up, or I will drink all of
your wine!) And then he hung up.

No thanks to Antoine, we somehow managed to find the small
stone house, nestled beyond the main road among olive trees and
brush. By this time it was well after dark. The only light you
could see for miles was a warm glow escaping from Le Cabaret.

Inside, there were small wooden tables scattered about the
dining room, which was actually Antoine's living room. We were
greeted by Antoine's wife, Émilie, who gave us a small twist of
her lips that almost resembled a smile. She sashayed over to a
table, and we followed, recognizing Christine seated there among
bottles of wine. Émilie dropped us off and swung her hips back
over to the kitchen.

"She looks like a Picasso painting, doesn't she?" Christine
said to us in place of a greeting. Indeed, Émilie had a narrow face
with a long nose, slender features, and olive eyes.

Antoine, a hurricane of a man, descended on our table. We
popped wine bottles, the corks rolling into corners of the floorboards that jutted up. In a bit of English for us, Antoine made one
thing quite clear: "There is no menu. I cook for you, and you have
no choice. Good?"

Lyle and I looked at each other. "Uh, yes," I responded.
"Good."

If someone didn't like his food, that was fine; they didn't
have to come back. There was no begging Yelp reviewers to take
down a bad comment or Googling the name of every person who
walked through the door. Antoine didn't care who came to see
him, because it was *his* show.

He resembled a worn sailor. His cheeks looked cut and hol-
lowed by the wind, and a gray beard climbed around his chin and
into a fantastic set of ears. "*Bon,*" Antoine said after emptying a
glass of Christine's wine into his mouth. "*Allons-y!*" He slammed

his big hands together in a loud, dull clap. The room, which held a few other patrons, jumped.

To our left was a tanned man, his round belly protruding between the tiny buttons that dotted his shirt. With Antoine's clap, a cigarette fell from his lips and landed on a little circle of skin that was poking out near his belly button. "*Oof!*" The tanned man stood up in a hurry. "*Ma cigarette!*" The guests all chuckled, their bellies rising and jiggling.

Christine took a wineglass from a nearby table and offered it to me. I happily accepted and watched as she poured a decent helping of her La Pinède into the goblet. We then lifted our glasses and Antoine scurried from the kitchen, not wanting to miss an opportunity to toast, his glass clinking all of ours just at the last moment. He then dipped down and looked at me, his eyes fixating on mine. "Look me in the eye! The French say, when you toast, you must, otherwise seven years of bad sex!"

A sip of the perfectly chilled La Pinède made us feel right at home. This is a wine that many sommeliers in New York overlook, as it is unapologetically affordable, highly quaffable, and from a nook of the world often forgotten.

Antoine effortlessly juggled four plates in his arms, setting them down in front of each of us with a toss and clatter. A freshly lit cigarette hung from his lips. As he distributed our plates a bit of ash flaked onto my first course. It was like when Jean-Paul Jamet poured a bit of mold into my wineglass on the slopes of Côte-Rôtie (*terroir!*). If anything, it was a refreshing change of pace from the stiff New York restaurants where if I spilled a drop of wine I would have my head chopped off. And to think, here Antoine was dropping *cigarette ash* in my *food*. I loved it.

Antoine described his journeys that morning, rolling up his pants and wading into the Mediterranean to grab sea urchins from the rocks. In front of us were the little tongues of those sea urchins, dressed only in olive oil and garnished with red onions and parsley he had chopped just moments before. As we scooped up the small bites, Antoine sucked on his cigarette and observed us, making sure we were correctly enjoying his food.

Antoine knew his food well because he had spent his whole life in this region, crafting these dishes. He would not accept an outsider coming in and trying to do it their way. *"Ils peuvent aller à McDo!"* he said, meaning that those types of guests can go to McDonald's if that is the experience they want. His eyes rested on my lips, slowly moving as the sweetness of the urchin danced on my tongue. A smile crept across his face as he offered a nod of approval. He walked back to the kitchen, grabbed a bottle of wine, and happily poured himself a full glass, drinking it by the hearth while singing along to a small radio propped up by the sink.

"Antoine scours the markets every morning. He will wake up early and drive all the way to Spain if he needs to," Christine explained, "to find the perfect ingredients each night for dinner. If he doesn't find what he wants, he won't open at all."

WE TOSSED OUR NAPKINS and, after licking our plates clean, declared defeat. It was a perfect meal. *"Pas de dessert?"* Antoine asked with a twist in his grin. We shook our heads, *No, no, please.* He added, "The same price anyway, no discount! *C'est prix fixe!* Maybe just cheese?"

Before we could protest, Émilie slipped our plates away and returned with chunks of goat cheese with blue veins running throughout the white cream. A drizzle of honey from a local beekeeper topped each serving. Even the smallest sliver of this cheese was wild—it tasted and smelled of the windswept grasses and sweet wildflowers that dotted the landscape.

Lyle, who was too enthralled in a conversation with Christine, left his cheese untouched. Antoine leaned over his right shoulder and exclaimed, "Not for you?" He motioned toward the cheese. Lyle mentioned something about his fullness and that he would try it soon, but too late! Antoine had already swiped it up in his palm and jetted the piece of dairy directly toward his mouth. He missed, though, and with a plop, the cheese hit the floor. *"Merde!"* Antoine exclaimed, and pulled the now-slippery chunk from the wooden floorboards. Without so much as an inspection, he popped it into his mouth, grinning at our shocked faces. Antoine was definitely not a New York restaurant owner.

Antoine pulled a chair from a nearby table and cozied up to us. "I've lived here for years, the floors will not be what kills me," he added while glugging a glass of wine to wash down the dessert. At this point, our table was filled with earthenware plates, linen napkins stained with red wine and oil, almost-empty bottles, and a smattering of crumbs. On the staircase behind us that led to Antoine and Émilie's living quarters, mortars and pestles made out of local red marble dotted each step. As the steps climbed, the marble creations became deeper and wider. Lyle, always looking for a new kitchen toy, tried to convince Antoine to sell him one.

Antoine scoffed. "You Americans . . . you cannot buy everything. Some things are just not sold."

I tried to take a photo of the mortar-and-pestle sets, hoping that maybe one day I might be able to find something similar for Lyle. Antoine became outraged that a cell phone was being used for photos in *his* restaurant. Within moments he turned around, bent over, and pulled down his pants. His ivory bum was pointed directly at my lens, his balls, tucked back between his legs, hanging like two walnuts in their shell. *Flash!*

Émilie rolled her eyes from the kitchen and lit a cigarette. Ragtime jazz began to spurt out from the radio. Antoine buckled his pants back up and laughed. To him, my taking a photo in his restaurant was as offensive as his showing us his testicles.

I thought about the stuffy Michelin-starred dining rooms where I had been a sommelier and how stale the service felt. Here, tucked away in the South of France, it felt like my first dinner party with Uncle Carlo and Aunt Sue. The warmth that radiated was what I wanted to capture in every dinner. Antoine didn't need fancy tablecloths or $600 bottles of wine to make his restaurant my favorite; it had *atmosphere*.

WITH LYLE, WE EXPLORED the world of *vignerons*. A *vigneron* is someone who tends to the vines and takes what Mother Nature gives them, trying their best not to mess it up. The wines are less human-made and more an expression of the terroir, a place and time.

It seems like between 2010 and 2015, all over the world, a craze for "natural" wines began. In a way, it makes sense. The market is seeing pushback after decades of chemical concoctions owning shelves and wine lists. The term *natural* is broad and un-regulated, which makes it even more confusing for the consumer. Some natural wine is good, and some is not. Even a talented wine-maker can fail to make decent natural wine if the weather doesn't cooperate. Unfortunately, a lot of natural winemaking is straight-up dirty. Wines are like women—we don't have to wear makeup to be beautiful, but we should probably shower.

Jean-Louis Chave from Hermitage in the Northern Rhône Valley told us, "Some people believe that if a wine is more rustic, it's more loyal to a sense of place. But I believe wine should have a sense of sophistication."

Still, no matter how sophisticated techniques become, wine-makers are still very much dependent on Mother Nature. Over dinner one night in the Loire Valley, Régis Minet told us that on April 27, 2016, he had painstakingly placed five hundred candles around his vineyards. He lit them all as night fell, a final effort in battling the below-freezing temperatures, hoping the candles would provide enough heat to protect his crop. He showed us a video of the most dramatic attempt I had ever seen at combating frost. The warm yellow dots of candles illuminated gnarled vines. The vineyard seemed full of twinkling stars.

"If it were minus-two degrees Celsius, it would have worked," Denis Jamain, a neighboring winemaker in Reuilly, added. "But the temperature dropped to minus-four degrees." Régis Minet lost 80 percent of his crop to frost that night.

Farther south in Burgundy, a combination of frost and hail devastated the vintage. Domaine Diochon in Moulin-à-Vent in Beaujolais noted, "The hail only lasted for twenty minutes but stole eighty percent of our production!" In Meursault, Jean-Marc Roulot would almost have preferred hail: "Frost is far more depressing than hail because it happens so early in the season. You still have to do so much work that year, knowing that there will be little in return."

When I stood in the humble home of Franck Follin-Arbelet in Aloxe-Corton, I could hardly believe his Romanée-Saint-Vivant Grand Cru cost upward of $1,000 a bottle! Where did that money go? His modest surroundings did not imply wealth but rather the life of a farmer. I quickly learned that this wine was made in tiny quantities, the profit hardly covering land taxes. I asked him what to expect from Burgundy after years of bad weather. Franck's steely blue eyes sparkled, he sipped on a glass of his pricey wine that barely paid the bills, and he said, "Do not expect normal. There is no normal, not anymore."

IN SAINT-JOSEPH IN THE Northern Rhône Valley, not far from Chave and Jamet, we visited Jean Gonon. Sommeliers in New York fight tooth and nail for allocations of his wine. Chave had remarked, "Jean's wines are fantastic, but they are not meant to be enjoyed like this—if you can even call it *enjoyed*. To be hoarded and crazily sought after like trophies. No, Gonon's wines are for drinking pleasure."

In 2008, Gonon, along with the whole region, had a terrible year. His white grapes were so destroyed that he went through the bunches and picked late-harvest berries for a sweet wine. "It was my idea . . . to try to make lemonade out of lemons, in a way," Gonon said. He tried to make the best out of a bad situation by creating a new and different wine. It was the only year he made this sweet wine. Sommeliers rushed to hoard this "rarity."

Years later, when we showed Gonon a bottle we'd found of this sweet wine, he cringed and said, "Ugh! Not that horrible thing! I hope never again to make that wine!" For him, the wine represented a lousy year. *How hilarious,* I thought, *that all of these cork dorks are going crazy over a wine not even the winemaker is proud of.*

I returned to Côte-Rôtie to revisit Jean-Paul and Corinne Jamet. Like everyone else in France, they had poor weather. Still, every morning they woke up, well before sunrise, and tended their vineyards. I thought about spending all day pruning grapevines, trying to balance and shift my weight on the cliff of Côte-Rôtie, and was sure I would never survive. In Sonoma, I had barely lasted one day in the vineyards, which were nearly flat.

Someone in the group asked, half jokingly, why they even still made wine. The work was laborious and heartbreaking, and the revenue hardly covered his costs. Jean-Paul didn't hesitate. He did his work because it had a purpose. Through his wine, he could make a meaningful impact all around the world.

I left Jamet feeling rejuvenated. His narrative made me feel justified. As a sommelier working in restaurants, I often asked myself, what was the point? On some days all of the hard work and abuse I faced as a young woman made it all seem not worth it. I calculated that around 70 percent of guests were discriminatory toward me, a ratio similar to what Mother Nature can take from winemakers.

I was stubborn, like Jean-Paul. He wouldn't let Mother Nature take from him what he loved. I couldn't let cruel or abusive guests and colleagues take from me what gave me purpose.

All of the little things, pruning each vine and touching each grape, were part of a bigger picture. Doing inventory in the wine cellar, putting away towers of boxes of wine, folding serviettes, editing wine lists—all of these things that nobody sees, they matter. When done well, those things allowed me to have a positive impact on people from all around the world. I could bring joy to people through wine, and the restaurant was my platform for doing so.

WITH LYLE, I SAW the *real* world of wine. Our trips weren't sponsored, and we paid our way equally, allowing us to experience regions on our terms.

Wine is also what led me to the world of artisans. Lyle read about an umbrella maker in Napoli who had been perfecting his craft for seventy years. We visited traditional cloth cutters on Savile Row in London. Next was a storied taxidermy shop in Paris. The opera in Venice. A vintage poster shop in Aspen. Record stores in the East Village in New York.

Through the lens of wine, I developed an appreciation for culture.

THE FLOWER

꽃

ALTHOUGH SIMON AND I CONTINUED to grow, Piora floundered. The chef wasn't particularly keen on Simon's belief in me and Chef felt he was at odds with our vision. After an especially brutal summer when all of our neighbors vacated the West Village for the Hamptons, the restaurant was devastated. Bar seats sat empty for hours, and the tiny space started to feel huge.

Frantic, I tried everything I could to get bodies in. Every week I threw an intricately themed wine party. I became a social media and PR maven, using every angle and business card I had collected over the past five years. Wesley would help me set up these elaborate parties, and Simon was impressed by the small uptick in business. For a while, the parties helped. Eventually, it wasn't enough.

I think things really started to go downhill when the grease trap began overflowing. A grease trap is a machine meant to filter all of the drippings, oils, and fats from a dishwasher into a big metal tin. Monthly, someone would come by to pick up the tin and dispose of it properly. However, due to some pipe problems, the grease trap wasn't functioning properly.

At first, like all things, the overflow happened only occasionally. Then it was monthly, weekly, and soon every day. Sidy, our dishwasher from Mali (home of Timbuktu), would have to lug downstairs, from the kitchen to where our grease trap was, a mop and bucket to soak up the swill. Usually, Sidy was all smiles and laughs. He never complained and worked harder than anyone else in the restaurant. However, mopping up the mush the grease trap vomited was unpleasant and backbreaking work. With every swipe of the mop, the oils slipped about everywhere. Sidy started to lose his spark.

During service, I would have to take off my shoes and wade through the sludge, grab a wine bottle from the cellar, and then wipe the grease from my toes and head upstairs to present to the guest their $500 bottle that had just come through a shitstorm. I thought back to my days at the Greasy Spoon and remembered our dishwasher, Antonio. Had I grown callous? Why wasn't I helping Sidy like I'd helped Antonio?

One day when the trap overflowed, Simon took off his coat and, in a full suit, started mopping up the spill. I watched as splatters of fat ricocheted onto his Hermès tie and Loro Piana shoes. I winced as it began seeping into the cuffs of his pants.

"Sometimes, you just have to get dirty," he began. "Whose job is it to clean up this mess? Not mine, not Chef's. Not Sidy's, and not yours. But then who should do it? Sidy, because he is lowest on the totem pole? No. We are a team, a family. We should all do it." After that, whenever the trap overflowed, I mopped it up myself. Simon also bought me rain boots.

DESPITE PIORA'S DOWNWARD SPIRAL, I was happy. My career suddenly took off; I had made a name for myself at Piora with a small but thoughtful list. Quickly, I started to win awards and receive press.

As I grew, Chef and Simon drifted further apart. Piora fell by the wayside as Simon began to focus his attention on opening up his dream restaurant—Cote, a Korean steakhouse. In Korean, *cote* translates to "flower," a natural progression after a blossom. Proud of what we'd accomplished together at Piora, Simon offered me a piece of the new company and an elevated role overseeing *all* beverages—from liquor to wine to water. He offered Wesley a position as manager at the new restaurant. The first time I saw Wesley in a suit, pressed shirt and tie gleaming, I cried.

But just as we were ready to open Cote, we had to close Piora. Another sommelier once told me, "Closing a restaurant involves such a specific skill set. It should be on your résumé, just like opening a restaurant." It's true; there are so many things to do, and in an emotional state quite the opposite of the excitement that comes with an opening.

A closing is sad, but there's almost no time to feel this between all of the work that goes into breaking the restaurant down. Simon had to answer to banks, investors, the guy who'd loaned him the espresso machine, insurance companies, Con Edison, and so on. Even cleaning out the wine cellar required multiple days of schlepping weighty cases up and down stairs and into U-Hauls. Chairs that had once cost Simon $500 were now worth $50. The table where Wesley and I would do our wine lessons was put in storage. Someone stole the electronics. Food started to rot in the fridge.

Our salad days together came to an end as we transitioned into the meat of our careers. "It's sad, especially because it was my first restaurant," Simon said, "but in a way, there is nowhere to go after the blossoming, and that's what Piora always was. We realized that we [he and Chef] were both young men when we opened and once fully grown we were just such different people. We didn't grow together but instead separately. Now that we have blossomed, the time is for the flower. For Cote."

SIMON NEEDED A CHEF for his new project, Cote. After years of searching he came across David Shim. Like Simon, David was from Seoul. When Simon first told him about his dream project, David thought Simon was insane. Simon talked with such confidence and big-picture ideas that David was worried. He thought it sounded too good to be true.

At the time, David was working as the chef at M. Wells, a Québécois steakhouse in Queens with a Michelin star. To Simon, David was the perfect candidate for Cote, since he had both Korean roots and Michelin-starred-steakhouse experience. So, Simon persisted.

David turned Simon down three times before he eventually gave in. A gentle giant, David reigned over us all at well over six feet but remained incredibly humble. Never before had I met a chef with zero ego. In Simon's home kitchen in Harlem, the two began to test recipes and ingredients. I can only imagine that Simon's wife, Nayun, was going crazy from all of the messes they created. When I once visited, the kitchen was filled with dirty dishes, vegetable peels littered the floor, and for some reason, the bathtub was filled with plums.

Simon and Nayun were also expecting their first child together. In a speech Simon gave later that year, he turned to Nayun and said, "Thank you for letting me be a bad husband, while you were pregnant no less, so that my dream restaurant could succeed."

However, way before Simon's dream came to life, he was still missing one key player. Simon had a chef and a beverage director but no one to help him run the show. Sure, Wesley was on board as a manager, but he was still very green. The fourth partner in the business had to be someone with a lifetime's worth of experience.

Simon was wise enough to know that even though he had opened and run Piora, there were things he could have done better. He needed a mentor, something a lot of newbie restaurateurs don't often consider. With padded wallets and fat egos, they think they have seen it all. Then, when the shit hits the fan, they don't know what to do. I admired that Simon was able to follow the same motto I'd first learned as a sommelier—*Be okay with not being an expert.*

He looked for someone who had had a positive impact on his career. He remembered that when he first began in hospitality, a man named Tom Brown had hired him as a manager at Blue Fin in Times Square. Tom, who had run restaurants in both New Orleans and New York, was now running the show at BR Guest, a hospitality group that included spots like Blue Water Grill and Dos Caminos. Simon knew Tom, with his twenty-five-plus years of experience and unwavering passion for hospitality, was his guy. But persuading Tom was not so easy.

Tom had a wife and two kids. He couldn't just up and leave his corporate job, even if BR Guest were selling out to the big Landry's chain. Although the concept of Cote and Simon's passion were inspiring, Tom had to play it safe. "Everything I do," he said, "it can't be for me. It has to be for my family."

As he had with Chef, Simon persisted. Finally, to make it work, he raised more money and found a way to offer his old boss what he needed.

With flippy brown hair and tortoiseshell glasses, Tom Brown became the "dad" of our group. And yet, he's still a kid at heart—

when he isn't in a suit, he wears graphic T-shirts and Vans. From Long Island originally, Tom has a slight New York twang, saying "cawfee" instead of *coffee*, with an animated smile. He hangs around telling jokes until things need to get done, then it is heads down and work hard. Somehow, Tom wrangled all of us crazy kids together.

WITH SIMON'S DREAM TEAM assembled, Cote could finally open. His concept was to completely rethink the New York steakhouse through the lens of Korean barbecue. Whereas at a New York steakhouse the meal is a gut bomb of thick steak, loaded baked potatoes, creamed spinach, and ice-cream sundaes, Cote would offer a more sustainable alternative.

Instead of rich sides, there would be pickled vegetables called *banchan* to help aid digestion, and in place of a hefty dessert, there would be a little cup of vanilla soft-serve drizzled with soy caramel sauce (an umami version of salted caramel). Simple yet refreshing. For the meat, everything would be cooked right in front of the guests, as at a high-end (and much sexier) Benihana.

Simon would get incredibly worked up talking about his concept. "At a normal steak place you order one huge big-ass cut, like a T-bone, and it lands in front of you like *boom*! Halfway through, the fat begins to congeal, the meat gets cold, and everything is tough. It's no longer sexy and fun. It's gross. So instead, here we will have little tiny bites grilled for you, with many cuts to sample—the flatiron, chuck flap, rib eye, filet mignon—and the guest can savor each morsel when it is ready. The meat is never cold and never congeals. Always it is fresh." Dinner and a show. We all believed that we could resuscitate a dying breed—the New York steakhouse.

Further, Simon wanted to bring the steakhouse to the people. Korean barbecue is lowbrow in many ways, whereas a steakhouse

can be seen as highbrow. Simon wanted Cote to sit somewhere in
the middle. He decided that our entry-level prix-fixe option would
be around $54 and would include everything—four cuts of meat,
kimchi, banchan, rice, stews, an egg soufflé, and dessert. He called
it the "Butcher's Feast." Honestly, there was nowhere else in New
York where you could get the quality of this meal for this price.

I TRIED NOT TO tell Tom, David, and Simon how scared I was. I
wondered if we would run out of money before we even opened.
I remembered the experience at RM and how the critics ripped
us apart. It was my second time opening a restaurant but my first
experience with skin in the game—I was a partner now.

This time, I wanted the restaurant to do well. Not just for
my bank account, but also because I believed in myself and these
three men. Not only did we want to make people happy and form
real relationships, but we also wanted to change the way meat is
produced, the way wine is drunk, the way staff is treated, and
the way dining is enjoyed. To put it quite humbly, we wanted to
change the world.

When it came to the beverage program, Simon had to think
philosophically about how it would work at Cote. He didn't want
to take the commercial route and throw a lychee martini into the
cocktail program and call the concept a "fusion." Instead, he
wanted the beverages to enhance the dining experience and help
drive revenue.

In Korea, people drink mostly soju. Unlike sake in Japan,
which is *brewed* from rice, soju is *distilled*. This means it is more
like vodka in style. I cringed at the thought of guests taking shots
of vodka with their wagyu beef and carefully pickled vegetables.
Simon agreed that soju was traditional but shouldn't be the focus,
as it doesn't enhance the flavors of the food like wine can. But how
does one pair wine with Korean food?

A couple of weeks later, after studying Korean cuisine and brainstorming with Chef, Simon had an idea. In Korean barbecue, all of the pickled vegetables, kimchi, and rice come out *before* the meat, which is said to get the stomach juices flowing, sort of like an aperitif. None of these items pair well with wine but getting rid of them would be getting rid of the heart and soul of Korean cuisine. Instead, Simon suggested putting them at the *end* of the meal.

"But wouldn't that be messing up the whole aperitif concept?" I asked, confused.

Simon insisted that the concept in itself was what needed reworking, not the foods. He went on to describe the qualities of the kimchi and pickles, which can also act as a digestif. "These KBBQ places want to give you the cheap stuff like vegetables and rice, hoping you will fill up on that and not the expensive things like meat. In fact, by giving the meat to the guest first, we are saying that we care about them and don't want to rip them off."

I puzzled over Simon's words. "Won't we *lose* money by having people fill up on meat and not the kimchi and rice!? We'll go out of business within a month!" I told Simon.

"No." He smiled wryly. "That is where you come in.

"I have a truly revolutionary idea," Simon continued. He explained that because guests would be enjoying so much high-quality beef right away, they naturally would drink more. Who can eat a whole steak without something to drink? The best pairing is wine and steak, and with more high-quality meat, people would want more high-quality wine. Simon was sure that what we lost on food, we would make up with beverage sales.

"The guest wins, too: more meat, and they get to enjoy wine," Simon added. "I am greedy *long-term*. Yes, I want to make money, but I also want to give guests the best experience and treat staff well. Then all together we will build Cote's success."

He had come up with a way to make a world-class wine program possible, honor Korean tradition, reinvent the steakhouse, allow the staff to make a decent living, *and* make guests happy by giving them the best value. It ended up working extremely well. He is a genius.

WRITING THE WINE LIST for Cote was incredibly eye-opening. How do these wines get from the vineyards to restaurants? At Piora, I had only begun to dip my toes into buying. At Cote, I was able to purchase millions of dollars of wine and liquor. It was a whole different game. I got a behind-the-scenes look at the politics involved. I chose to support small producers instead of companies that were offering "pay to play."

Before Cote opened, I traveled to France and had growers bottle specific wines for the restaurant. By going directly to the source, I was able to negotiate the best price. I instructed that all of the wines were to be bottled in magnums (twice the size of a standard bottle). Since there is less exposure through the cork to oxygen, the wine inside the bottle stays fresher for longer and tastes better. All of our wines by the glass at Cote are poured out of these magnum bottles—my way of showing the guests that I care about them.

Big liquor companies, smelling the opening of a new account, started to bully me. A "key account manager" came in one night after the opening. He called me over to his table, his heavyset body barely fitting in his chair. "Tonight," he said, "I brought in my family. Don't embarrass me in front of my family."

I felt like I was in *The Godfather*! He went on to demand more of his wines on our list. "And let me tell you something, I live one block away, our offices are one block away, our brand manager's office is one block away, you're surrounded, kid . . . you're surrounded!" Like Simon taught me, I stayed strong. The sharks didn't stop circling, but I learned not to be scared of them.

AS THE BEVERAGE DIRECTOR, I had to put together a team of sommeliers, bartenders, and bar backs. For the head bartender role
I interviewed over fifty candidates, for the sommelier roles over
one hundred people.

I was so grateful that I was a bartender before I became a sommelier. Working at Lattanzi taught me speed and that service is
about seduction. Good drinks are not just about the ingredients,
but about the presentation and ceremony that surround them.
Learning the classics from Sean Muldoon, along with consistency, was incredibly helpful. Since our time together at Harry's,
Muldoon had opened his dream bar, the Dead Rabbit, which had
won the title of "World's Best Bar" (a prize given by the Spirited
Awards at the heralded Tales of the Cocktail festival). Attention
to detail did pay off.

At Aureole, working with the bartender there (also Sean) had
taught me that, no matter how busy we were, the guest always
came first. For a server, a firm handshake and acknowledging a
guest are more important than making a drink. From all of these
experiences, I wanted to manage a team of bartenders and bar
backs with empathy. I knew how suffocating the bar can feel,
being stuck in the same spot for hours, like a cook, churning out
creations. Then, on top of that, you have to be warm to guests
who are demanding, and there is no escape! You can't hide in the
kitchen. It is an enormous amount of pressure.

In bartenders, I looked for humility, proficiency, and presentation. At Cote, they would be one of the first faces you saw upon entry.

I was shocked by how few good sommelier options there were.
I now realized why I had been hired at Aureole, even though I
had so little experience. I talked about making people happy and
had researched the role before my interview. Some of the people I
interviewed for Cote had never even heard of Simon! Why work
for someone you know nothing about?

Others refused to interview with me at all. One older gentleman walked in for the interview, asking after the beverage director. When I introduced myself, he retorted, "No, *you* must be confused. I am looking for the sommelier." Again, I repeated my introduction and assured him that I was who he was looking for. "I don't think so, sweetheart," he commented, before turning around and leaving.

On another interview, the man seemed to think we were on a date, getting too comfortable. "You look beautiful in that sweater," he said, adding, "So . . . do you live around here?" For weeks afterward, he kept trying to "meet up for a drink."

My general rule was that if the interviewee said something negative within the first five minutes, they were out. Grumbling about their last job, complaining about the weather—these were all signs of underlying unhappiness, of someone who couldn't deal with making three-hundred-plus people happy every night.

However, I tried to remember how I'd first felt at Aureole. I knew interviews could be daunting and wanted to show those coming in that at Cote we were human. I offered them water and asked them about themselves and *who* they wanted to be.

Eventually, after a grueling number of interviews, I finally put together a team of beverage professionals. I was taken aback by how many women were interested in the role and entirely overqualified for the position.

Over the next year, I continued to hire more women and minorities. Some started as servers, like Wesley. I tutored them privately and promoted them to sommeliers. Along with the other partners, I kept a close eye on our team, looking for burgeoning talent ready to blossom. Bussers became bar backs, hostesses became maître d's, and servers became managers.

WE OPENED COTE ON June 8, 2017. The days before were spent poring over the nitty-gritty of making the restaurant functional.

Tom spent hours on the phone with Con Edison, begging them to turn on our gas. Simon tried to stretch the funds from our dwindling bank account just a tiny bit further. Wesley trained the whole team on the difference between *chojang* and *ssamjang* and how to grill all of the different cuts of meat tableside. David taught his cooks all of the recipes and how to butcher whole animals. He filled the dry-aging room with meat we could not yet afford. Sidy, our dishwasher from Piora, now tutored all the porters at Cote in how to run the dish pit. With delays, my beverage budget had been cut almost in half. To fatten up the wine list, I got creative and worked with private clients on consignment. We all prayed we wouldn't go out of business before we even opened.

Then a torrential downpour hit New York. The streets flooded with a rainstorm no one had seen coming. That morning, David noticed some water leaking into the kitchen in the basement. Trickles of drain water began to splash onto the brand-new appliances. Within a few hours, thousands of dollars of shiny equipment was drenched. Simon and I watched as waterfalls poured from the ceiling, unable to do anything.

"What's that?!" Simon pointed to a floating brown piece of mush. It circled and then plopped onto the kitchen floor. I looked closer. David and Tom inspected the glob.

Could it be? No way. Yes way.

More turds squeezed from the tiles and into David's brand-new kitchen. The four of us all watched in disbelief. The world was literally shitting on our dreams.

AFTER A METICULOUS (AND very expensive) sterilization of the kitchen, repairs began. The water damage set us back by a few days, if not weeks. I don't know where Simon found the money, but he did. His calm disposition was only matched by his resourcefulness.

On our first night, we started slowly with eighty guests. Grills caught on fire, the air-conditioning barely functioned, guests spotted spelling mistakes on the menu, a sommelier served the wrong bottle of wine, we broke an entire rack of wineglasses, the kitchen vents stopped working, and every single one of us was drenched in sweat. It was pure chaos, and at the end of the night, management all sat down together. We were in the basement, gathered in a circle, and utterly defeated. It was the worst dinner service we had ever worked. What were we doing? We felt like a bunch of kids playing restaurant, instead of the group of trained, seasoned professionals we were.

But we talked it out, got our spirits up, and kept pushing through. Luckily, things got better. "To achieve the impossible, we need to give the impossible," Simon said. All of us put in our whole selves.

As the beverage director and a sommelier, I worked two jobs. Imagine if the person who bought all of the dresses for Bloomingdale's also worked the floor to sell those clothes. I spent all morning and afternoon ordering wine, going through hundreds of emails, researching the market value of wines, studying recent producer and vintage reports, compiling the curriculum for staff education, organizing inventory, putting away towers of wine boxes, updating the wine list, etc. Then, at night, I worked service, selling wine, making guests happy, and managing staff. My days would start at six A.M. and creep well past midnight.

For the opening, I worked more than I had at Marea and Aureole, but there was a difference. I kept my humanity because I was working toward something with purpose. When I was tired, Tom told me to take a break. David fed me bowls of kimchi and rice. The sour pickle notes of the kimchi brought me back to my childhood, when, starving, I would survive for days on pickle juice. *Look how far you have come*, I thought. I was no longer facing starvation or surviving on "low-income" lunches. My dreams of dinner parties had now grown into something far beyond what I'd imagined. I now *owned* part of a restaurant!

As a team, we were there for one another. Simon boosted me with pep talks. Wesley continued to inspire me. "In Korea, we have a saying," he told me one day. "*If not with the teeth, then with the gums.*"

Then the restaurant started to get fantastic buzz. Even in the midst of summer, when every other restaurant in New York slows, Cote was on fire.

NEXT CAME THE BIG fear: reviews. I flashed back to my days at RM and how the one bad review from Pete Wells broke us. I was terrified the same thing would happen at Cote. We believed in this concept, but would others? Simon encouraged us all to acknowledge the reviewers who began to trickle in. "I am done pretending to play the game. They know we know. Let's treat this like what it is—a business." Simon added, "Reviewers see themselves as gardeners. They are here to pull out the weeds and water the good plants. We want to show them why we are not a weed. Show them why we love what we do and what this restaurant is all about; let's not hide. Cote is not about hiding."

I watched as Simon went right up to Ryan Sutton from Eater and Zachary Feldman from the *Village Voice*, shook their hands, and introduced himself. Thankfully, we received glowing reviews from both. (Sutton's review was headlined "Korean Barbecue at Cote Stands Up Against Any Steakhouse in Town—Three Stars for the Flatiron Newcomer"; Feldman's was headlined "Korean BBQ Meets Classic Chophouse at Cote," and he noted, "It's a knockout combination.")

Next came the big guns. Adam Platt was hard to miss, as he towered above everyone else at almost seven feet tall. Those in the industry had told me that he was notoriously grouchy and to be careful. As I walked over to his table to offer beverages, I shook with fear. What if he didn't like me? What if he didn't like our wine or cocktail list? Will I have let everyone down? His guest complained that there was nothing he wanted by the glass.

Adam Platt butted in. "Careful. She is not one to be trifled with." I was entirely caught off guard. *She?* Adam Platt knew who I was? What's more, he thought it best not to mess with *me?* I had made it.

Adam Platt gave us a singing three-star review in *New York* magazine, a rarity. He even applauded the wine list. His review was headlined, "Cote Offers Korean Barbecue with the Soul of a Fat-Cat American Steakhouse," and in it, he said, "They've created a steakhouse disguised as a Korean barbecue joint (or vice versa), a satisfying hybrid that instead of feeling like gimmickry or an exploitation of these two familiar genres, is an improvement on both. . . . Beverage director Victoria James has compiled an impressive list of trophy bottles."

Then came the biggest gun of all. We all kept our eyes peeled for Pete Wells. I knew that if Pete Wells gave us a bad review, Cote was finished. Finally, one day we caught him in the middle of his meal. He had snuck in as a late joiner. I had studied the photo we had of him and tried to remember what he'd looked like when I'd spotted him at RM. He looked completely different! A master of disguise, Wells had gained weight, had shorn his beard, and sported a thick set of glasses.

I noticed that Wells was looking at the wine list. I felt my insides start to tighten. I walked over and asked if he needed any assistance. He pointed to an affordable bottle of Bordeaux. Of course, he had to pick a wine that we had just sold the last bottle of the night before. I was furious at our printer, which had decided to stop working right before the dinner service, making our wine list obsolete. I was angry with myself. Here was our one opportunity and I might blow it. I tried to lead him to another wine effortlessly. I channeled Franky, Enzo, Marianne, Mimi, George, Jane, Richard, and everyone I have ever admired. Luckily, he agreed.

When I returned to his table with the wine, I found myself clutching his arm, almost as if to say, *I am human, we are human, please be kind to us*. As Simon advised, I didn't hide. I introduced myself and highlighted what our wine list at Cote was all about— small producers and big bottles.

Cote wasn't another jewel in some far-off owner's crown, another concept with big margins and low pay for the staff. Cote was Simon's baby—*our* baby—that we had all poured our hearts and souls into. We couldn't get a bad review. We just couldn't.

WHEN OUR *NEW YORK* *Times* review came out, the whole team burst into tears. Cote had received two stars and a Critic's Pick ("This May Be the Best Beef at Any Korean BBQ"). What was more, Wells mentioned me by name, something he almost *never* does with sommeliers. *But Victoria James, who wrote the list, found some pockets of affordability in Beaujolais, Southern France, Corsica, and Switzerland, and she makes a small adventure out of the wines by the glass, all poured from magnums.*

Then something even more magical occurred. We had barely been open for longer than a few months and had no idea our little restaurant stood a chance. But it happened. Cote received a Michelin star!

When the announcement was made, I burst into tears yet again. My whole body began to shake, and in the early morning, we popped a bottle of champagne.

That night at the awards ceremony, I saw the GM from Aureole and the DOP from the Altamarea Group. The following year, Aureole quietly lost its star.

Since my tenure at Marea, all of the four managers had been let go and the GM had been shipped off to work on a new project. George, the beloved maître d', had been pushed out.

At the Michelin ceremony, the Aureole and Marea leaders kept looking at their watches and seemed bored. They were also there to collect Michelin stars. And here I was, with the Cote team, receiving our first Michelin star together.

We were elated. Somehow, we had done it. Cote had not only managed to survive review season; we'd come out on top.

THE CRITICS WEREN'T MY only nightmare, though. I was also juggling a whole staff. Unlike at Marea and Aureole, there is no class system at Cote. The partners and management do not see themselves as "above" everyone else. Still, sometimes we do have to be the boss.

When I had to let go of a bar back after performance issues, he angrily lashed out, "You are going to get raped!" His words felt branded onto my skin with a hot iron. I thought back to the diner, to the trip to Chile, to those times in the wine cellar, and to all the times I had been assaulted in the service industry. All of the fear, feelings of worthlessness, and shame returned.

For months, I received haunting phone calls with vivid accounts of my whereabouts and continued threats. At first, I kept all of this a secret, ashamed that I was being targeted. Finally, I told Wesley, Tom, and Simon, who leaped into action. Wesley always escorted me outside into a taxi after work. If I was closing the restaurant, he would make sure that there were other people around to help, just in case. Over time, the threats dissolved and the support of the team made me stronger.

One night, I learned that a guest had manhandled one of our female staff members. We only learned about the incident days later, as the woman had been too scared to tell anyone. I understood her fear and my heart sank. I never wanted anyone at Cote to feel the way I had felt growing up in the restaurant industry. I brought up the incident and my fears to Simon and Tom. I was shocked by how quickly they came to the defense of the team and the women they worked with.

"Cote from here on out will have a zero-tolerance policy," Simon told me. "If a guest or coworker physically or verbally harasses a Cote team member, they will be removed from the property. I don't care if I have to call the police!" When this same guest later tried to make a reservation at the restaurant, he was refused entry.

I realized how lucky I was to be working with Simon and Tom. They were two anomalies in a restaurant world that was primarily run by chauvinistic male tycoons. With them, I finally learned how to stand up to bullies. I was not my mother, suppressed into silence by my father. Simon and Tom gave me a voice.

In my early restaurant days, I'd wished those in charge made me feel safe. To give our staff what I had always wanted, I made sure to announce from the start, "Cote is not a brothel, it is a restaurant. No one should ever be made to feel uncomfortable by a guest or fellow teammate. If this ever happens, let management know right away, and we will investigate on the spot. If you are uncomfortable talking to management, here is the information for our HR department."

My younger sister Laura continued to push me as reports of abuse from all over the restaurant industry came to light. "You now have the power to make a *difference*," she said. In a world where men hold the power, another voice needed to be heard. "Don't waste this chance," Laura continued, "create a restaurant for our daughters."

Finally, after years of abuse in restaurants from coworkers, bosses, and guests, I felt empowered to make a change.

IN A SAFE ENVIRONMENT, healthy curiosities grow. I saw that many
of our team members wanted more. I started a ten-week class series, like I had done with Wesley at Piora. The wine classes were
free to everyone on the staff. Bussers, food runners, servers, and
bar backs all signed up. Wesley sat in on the lessons for support,
cheering me on. It was no longer just he and I, but a whole room-
ful of students.

One of our food runners told me that when he was a dishwasher, he started to become interested in wine: "I would smell
the dirty wineglasses and try to remember all the different smells."
He went on to say that he'd never thought he would be able to
learn about wine. To him, it seemed too fancy, too expensive,
and too complicated—a sentiment I remembered from being a
nineteen-year-old bartender. The classes not only gave our team
a deeper understanding of wine, but it also showed them that we
cared about their growth.

Inspired by these classes, I decided to start Wine Empowered, a nonprofit for minorities and women in the hospitality industry. Later, Cynthia, one of the sommeliers I had hired, and
Cote's general manager, Amy, joined as cofounders. When she
was twenty, Amy had been a sommelier in Shanghai and then
moved to New York, working her way up in the restaurant world.
As young Chinese women, Cynthia and Amy shared my vision of
diversifying the wine world. We went to the margins of this society and brought the people who had been deemed insignificant
inside. The more diverse a community, the healthier it is.

Coming of age in the restaurant industry wasn't easy for
me. However, I know that many continue to struggle infinitely
more than me because of their sexual orientation, skin color,
religion, or immigration status. Wine Empowered brings free
wine classes to those who wouldn't usually be able to afford
the education or wouldn't normally receive an invitation into
the "pale, male, and stale" wine community. It gives them the

chance to break the cycle, putting more women and minorities in positions of power.

The classes are intended to offer a safe place where women and minorities can speak freely and not have to worry about being sexualized or belittled by their peers. Unlike (as I had experienced) those who are only in teaching for the money and control, we focus on empowering others. Wine doesn't have to be fancy; it shouldn't be exclusive to the wealthy. Just like art and music, it's something everyone deserves to experience.

A MANTA WEDDING

THE SUMMER AFTER COTE OPENED, Lyle asked me to marry him. Happily, I said yes. And one year later, I was able to say "I do."

We embraced my roots and held the wedding celebrations in the family *castelli* in Piemonte. I thought back to when Uncle Carlo first told me about these, that our de Rege ("of the king") family came from a line of aristocrats that lived in castles. To a little girl, it seemed like such a fairy tale. And yet, here I was, twenty years later, with everyone I loved in Castello della Manta.

Laura was my maid of honor and Angela my bridesmaid. Timmy was now Tim, all grown up. Aunt Kathy came from California with her family, Aunt Betty from Washington, DC. Two of her granddaughters were flower girls.

Our cousins Baron Aimaro Oreglia d'Isola and Baroness Consolata d'Isola Solaroli at Castello di Bagnolo showed us photographs of my great-grandmother Contessa Laura de Rege on her wedding day. In the grainy black-and-white photos, I saw traces of myself and my sister. They organized a big party at Bagnolo for our rehearsal dinner.

Aunt Sue and Count Carlo de Rege welcomed us warmly at Castello della Manta, where the wedding ceremony and reception were held. They helped us understand complicated Italian bureaucracy and how to find a good caterer. Their granddaughter, Phoenix, was also a flower girl.

Hours before the wedding, I walked through the Salone Baronale in my gown and paused. I looked around at the ancient frescoes Uncle Carlo had told me about years earlier. I thought back to the empty white square on our wall when we had returned to our house in New Jersey without our mum. All of the prints from Manta she had taken, and the blank space just remained. It seemed that what had once felt like an infinite emptiness was now forever filled.

Now here was the original fresco, depicting Teuta, queen of the Illyrians, or "the Pink Lady," that my grandmother had loved best. Teuta's outstretched hand no longer seemed to say *Come with me*. Instead, she looked like she was waving, as if welcoming me back home.

"I WILL TELL YOU why this is so important to me," Uncle Carlo started in a speech during the wedding dinner. "This is the house, the home, the castle that I grew up in. My wife and I love it, as do my children, and it is just so important that one of our cousins is getting married here. Victoria's grandmother Anna was my big sister," he said, his voice quivering, "which is why the bond here"—he looked at me—"is so strong."

I later remarked to his children, Chiara and Francesco, that I wished Anna were there for the wedding. I wanted to tell her that I had listened, that she was right—making others happy had made me happy.

Francesco and Chiara responded, "But she is here. Your *nonna* is right here." And they pointed to my heart.

LYLE AND I WERE amazed that so many people made the trek to the small rural village in Italy. His family, friends, even Kermit Lynch's wife, Gail, and son, Anthony, came.

A friend of mine, Judi, who used to work with me at Aureole, made my dress by hand. Of course, Richard was there. Jane, who had passed her master sommelier exam and now lived in Australia, came. Philip "the Ritz" Dizard seemed to have flown in on a bottle of champagne.

From Marea, Lizzy Jo, who now owned her own wine shop, and Alexander, who was now a sommelier in Berlin, were there. Marianne lived in Paris with her husband and drove over in a stylish Fiat convertible.

Simon and his wife, Nayun, were there, too. The rest of the Cote team held down the fort in our absence. During the dinner, Simon got up to give a speech.

I first met Victoria on a job interview. I was looking for a wine director and across the table was Victoria. A twenty-four-year-old woman. A beautiful woman.

She had worked for some of the most amazing Michelin-starred restaurants in New York. Everyone talked highly of her as a great sommelier. But she was about to be presented with a new, huge challenge.

A sommelier is a kind of salesperson, so if you sell well, you are a great sommelier. But a wine director not only has to sell well but is responsible for curating the wine list, and also making a profit. I was concerned. Is she going to be able to do this?

And I looked at her—she has got something that I don't know. So we took a leap of faith. And boy, was my concern not necessary or what?

So soon after she took on the position, great accolades started rolling in. To name a few: *Forbes* 30 under 30, *Food & Wine* Sommelier of the Year. When faced with a challenge, she didn't just overcome—she was victorious.

And last year we opened our second restaurant, Cote. Another challenge for her. She was going to be a beverage director, responsible for everything that people drink, including cocktails, wine, spirits, water, and coffee.

So I was concerned. But again was that concern not necessary. Thanks to her amazing efforts, and everyone else's at Cote, just four months after opening we got a Michelin star.

All of those accolades are amazing, and we are so grateful. But most importantly, every person who Victoria touched, every customer, every staff member, she brought happiness to all of them. She was presented with great challenges, so many challenges in her life, and every single challenge she didn't just overcome, she was victorious.

Regulars of mine from Aureole, Marea, and Piora, whom I now considered friends, all came. Winemakers whom Lyle and I had visited at their domaines now visited us. Gifts of cases of wine were sent to the wedding from all over the world.

We were so honored by all of the wine given and all the *vignerons* in attendance. But there was one wine in particular that Lyle and I treasured—the Collioure from La Tour Vieille. It was the same bottle we'd drunk on our first date and the magical place we had visited together years before. Christine had driven all the way from her small corner of France by the Spanish border, with a car full of magnums. In his vows, Lyle even spoke of what this wine meant to him on our first date.

> We shared a magnum of Collioure Rouge with my amateur rendition of Zuni Café's roasted chicken and bread salad. A wine like this is deceptively simple, and there's a lot more to it than just the wine. So when you "got" this, I knew it was right.
>
> This first date was on a full moon, like tonight, but it's hard to even think of this as a first date because for me the date hasn't ended yet, and it never will.

Before the wedding, my younger sisters had helped me get ready. Laura had curled my hair, and Angela had steamed my dress. Angela was not just a bridesmaid but a little woman. Her thick black mane showed her Brazilian roots, but in her eyes and face, I could only see Grandma Willie. She surprised me with an impressive level of confidence for a thirteen-year-old, standing in front of a room and saying,

> Victoria, I just want to let you know how much of an inspiration you are to me. You always work for what you want and don't stop until you get it. I look up to you as a big sister and most of all a person.
>
> You taught me how to be confident in myself and to be proud of who I am, to be the bigger person in tough situations.

Behind Angela stood Laura, who rubbed her back to keep the nerves away. Just as I had watched over Laura, she watched over Angela.

Then Laura gave her speech. She stood powerful, unwaver-ing. Laura was now in her twenties, studying and living in Italy. It was the biggest crowd Laura had ever spoken in front of, but at that moment I felt it was just us. There seemed to be an invisible cord that ran between us, one that had always been there. My aunt Kathy reminded me of how we'd both gotten here: "You saved each other. You gave her a role model, and she gave you a purpose."

Victoria—you are my best friend and a strange quasi-mother figure to me.

When I was born, you were just seven, but you cared for me as if I were your own.

In all my life, you have been my go-to emergency con-tact. You have given me the clothes off your back, figura-tively (but literally, I have built my closet out of the clothes you have gifted me).

For most of my life, I had thought of you as being this unbothered person, someone that couldn't be shaken even with our tumultuous upbringing. And I thought that if only I could be as strong as you, I would be okay. Or I would be more than okay.

You have kept me hopeful, loved, comfortable. And when we got a bit older, around the time I was in middle school and you were in college, I think that is when you really let me get to know who you were. And I gained a best friend because of it.

I thought of the baby I'd held in the hospital and never wanted to put down. The little girl whose hair I would stroke until she fell asleep. Her bright blue eyes twinkled today as they had then, reflective pools of light. Then they'd said, *Up, up,* and I would bend down to carry her. I realized that at some point she had started carrying me. I wonder when it happened, exactly when it went from my carrying her to our carrying each other. Over the years, when I felt weak, she would almost seem to bend down and say to me, *Up, up.*

I discovered that you were a bit more affected and human than you led other people to believe. This secret vulnerability made me love you more than I thought possible.

Considering that all odds were against us, you built us a life that was filled with Sunday dinners, hitchhiking across the Amalfi Coast, Negronis, the best of it. And understandably all of my best personality traits come from you.

From me? I thought. *Those are from you, Laura. You gave me unconditional love when I was a washed-up diner waitress who smoked heroin out of an old apple. Your tiny arms hugged my tortured body, abused by men and strangers, healing my saddened bones.*

I still aspire to be as poised, loving, and caring as you. Because you have taught me unconditional love—from loving me as a crying baby to the crybaby I still am today. And now you offer that same unconditional love to Lyle. Who I think knows he is the luckiest man.

All the makeup that Laura had helped me put on that morning seemed to now wash off in waves of tears. We'd grown from little girls who gave each other purpose to young women, each shaped by the other. Every ounce of love I had given Laura had come back in pounds.

THEN THERE WAS TIM. He stood up proudly, his over-six-foot body rising high above the crowd. I could tell that he had trimmed his usually unruly beard for the occasion. He played a song he had prepared. Right before, he said a few words that brought a hush upon the *castello* and sent me into quiet, gut-wrenching sobs.

> We don't necessarily always get the opportunity to
> share what we mean to each other. Throughout my
> life, you have been many things to me.
> You've been my protector,
> my partner in crime,
> my friend.
> My teacher,
> my role model,
> my hero.
> You've been my inspiration.
> My encouragement.
> You've picked me up off the ground when I was hurt
> and broken.
> You brushed me off and helped me get back on the
> horse at some of the worst and hardest times of
> my life.

Tim, little Timmy, who climbed tall oak trees, who writhed in his dinosaur pajamas when scrambling eggs, who hugged me when I got my first job, who smoked pot with me, and who was tied down on a stretcher with thick gray straps. I knew how much Tim meant to me, but I had never stopped to think how much I meant to him.

Then Tim went on to talk about Lyle.

Victoria asked me, "Tim, what did you think of Lyle?"
I thought about it, and you know, he's handsome, he has a great family, he is successful, he's obviously intelligent,

he's funny, and those are all important things. But it wasn't the most important thing to me.

The most important thing to me was something that I saw when I saw them for dinner that evening and what I still see today—it's the way they look at each other, the way they talk to each other, the way they act around each other. They make each other happy. They love each other. They are good to each other.

As long as you make each other happy, as long as you are good to one another, he is everything I could ever want.

Tim illustrated that I had finally found someone who cared about *my* happiness. Then Tim sat down at the piano his ancestors had played for years. And everyone was spellbound by his rendition of Louis Armstrong's "What a Wonderful World."

Tim was doing what brought him great joy: playing the piano. The ban from childhood was over. I looked around for my father, and saw that he had joined in with the whole room, singing at the end, *"And I think to myself . . . What a wonderful world."*

After all of the speeches from my siblings, my father was quiet. By praising the fact that I had been there for them, I could tell he felt what they *didn't* say about him. These words, and the fact that I didn't want anyone to walk me down the aisle, must have hurt his feelings. His quiet sadness filled me with compassion. The turmoil of my childhood seemed a lifetime away.

My father didn't drink all week, a decision I knew he'd made for me. He admitted that his struggles had affected us growing up and that he wished he had been more flexible, not as strict. Most important, he now realized that his behaviors were all signs of an addictive personality disorder and said that he was consciously trying to be a better parent, for Angela.

During the wedding festivities, Lucy and my father were helpful, both of them fueled by excitement and pride. I gave them the task of the seating chart, and Lucy owned it. Soon, she was telling the caterers who was boss, and I loved her for it. My father ran any and every errand I needed, including trying to find a steamer. Every store in the Italian countryside is closed during August, so this really was an impossible task. Somehow, he managed to find me one. In my surprise, I mentioned to my aunt Betty how giving my father and Lucy seemed now, how much they had changed.

She responded, "Sometimes people need time. You idolized my mother, Willie. To you she was the best grandmother, but to me, she hadn't been a very good mother. She wasn't there for me growing up. It wasn't until I had children that we started to form a bond."

I realized that with time and a new generation comes a veil of forgiving. My father had changed, and so had I—I wanted to show him that I forgave him. Franky's love cycle had taught me *how* to love people even when it is difficult, and *why* those are the people we should give the most love to.

During the father-daughter dance, my father first spoke of his new job and how he was traveling all over the world. Then he seemed to catch himself. He realized he had been talking about his career. After a pause he allowed himself to show tenderness.

"You were always able to take a bad situation and make it into something good. Never lose that trait. But know that if you ever need anything, I am here now."

AND THEN THERE WAS Mum. She seemed to float around the *castello* like a ghost. I struggled to recognize her after all these years. Since I was a child, I had only seen her a handful of times; these were mostly court-appointed sessions or awkward afternoon visits. Even now, her head seemed elsewhere.

When Lyle was dancing with his mother to Chuck Berry's "You Never Can Tell," everyone seemed unable to resist the music and joined in. Lyle and his mother had prepared by watching John Travolta and Uma Thurman do the twist to the same song in *Pulp Fiction*.

Even Count Carlo shook his whole body, his knees and elbows following enthusiastically, while Sue was twirling so rapidly her silk scarf came undone. The twelfth-century *castello* transformed into a sock-hop party.

Since Lyle was dancing with his mother, I looked for mine. She was over by the dessert table, nervously pretending to pick at the sweets. Her hair was stacked on top of her head and she wore a dress I could tell she wasn't accustomed to yet. I felt a tug inside.

I parted the dance floor with my long white gown and train, walking directly toward her. "Let's dance," I said, smiling.

Up until now, I had admittedly been avoiding her during the wedding. I didn't know what I could say to this strange woman who was supposed to be my mother. I didn't have the words.

"Darling, I don't know how to dance!" Mum replied skittishly, looking around at swiveling hips and a couple of characters holding their nose and doing the swim.

"Don't worry about the *how*," I said, taking her hand in mine. *Stacked bones, tired face / A tiny waist I couldn't hold / Because I had tried / And you would never / Hold me / back*. My childhood poem flashed through my head. She seemed so brittle, and I was worried my tight grip would hurt her.

Soon her delicate fingers twisted in mine and held on. Mum's updo bopped back and forth; her movements quickened. She looked the same as the woman in the peppermint shirt who had run after us in the blue van.

At that moment we were like my two grandmothers, the contessa and the cotton picker. Whether in a kitchen or a *castello*, dancing to Don McLean or Chuck Berry, in the music was that feeling, that exhilaration of familiarity that tied us together.

I looked around the room at all the people brought into my life through wine. And now here, with my mum, who didn't drink, we were coming together through music. Her absence over the years had hurt me, but there on the dance floor in the place her own mother had found happiness, I found a way to love her.

Acknowledgments

I hope my story will give young women all over the world courage to share their stories, take charge of their lives, and empower others. Let's stand together for social justice and create positive change. Wherever you are, don't let anyone stop you from telling your truth.

This book took over five years to write but so much longer to develop. As a result, there are a lot of friends, family members, and colleagues to thank.

Thank you first and foremost to my loving husband, Lyle, for giving me the courage and support to dedicate myself to this project (and for walking Rocco on days I was glued to my computer). Your unconditional love, even when I am sharing more of myself with the world than with you, is forever appreciated. I love you and I carry your heart—I carry it in my heart.

Thank you to my sister Laura, who read the first "vomit draft" and taught me the importance of an Oxford comma. You believed in this book even though it made you uncomfortable. There is no way for me to tell my story without including a bit of yours. Thank you for allowing me to give something to the world that is not mine to share.

Thank you to my brother, Timothy, for permitting me to write about difficult parts of your life. Your kind words of encouragement also gave me the strength to continue.

To my littlest sister, Angela: You continue to inspire me with your wit and love for life. Angela, Timothy, and Laura—you are my reason for being. I love you all so much.

To Jana, who has fixed way more than my body over the years: Your words of wisdom are even more powerful than your needles.

To my mum: Thank you for sending me your private journals, court transcripts, police records, and, of course, an endless supply of "cute quotes" and photographs. I was blown away by how well you documented the time you spent with us through your camera lens. This is a beautiful way to show love, isn't it? Ours was a hard story to tell, but I thank you for your support.

To my father: This couldn't have been an easy book for you to read. Thank you for your support and love. I am so impressed by your growth and how far we have both come, together.

To all of the first readers and "editors"—Balachander Krishnamurthy (and all the FOBS): Thank you for all of your DRD notes and for telling me what I needed to hear. To Richard Anderson, who continues to tell it to me like it is. To Judi Olson for not only handcrafting the most beautiful wedding dress I could possibly imagine but also giving me perspective on all of our Aureole experiences. To Bianca Bosker for being an early supporter. Marianne Fabre-Lanvin, you are simply wonderful and gave me so much hope. To my mentor, Rita Jammet, for your never-ending kindness and unwavering positivity. And to my dear friend Aileen Robbins, whom I loved so much: I wish you could see that this little book made it! Thank you for editing the heck out of the manuscript even when you were battling cancer. I miss you so much.

Thank you to my aunt Kathy and aunt Betty. To my grandmothers, you both made me the woman I am today. To the de Rege family. To my high school English teacher Mr. Wagenblast— thank you for encouraging me to write.

To the Wine Empowered team—Amy Zhou, Cynthia Cheng, Suzanne Walker, Patricia Murphy, Jeff Reed, and Gabrielle Simon: Thank you for supporting and believing in one young woman with a dream.

To the whole Cote core family—Tom Brown, Tom Piscitello, Wesley Sohn, Amy Zhou, David Shim, Heather Carlson, Seung Kyu Kim, John Drewniany, Jillian Tuttle, and, of course, Simon Kim: Thank you for believing in me and all of your endless love. Let's keep slaying those dragons together. Thank you to the entire Cote team—every sommelier, bartender, bar back, server, server assistant, reservationist, host, cook, porter, and dishwasher. To our dynamic sommelier team—Marina, Amanda, and Daniel: Thank you for holding down the fort and loving guests. A special thank-you to Sidy.

Thank you to all of the regulars who have followed my career and supported it—from Lattanzi to Cote. A special shout-out to a few longtime regulars—Roger Park, Elise Pagano and Matthew Graziano, Jake Fisher and Lauren Lucas, Michelle and Jeff Greenip, Michael and Beth Nochomovitz, Hutham Olayan and Robert Raucci, Bill Motherway, and the whole Lyons family. Without guests to serve, a sommelier is useless. (Bonus points when they're super cool.)

Thank you to my brilliant agent team, Allison Hunter and Clare Mao, and to Gabriella Doob, Miriam Parker, and the entire editorial (and legal!) team at Ecco. Most of all, thank you to Daniel Halpern for having confidence in me as your sommelier, and later as one of your authors. I wouldn't trust anyone else with my story but you.

And to everyone in the restaurant industry who believed in me and was kind, thank you. I couldn't have done this without your help.